BELLEVILLE

· LOYALTY · TRADITION · PROGRESS ·

BELLEVILLE

~ A Popular History ~

Gerry Boyce

NATURAL HERITAGE BOOKS
DUNDURN PRESS
TORONTO

Editor: Jane Gibson
Copyeditor: Chad Fraser
Design: Courtney Horner
Printer: Transcontinental

Library and Archives Canada Cataloguing in Publication

Boyce, Gerald E., 1933-
   Belleville : a popular history / by Gerry Boyce.

"A Natural Heritage book".
Includes bibliographical references and index.
ISBN 978-1-55002-863-8 (pbk.).--ISBN 978-1-55488-412-4 (bound)
   1. Belleville (Ont.)--History. I. Title.

FC3099.B46B68 2008   971.3'585   C2008-903972-6

1   2   3   4   5   12   11   10   09   08

Conseil des Arts   Canada Council
du Canada   for the Arts

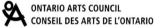

ONTARIO ARTS COUNCIL
CONSEIL DES ARTS DE L'ONTARIO

We acknowledge the support of the **Canada Council for the Arts** and the **Ontario Arts Council** for our publishing program. We also acknowledge the financial support of the **Government of Canada** through the **Book Publishing Industry Development Program** and **The Association for the Export of Canadian Books**, and the **Government of Ontario** through the **Ontario Book Publishers Tax Credit program**, and the **Ontario Media Development Corporation**.

Care has been taken to trace the ownership of copyright material used in this book. The author and the publisher welcome any information enabling them to rectify any references or credits in subsequent editions.

J. Kirk Howard, President

Printed and bound in Canada.
Printed on recycled paper.
www.dundurn.com

Published by Natural Heritage Books
A Member of The Dundurn Group

Cover Photo Credits:

Top Left: Downtown Belleville, photograph, looking south from Bridge Street West, 2006. *Courtesy of Doug Knutson, Windswept Productions.*

Top Right: *Belleville; Mouth of the Moira River, Bay of Quinty in the distance,* circa 1830, painted by Thomas Burrowes, described in detail on page 66. *Courtesy of Archives of Ontario, Burrowes Collection, C 1-0-0-0-109.*

Bottom Left: *Belleville: Looking East,* circa 1830, painted by Thomas Burrowes from near the west end of the Bridge Street bridge, described in detail on page 51. *Courtesy of Archives of Ontario, Burrowes Collection, C 1-0-0-0-110.*

Bottom Right: Photograph of the Bridge Street Bridge and the Moira, 2006. *Courtesy of Doug Knutson, Windswept Productions.*

Back Cover: Belleville: Front Street with City Hall in the distance. August, 2008. *Courtesy of Gerry Boyce.*

Opposite title page: City of Belleville Armorial Bearings granted by Her Majesty's College of Arms in 1982, reflecting the city's Aboriginal and Loyalist heritage.

Dundurn Press	Gazelle Book Services Limited	Dundurn Press
3 Church Street, Suite 500	White Cross Mills	2250 Military Road
Toronto, Ontario, Canada	High Town, Lancaster, England	Tonawanda, NY
M5E 1M2	LA1 4XS	U.S.A. 14150

Lovingly dedicated to the memory of my parents Egerton & Rowena Boyce (who instilled in me a love for history); and my aunt and uncle Judge Gerald & Eva Smith (who shared an enthusiasm for history in Lennox & Addington County); and in appreciation to my wife Bev and our children, Duncan, Egerton, Thomas, and Susie (who actively encourage me in my historical activities).

CONTENTS

ACKNOWLEDGEMENTS

BEING AN AUTHOR can be a lonely occupation at times. Fortunately, there are people and institutions that can help, and I am indebted to many of these for their assistance over the past half-century:

Staff at the following research facilities beyond the borders of Belleville helped to identify useful sources of information and allow for the inclusion of pictures: Library and Archives Canada (Ottawa), the Archives of Ontario (Toronto), and Queen's University Archives (Kingston). At Belleville, staff at the Belleville Public Library (in particular Reference Librarian Elizabeth Mitchell), Glanmore National Historic Site (Curator Rona Rustige), the City of Belleville, the County of Hastings, and the Hastings County Historical Society (operators of the Hastings Heritage Centre) have gone out of their way to provide assistance. Among the historians who helped are C.W. "Bill" Hunt, Lois Foster, and Orland French of Belleville, and Michael Peterman of Trent University. Anthropologists Ann Herring and the late Shelley Saunders of McMaster University, as well as archaeologist Heather McKillop of Louisiana State University, provided assistance with the St. Thomas' Anglican Church Cemetery section. Doug Knutson has been invaluable in connection with selecting pictures.

Bev, my wife, has been an excellent proofreader and prompter throughout the writing process. Bruce Retallick, my former student at McArthur College of Education and former head of the history department at Belleville Collegiate Institute and Vocational School, came to my rescue after a recent jogging mishap put me out of commission for a time. Bruce supplied inspiration, drafted some key sections (including the Epilogue) and aided in the selection of visuals.

Thanks to Barry Penhale, friend and publisher, for suggesting that I write about my adopted home city, and to Jane Gibson for providing considerable help during the publishing phase. Much appreciation also goes to the editorial staff at Dundurn Press for all their encouragement in bringing this work to fruition.

INTRODUCTION

THE CITY OF Belleville is a historic and attractive community on eastern Ontario's picturesque Bay of Quinte. Established in 1816 as a town site, Belleville has undergone significant changes. Today, it is a vibrant community offering many advantages to its citizens and visitors.

This book is not a complete history of the city. Such a history, with lists of former mayors and councillors and summaries of all the achievements of churches, service clubs, and other groups, would fill many volumes. Rather, it is a personal commentary on some of the most important and interesting events, personalities, and places from the community's long and eventful past. The material is largely in chronological order. However, some topics, such as the "Mighty Moira," cover a long time period, reflecting the flow of history and the many links between past, present, and future. The earlier portion of the book maintains imperial measurements in keeping with the time frame, then shifts to metric in keeping with the change in methods used in different points in history. Likewise MLA is used to designate a member of the Legislative Assembly during the time of its usage, and is followed by the use of MPP for the period following the mid-1970s. The names of newspapers have changed over time, but for consistency the following usage has been maintained in context: *Kingston Chronicle and Gazette, Kingston Chronicle*, the *Intelligencer* and the *Ontario*.

The publication marks the fifty-fifth year of the author's study of Belleville's history. It began in the summer of 1953 when I approached Bill Stovin, the manager at local radio station CJBQ, to see if there might be a summer job for a university student, perhaps writing stories about Canada's history. They did not need such a person. However, because of an announcer's sudden departure, I was hired as an announcer-operator.

When it became apparent that this was not my forte, and when an experienced announcer was found, Stovin offered me work in the continuity department (writing commercials) and doing market research and similar studies. He wanted data on the local market for potential advertisers. Accordingly, I searched government reports, 1951 census data, and historical publications (of which there were very few).

A by-product of this research was a series of CJBQ spot announcements, known as "Quintisms." A bell would ring and the announcer would ask, "Did you know that Captain John W. Meyers was the founder of Belleville?" or "Did you know that there were x number of sheep in Hastings County in 1951, according to the recent census?"

Quintisms did not survive. However, my research into local history did. The establishment of the Hastings County Historical Society (1957), the opening of the Hastings County Museum (1961), and the publication of several books on this area — beginning with 8,000 copies of *Historic Hastings* (1967) — attest to that.

My original plan was to title this book *Belleville: What the Chamber of Commerce Doesn't Tell You* and then relate some of the unfortunate aspects of its history. However, that would have excluded the many positive moments in our history. Accordingly, *Belleville: A Popular History* will focus on both the glorious and not-so-glorious moments.

Originally, Belleville was part of the Township of Thurlow. That political tie was broken after Belleville became a town and had its own seat on Hastings County Council. The link was re-established when the citizens of Belleville and the Township of Thurlow voted to amalgamate to become the new City of Belleville, effective January 1, 1988. This book will include frequent references to Thurlow Township (now known as Thurlow Ward); however, the emphasis will be on that part of it known as Belleville for almost two-hundred years (and now referred to politically as Belleville Ward).

1
THE BEGINNING

Location, Location, Location

SOME REAL ESTATE companies claim that location is the main selling point when it comes to property. The same claim was true in the past when it came to determining where to settle in an unsettled land. Belleville enjoyed — and still enjoys — many advantages. The most important is its location on the Bay of Quinte at the mouth of the Moira River. Nature provided a sheltered, though shallow, harbour, and good communication by water (or ice in winter). The narrowness of the river's mouth made bridge-building relatively easy. Whereas the northern two-thirds of Hastings County are covered by the ancient rocks of the Canadian Shield, the southern third is part of the St. Lawrence Lowlands. Much of the area near Belleville consists of fertile agricultural land. Available timber, mineral resources in the nearby Shield, and scenic vistas are also important.

At the same time, nature provided some obstacles. Ice jams and flooding destroyed more than one bridge across the

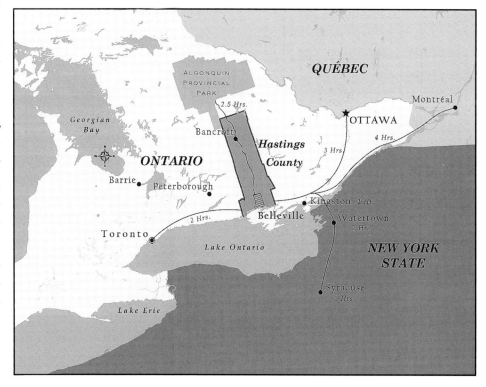

Belleville's central location with respect to Ontario, Quebec, and New York State. Courtesy of County of Hastings Planning and Development Department.

Moira River. Also, the Prince Edward Peninsula, which juts out into Lake Ontario, led many travellers and prospective settlers moving west from Kingston to bypass the Belleville area.[1]

Aboriginal History

WHEN I WAS preparing *Historic Hastings* more than forty years ago, I wrote that our knowledge of the earliest inhabitants of Hastings was "based on the work of the archaeologists, the accounts of early white explorers, and the traditional legends of the Indians. Unfortunately," I continued, "the archaeologists have neglected our area, the white explorers did not touch the county until the early seventeenth century, and the legends are not always reliable."[2]

Fortunately, this statement can be modified somewhat as the result of work by two archaeologists from outside the area who have shed more light on our aboriginal history.

The first was Russell J. Barber, a talented graduate student from Harvard University's Peabody Museum. Barber spent parts of two summers in the Belleville area.[3] In 1975, he conducted a preliminary surface survey of known and potential sites in the non-Canadian Shield portion of the Moira Valley. He identified one site in lowlands next to the Moira River at Foxboro, where another archaeologist had made a test excavation in 1967. Unfortunately, the area had been extensively disturbed over the years through ploughing and road construction. Several collected artifacts indicated that the site had been occupied briefly by Archaic, Point Peninsula, and Iroquois settlements.[4] Given the small number of artifacts found and the flood potential of the Moira, these occupations likely took the form of camps, as groups of people migrated through the area, rather than permanent settlements.

Barber's 1975 survey was important because, in his words, the Moira Valley had been "archaeologically unknown." He hoped the surface survey would encourage in-ground exploration. In fact, Barber returned the following August and organized the Moira Valley Archaeological Survey. Supported by Harvard University, the Ontario Ministry of Education's Experience '76 Programme, and the Hastings County Board of Education, a team of archaeologists, university and high school students, and volunteers examined a large series of man-made small mounds near Stoco Lake. Although the excavated mounds yielded no artifacts, Barber suggested that they probably were intended to function as monuments or cenotaphs by people of the Point Peninsula culture in the early centuries A.D.

Hugh J. Daechsel of McMaster University carried out a further study of the Moira Valley in the summer of 1984.[5] His survey located seventeen prehistoric sites of which ten were test excavated, yielding over 16,000 artifacts. The team's primary camp was situated at the H.R. Frink Outdoor Education Centre and much of the effort was concentrated in the Plainfield and Parks Creek areas of Thurlow Ward. The Daechsel team located four sites with Archaic components (7,000 B.C.–1,000 B.C.), several with Middle Woodland (400 B.C.–800 A.D.) components, and nine with Late Woodland (800 A.D.–1600 A.D.) components.

Although Daechsel's survey focused on the location of prehistoric sites, the team found evidence of historic use of many of the sites dating from the mid-nineteenth century. However, there was no archaeological evidence for the period extending from 1500 A.D.–1650 A.D. Daechsel concluded that "prior to the settling of the area by Loyalist groups in 1783 there was limited European as well as aboriginal activity" in the Moira basin.[6] He estimated that four or five field seasons, including both survey and excavation of selected sites, would be required to provide a comprehensive assessment of the cultural history in the Moira drainage basin.

Barber and Daechsel proved that the Moira River had been a travel route for aboriginal peoples for many hundreds, even thousands of years. What they could not determine — or even attempt to determine — was whether there had been an aboriginal settlement at the mouth of the Moira River. Two centuries of white settlement had removed or covered any evidence.

What is known is that there were some aboriginal burials — possibly from fairly recent times — near the mouth of the Moira River, in what is now the heart of Belleville. In fact, when the United Empire Loyalists began to arrive after 1784, the government refused to allow them to settle on this land (lot 4 in both the first and second concessions of Thurlow Township) and reserved it for the Mississauga, who had used the site for various purposes for about a century. A notation on a copy of the 1787 survey plan of Thurlow indicated that this land was "Reserved for Indian Burying Ground."[7] Unfortunately — or perhaps fortunately — none of the early maps that indicated the presence of an "Indian Burying Ground" showed exactly where it was located. Had the site been specified, persons looking for Indian artifacts might have vandalized it.

Evidence for the existence of a local Indian burying ground came from author Susanna Moodie, who arrived in Belleville in 1839. She later wrote:

> On that high sandy ridge that overlooks the town eastward — a tangled maze of hazel bushes, and wild plum and cherry, once screened the Indian burying-ground … We will suppose ourselves standing among the graves in the burying ground of the English church … the quiet dead sleeping at our feet. The white man has so completely supplanted his red brother that he

has appropriated the very spot that held his bones; and in a few years their dust will mingle together, although no stone marks the grave where the red man sleeps.[8]

Obviously, Moodie was aware of an Indian burying ground on the town's East Hill.

There had been a long-standing belief that an Indian burial site was located on Zwick's Island. However, when that site was developed as the centre of a major park system (commencing in 1967 as a project to mark Canada's centennial), no evidence of any burial site was uncovered. Over the years, Belleville residents have picked up the occasional arrowhead, implement, or pottery shard. This proves that First Nations Peoples and their ancestors passed through this area, but there is not nearly as much evidence as there is in Prince Edward County. For example, the nearby sandbanks, some within Sandbanks Provincial Park, yielded wonderfully preserved ceramic pots, and the Reverend Bowen P. Squire uncovered a variety of artifacts at the Squire Site near Consecon and elsewhere in "The County" (as Prince Edward County residents refer to their home).

Nevertheless, there were people who believed that there had been aboriginal settlements at the mouth of the Moira. One believer was Wallace Havelock Robb, a native of Belleville whose views will be noted later. Evidence of an eighteenth-century Mississauga village at the site is found in an early settlement map showing collections of huts near the mouths of both the Moira and Salmon rivers.

Almost 150 years ago, Thomas C. Wallbridge, a Belleville businessman, amateur scientist, and future parliamentarian wrote "what must be among the earliest published accounts of archaeological excavations undertaken in the province of Ontario — if not Canada."[9] Wallbridge described and illustrated the results of his trenching through "several examples of a distinct class of late Middle Woodlands mounds largely found along the south shore of the Bay of Quinte." In August 1859, he opened five of the five-foot-high mounds and estimated that there were perhaps a hundred such mounds in Prince Edward County, the majority located in Ameliasburgh Township along the south shore of the bay between Massassauga Point and Rednersville. Believing that the mounds were related to similar mounds in the United States that had yielded spectacular finds, he was disappointed by the "apparent sparseness of artifacts or burials." Most of the Quinte Mounds were simply piles of fire-cracked rock, charcoal, and ashy soil. Wallbridge wondered what these mounds were for and why they were apparently found only on the south shore of the Bay of Quinte and not on the north shore in or near Belleville.

Recently, archaeologist David A. Robertson studied the literature relating to these burnt stone mounds and similar mounds in the Perch Lake region of Jefferson County (New York) as well as in England and Ireland. He found that they have been identified variously as burial mounds, hut rings, the remains of circular lodges that were the antecedents of the long house, sweat lodges, and the remains of fire rituals. He suggested that they "are more likely to be the remains of seasonally occupied large-scale cooking or food processing sites," perhaps involving hot-stone boiling techniques.[9] It is also possible that some mounds "acquired symbolic significance." Today, it is generally agreed that the Quinte Mounds were quite different from the Serpent Mounds near Rice Lake, which were intended as primary burial sites. The Quinte Mounds were not intended primarily as burial sites, although later groups used them for that purpose. Without the efforts of Thomas C. Wallbridge in researching and writing on these mounds in the 1850s, we would have little or no knowledge of them. They disappeared not long after his research was completed.

Unfortunately, Belleville has had very few amateur archaeologists who have studied aboriginal settlements. Regretfully, most have chosen to study Prince Edward County rather than the Belleville area. For example, in the 1950s, M.C. Cummings and his wife helped the Reverend Bowen P. Squire conduct research at his Consecon site and elsewhere in Prince Edward County. Perhaps in the future, the Cataraqui Archaeological Research Foundation, which has carried out extensive research in the Kingston area, can take steps to expand its occasional sorties into the Belleville region. To date, most of the foundation's activities near Belleville have been limited to examining a few sites and buildings from the period of white settlement.

Samuel de Champlain: "Discoverer" of Belleville in 1615?

ON THE FIRST page of his *City of Belleville History,* published in 1943, Belleville historian, lawyer, and former mayor W.C. Mikel wrote that "Belleville … was discovered by Samuel de Champlain, the great French explorer when he discovered the Bay of Quinte." Seven pages later, Mikel noted that Champlain was "supposed to have visited the Indian village of Asaukhknosk, now the City of Belleville." Then, on the next page, he explained that "No one definitely knows that Samuel de Champlain … actually stopped at 'Asaukhknosk' but as it appears to have been an active Indian centre the assumption is made that he did stop at this point."[10] One author with three different answers to the question in the space of eight pages!

Obviously, Mikel was uncertain as to Champlain's connection with Belleville. Possibly his

For many years, this engraving was accepted as a true likeness of Champlain. However, biographer Joe C.W. Armstrong described this famous depiction as "one grand artistic hoax," looking "more suitable for a cereal package." Armstrong pointed out that the only certain images of Champlain are the crude self-portraits to be found in three battle scenes, where Champlain appeared in full armour. Courtesy of Library and Archives Canada, C-6643

positive assertion on page one that Champlain did discover the site was an attempt to promote book sales by closely linking the community to the famous explorer. Perhaps his conscience and the lack of historical evidence for the claim caught up with him in the later references.

In addition, Mikel's reference to Champlain "discovering" the site was inappropriate. How could the explorer "discover" a site that had been discovered and visited for centuries or even thousands of years by representatives of the First Nations?

Our knowledge of Champlain's link with Belleville is based on two sources: his journals and his maps. From his journal, we learn that he descended the Trent River system with a band of allied Huron Indians on his way to attack an Iroquois village south of Lake Ontario in 1615. En route, he described the countryside in the vicinity of the lower Trent as "green and pleasant. The trees overhanging the banks look as if they had been planted by a landscape-gardener. Vines and fruit trees were growing everywhere and game was plentiful in season."[11] However, there is nothing in the journal to support the view that he passed by or stopped at the mouth of the Moira. Similarly, there is no evidence to support the once-popular notion that he ascended Mount Pelion, at Trenton, to view the surrounding countryside.

Nevertheless, Champlain scholar Joe Armstrong echoes the traditional assumption that the war party "exited through the Trent River into the Bay of Quinte at Trenton, Ontario."[12] If that assumption is correct, Champlain probably would have been the first European to view the site of Belleville.

Certainly, Champlain's map of 1616 does suggest that he was at least familiar with the presence of a river in the vicinity of the Moira. He may have gained this knowledge when he spent five weeks (from late October to early December 1615) at a lake north of the Bay of Quinte recuperating from wounds suffered in his attack on the well-fortified Onondaga village. Local historians disagree about the actual river he ascended and the lake where the war party camped.[13]

Champlain's account of his trip down the Trent system and his stay north of the Bay of Quinte contains excellent references to the hunting and fishing lifestyles of the aboriginal peoples who travelled through this area. He stressed a changing population pattern when he wrote, "The whole area was once occupied by the Hurons, but they have been driven out by the Iroquois."[14] The pattern would change again with the arrival of the Mississauga in the early 1700s.

A Mission at Belleville?

IS IT POSSIBLE that Belleville was the site of an early Roman Catholic mission to the First Nations? Some early French maps show the Quinte (or Kente) Mission located near this site in the late-seventeenth century. However, more maps show the mission at other locations in Prince Edward County, and in neighbouring sections of Hastings and Northumberland counties.

Fortunately, we know quite a bit about the Quinte Mission — its background, operation and abandonment — largely because of surviving correspondence.[15] A band of Cayuga Indians, who had arrived in 1665 from south of Lake Ontario, where they had been harassed by enemies to the south, asked the French at Montreal to send missionaries. Anxious "to expand their influence to the west," the French readily agreed. Bishop Laval instructed two Sulpicians, M. Trouve and M. de Fenelon, to undertake the mission. They were instructed "to allow no savage to die without baptism in so far as that is possible."[16] In addition, they were granted a land concession with the right to erect the necessary buildings, to farm, and to fish in the waters from the Bay of Quinte to Georgian Bay.

The missionaries left Lachine on October 2, 1668, and, after twenty-six days of travel, reached their destination, the village of Kentio (Quinte). The mission met with early success, baptizing fifty children in its first winter. Financial assistance was provided for permanent buildings, and the rector of St. Sulpice in Paris sent out cattle, swine, and poultry. Visitors included explorers Joliet and Galinée in 1669 and La Salle in 1672.

Unfortunately, the Cayuga were reluctant to listen to the gospel and follow its teachings and this, coupled with the fact that the Cayuga wished to desert the Bay of Quinte area for more profitable hunting grounds further west, doomed the mission to failure. The chief blow to the hopes of the Sulpicians was Governor Frontenac's decision to build the first French fort at Cataraqui, and not at Quinte as had been hoped. The result was that the Montreal congregation approved the closure of the mission in March 1680, and the missionaries left the Quinte Mission soon after.

As to the exact location of this interesting, but unsuccessful, mission, it is impossible to reach a positive conclusion. The jury is still out, and there is a slim chance that it was at the mouth of the Moira River.

The Cayuga village at Kentio as it may have appeared in the mid-seventeenth century from a pen-and-ink sketch by the Reverend Bowen P. Squire, archaeologist and artist. Courtesy of Hastings County Historical Society, Reverend Bowen P. Squire Collection, HC-2018, Neg. Indian-6.

A Poet's View

ONE PERSON WHO actively promoted the view that the Indian village of Kente was at the mouth of the Moira River was Wallace Havelock Robb. The son of a prominent Canadian National Railway official, and the brother of noted inventor Morse Robb, Wallace Havelock Robb grew up on Station Street in Belleville. Moving to a picturesque site a few kilometres east of Kingston, he established Abbey Dawn, which he promoted as his "sanctuary home" and "Tourist Mecca." Here, he mounted a special bell, *Gitchi Nagamo*, which he described as the "World-famous Poet's Bell, symbol of the Bluebird of Happiness."[17] Sometimes known as "the Homer of Canadian literature," Robb studied Indian legends and lore and helped to popularize the legend of Deganawedah, the Huron Indian born to a virgin mother near Deseronto, who is regarded as the traditional founder of the Iroquois Confederacy.

Robb's research, time spent among the Mohawk of the Bay of Quinte, and poetic intuition convinced him that Kente was at the mouth of the Moira. He wrote, "Kente, the village of the far Keepers of the Flint was located at the mouth of the Sagonaska River. Time was, when the village had moved hither and yon … but now the village of Kente was at the Sagonaska."[18] In the introduction to *Thunderbird*, his historical novel of life in this area many centuries ago, Robb included a "Map of Quinte Mohawk Lore." He also sketched the layout of the village, located on the east bank of the Moira.[19] A horseshoe-shaped arrangement of lodges flanked the council fire, drum, and tree that stood in the middle of the "forum," while pine trees were in the background. Moreover, Robb went so far as to describe the presence of a Viking youth, Ron-wa-ya-na, who was a Mohawk captive. Much of the action in *Thunderbird* took place at Kente, including a potlatch-type ceremony in which O-je-kwa ("Hardwood Arrow") gave away all of his possessions through gambling games.

Although Kingston's Abbey Dawn is no more, its tradition lives on. In Yarmouth County in Nova Scotia, one-time Belleville-area resident Klaas Tuinman established Dawn Cove Abbey in 1995 as a "community in memoriam as a tribute to Abbey Dawn of Kingston," and in honour of his friend, the late Wallace Havelock Robb, a distinguished native son of Belleville.[20]

Section of a map by John Collins, deputy surveyor general, 1785, showing Great West Bay, the section of the Bay of Quinte between Carrying Place (left) and Mohawk Bay and the Napanee River (right). The Sandbanks and West Lake are shown at the south. Courtesy of Library and Archives Canada, NMC-3195.

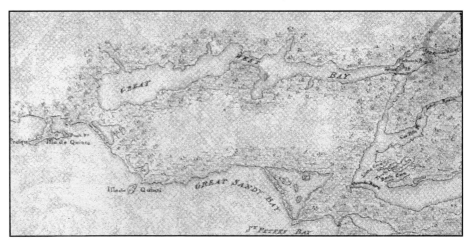

The Mississauga

AN EARLY MAP of the shores of the Bay of Quinte shows two Indian encampments near the mouth of the Moira and Salmon rivers.[21] These small settlements were created about 1700 and were evidence of the success of the Mississauga from northern Ontario in replacing the Iroquois who had occupied these lands for some time previous.

The Mississauga belonged to the Ojibwa or Chippewa group, branches of the Algonquian linguistic family, which stretched from the Atlantic seaboard to the Rocky Mountains. Unlike the Iroquoians, who relied heavily on agriculture as well as on hunting and fishing for their survival, the Mississauga relied almost exclusively on hunting and fishing. They "called themselves 'Anishinabe,' in its plural form 'Anishinabeg' — 'human beings' or … 'men par excellence.'"[22] However, the whites described those Anishinabeg living on the north shore as Mississauga. This name had been first recorded by the Jesuit fathers in 1640 to identify an Ojibwa band near the Mississagi River on the northwestern shore of Lake Huron. The change in name puzzled the Ojibwas living in the Belleville-Kingston area, who believed that it probably came from the many rivers (the Moira, Trent, and Gananoque) that flowed through their hunting territories into Lake Ontario.[23]

After the withdrawal of the French from the Quinte area in 1760, during the Seven Years War, the Mississauga made an alliance with the English. The Mississauga's reliance on European trade goods — notably iron axes, durable iron kettles, and guns — increased greatly during the American Revolution. This dependency contributed to their decision to allow their British allies to settle among them after the revolution. Britain needed land for the Loyalists, those Americans and Iroquois who had fought on the king's side and wished to remain under the British flag. Unfortunately, the Mississauga and the British viewed these land surrenders differently. There was nothing in the Mississauga tradition or experience that enabled them to imagine the private ownership of land or water by one person. They had regarded French presents "as a form of rent for the use of the land where the French posts stood and as a fee for the right to travel over their country."[24] After surrendering lands in the Quinte region to the British, the Indians regarded these surrenders "as giving only tenant status to the British, the right to use the land during good behavior."

It was Captain William Crawford, a Loyalist officer who had accompanied the Mississauga on several raids during the American Revolution, who negotiated the surrenders of the lands along the Bay of Quinte.[25] On October 9, 1783, Crawford reported that the Mississauga had surrendered the lands between the Gananoque and Trent rivers "within eight leagues from the

Royal Regiment of New York, he served in the siege of Fort Stanwix (Rome, New York) where he was wounded and taken prisoner. Local American historians link him with an alleged "act of shameful cruelty," since he is said to have encouraged his Indian allies to kill prisoners. Following two years on parole at Montreal, he joined Joseph Brant on a scouting expedition in the Mohawk Valley. His journal of that event indicates that he was "a man of some education and ability."

Following the war, Singleton occupied land in Fredericksburgh Township, where he and his brother-in-law, Israel Ferguson, became trading partners. There is strong evidence to suggest that he had a trading post near the mouth of the Sagonaska (Moira) River in the summer of 1785, thus becoming the first resident merchant. The "Hungry Year" of 1788, caused by drought and a poor crop, and complicated by severe winter weather, had disastrous consequences for Singleton. His customers were unable to make payments, forcing him to mortgage or sell land. Knowing that he was due 3,000 acres, because of his officer's allowance, he petitioned the government for 3,000 acres in Ameliasburgh Township, directly across from his trading post. Unfortunately, before the government could respond, tragedy struck. Early in September 1789, Singleton set out by bateau for Kingston to obtain trading goods and to appear as a defendant in a civil court case. En route, he was taken ill and, despite medical attention from the Tyendinaga Mohawk and a Kingston doctor, he died. His untimely death, perhaps brought on by the privations of the "Hungry Year," meant that the river and site soon took on their modern names — Moira and Belleville. No longer would they be known as Singleton's Creek and Singleton's.[1]

Captain Singleton's death was probably a factor in Captain John W. Meyers' decision to relocate from Sidney Township to the Moira River. Among all of the early settlers, Meyers is certainly the one who has attracted the most interest. Jane Bennett Goddard of Grafton, Mary Beacock Fryer of Toronto, and Connie Brummel Crook of Peterborough have all written extensively on various aspects of Meyers' life.[2] Goddard's book, *Hans Waltimeyer,* described by the author as a "monumental endeavour," is the largest and most artistically produced volume. Produced in large format as a duplication of an old record, the 545-page volume is based on a variety of sources, ranging from government documents to family anecdotes, legends, and traditions.[3] An appendix provides brief notes on many of the leading contemporary men and women. In addition to these books — both biography and historical fiction — Doug Knutson of Windswept Productions (Belleville) has spent several years working on a filmed version of Meyers' life.

All the accounts of Meyers stress two major themes: his heroic actions during the American Revolution and his role as the founder of Belleville. His principal roles in the revolutionary war were as a recruiting officer and then as a spy, gathering intelligence and carrying dispatches through hostile territory. "On each hair-raising expedition he managed to elude rebel troops" while fulfilling his mission.[4] So feared was Meyers as an enemy agent in New York State that mothers warned their children that if they were not good, Hans Waltimeyer (the Germanic name for John Meyers) would eat them up.

After the end of hostilities, Meyers spent time in Quebec and Cataraqui before moving in 1786 to what would become Sidney Township. There, he attempted, unsuccessfully, to develop a saw- and gristmill on his farm. By 1790, he had moved to land immediately east of the Mississauga Reserve near the mouth of the Moira, and, in that year, built the district's first dam and mill complex. A store and other businesses followed the saw- and gristmills, forming the nucleus of Belleville. From about 1793 until 1816, both the river and the settlement were often referred to as Meyers' Creek, although the official name for the river during the latter part of the period was the Moira (after Francis Rawdon-Hastings, the Earl of Moira) and the community often was called the "Town of Moira" or the "Village of Thurlow," until it received its present name.

Meyers had hoped to build his mill closer to the river's mouth, where there was a better site, and had worked out a 999-year lease with the Mississauga; the Indians would receive an annual payment of "one Gallon of Rum and Fifty weight of Flour." The government, however, refused to recognize the lease.[5] Petitions by his customers and neighbours also failed to persuade government.

Meyers was responsible for many "firsts" in the community. For example, he built the first brick house, on the hill overlooking his mills, from bricks baked on Meyers' land in Sidney Township. In 1801, he became the first master of the local Masonic lodge. In 1820, he chaired the meeting that led to the first county fair on October 1, 1821 and, at that fair, won three awards for livestock. Meyers was active in many other areas, including the Hastings County Militia (serving as a captain from 1798–1812), law enforcement (serving as justice of the peace from 1788 until his death), religion (helping to establish St. Thomas' Anglican Church), and politics.[6] Above all, Meyers was a successful businessman. When he died, he owned in excess of 3,000 acres of land and his estate was valued at more than £12,000.

Heritage industrial building on the site of Captain John Meyers' 1790 mills. The building was saved from demolition or conversion to a small picnic facility by members of the Quinte Construction Association who, convinced by Alderman Kay Manderville that it could be preserved and used as an office building, donated their time and materials to save the structure. Photo by author.

Even after his death, legends attached to Meyers attract interest. The most interesting one is the Legend of Meyers' Cave or Bleecker's Lost Silver Mine. The location of this site, rich in silver and originally known only to the Indians, was said to have been revealed to Captain Meyers or a member of the family shortly before his death. The site was said to have been in the vicinity of Lake Mazinaw. There are several versions of the legend and speculators have tried to determine, without success to this time, the exact location.[7]

In recent years, Meyers remains the centre of controversy. After the Ontario government erected a plaque honouring him at the entrance to Victoria Park in 1959, concerns were raised about the accuracy of some of the details. For example, it has been a family tradition that Meyers was the first slave owner in the district to free his slaves. Unfortunately, there is no documentary evidence to support this claim. As a result, in 1978, the government replaced the Meyers plaque with one commemorating the founding of Belleville. In 1990, the various parties came to agreement over the wording for a new Meyers plaque and it was erected in a very appropriate location near the site of his original mills. Following the plaque dedication, his descendants held a major banquet at which, by a vote, they determined that Meyers' middle name was Walden, not Walter or another variation. The same day, the family also dedicated a memorial at White's Cemetery near Bayside. This memorial honoured Meyers and his family, as well as the Indians and Black slaves who accompanied the Loyalists to this area after the revolution.

CAPTAIN JOHN W. MEYERS 1745-1821

Meyers gained fame as a loyalist spy during the American Revolution. He recruited soldiers, gathered intelligence and carried dispatches through enemy lines for the British army in his native New York. Exploits such as his daring attempt to capture rebel General Philip Schuyler in 1781 made "Hans Waltermeyer" a legendary figure in the folklore of the times. After the war, Meyers moved north to British territory and bought this site for a grist mill in 1789. He traded furs, ran merchant vessels, and built a sawmill, distillery, fulling mill, and inn nearby. The surrounding community became the town of Belleville in 1816. Meyers was one of many loyalists whose defeat in war led to the beginnings of permanent settlement in what is now Ontario.

Ontario Heritage Foundation, Ministry of Culture and Communications

Plaque erected to honour Captain Meyers by the Ontario Heritage Foundation, 1990. Photo by author.

One biographer summed up Meyers in this way: "What confirms the personal stature of John Walden Meyers more than anything else is one simple fact: he was so talked of in his own lifetime that even before he passed to his final rest he passed into the folklore where he lives today."[8]

Two of Captain Meyers' business competitors were the McNabb brothers — James and Simon.[9] Unlike Meyers, their stories have yet to be written in detail. However, at least one member of the McNabb clan has actively promoted the pair as very important early settlers and sought to restore their reputations.[10] Phyllis H. White of Peterborough, who married into the McNabb family, discovered that the books about Meyers by Jane Bennett Goddard and Mary Beacock Fryer were the main sources of information on the McNabbs. Further, she believed that Goddard and Fryer had rejected the McNabb family's tradition of Loyalist status and had portrayed the two youngest sons as "pariahs in the town of Belleville." Moreover, the writers had disregarded "the wealth of information available through both the usual archival sources and the early histories written by respected authors such as William Canniff…."[11] Given White's summary of documentary evidence, it will be interesting to see if Goddard and Fryer will modify their views on the McNabbs.

Like Meyers, the McNabb brothers played major roles in Belleville's development. Shortly after his arrival in Thurlow in 1803, James McNabb purchased the lot immediately west of the Mississauga Reserve and constructed a saw- and gristmill and a cloth factory. A bakery soon followed. The McNabb brothers carried on an extensive lumbering and trading business and shipped such goods as fur, potash, and lumber to European markets. In 1810, the brothers dissolved their shipping partnership. Simon continued with his commercial activities and was also named the first postmaster at Belleville and collector of customs at the mouth of the Moira in 1816. These appointments were probably facilitated by James "focusing his interests on political and civic areas."[12] In addition to serving as a magistrate, James represented Hastings in the Legislative Assembly from 1808–12, and Hastings and Ameliasburgh Township from 1816–20.

It is interesting to observe that there were examples of co-operation between the McNabb brothers and Meyers. The notable exception was a serious conflict that arose from the War of 1812–14 and resulted in a petition asking government not to grant any further "honours" to Meyers, whom, they and other citizens alleged, had betrayed the Crown.

The Chisholm-McDougall House on Dundas Street West is perhaps the oldest surviving home in Belleville, probably dating from the 1790s. Unfortunately, the Wilmot Plan of 1816, which showed and dated early buildings, did not extend beyond the original town boundaries. Courtesy of Library and Archives Canada, PA-26837.

Yet another successful Belleville storekeeper was William Bell, who opened a small store on or about September 7, 1787, and introduced apple trees to the Belleville area in 1791.[13] Other important early settlers were Doctor Seth Meacham, the first physician, who arrived about 1801; storekeeper Captain John McIntosh; and blacksmith Roswell Leavens. These were a few of the enterprising people who began the process of establishing a thriving community at the mouth of the Moira.

The Illustrious Mrs. Simpson[14]

MARGARET SIMPSON WAS Belleville's first successful businesswoman. She was the first woman to be issued a tavern licence by the magistrates of the Midland District, which made her one of the leading businesswomen in the Quinte area, since the district included four counties: Frontenac, Lennox and Addington, Prince Edward, and Hastings.

Born in Scotland, Margaret and her first husband, John Russell, arrived at Kingston in 1791. John died soon after their arrival, leaving his widow to tend four children. On November 14, 1793, she married widower James Simpson and the couple and their children moved to Meyers' Creek in 1797, almost twenty years before the town plan for Belleville was laid out. The Mississauga granted them permission to reside on the east bank of the Moira, for which they paid the Mississauga an annual rent. On land near the corner of the present Dundas and Front streets, the Simpsons built a 12 x 20–foot log house in which they also kept a tavern. The log shanty, one of the earliest in the community, had no floor. Mrs. William Ketcheson, an early visitor who stayed there overnight, noted that Simpson had a barrel of beer in the middle of the house. Apparently he sat by the barrel all night, drinking and singing. The brew was said to be home-brewed, but certainly intoxicating.[15] Within a short time, a number of breweries and distilleries had commenced operations and begun to supply the tavern's needs. For example, William Bell's account book for 1806 showed that he sold several gallons of whisky at five shillings a gallon, certainly a bargain price compared to 2008.[16]

Two years after their arrival, the Simpsons built a framed house and, the following year, a framed stable, both with Indian permission. Unfortunately, James died in July 1802 and Margaret, with the help of her children, was left to carry on the business for twenty years, possibly with the help of a female slave. According to Alexander Oliphant Petrie, who arrived in 1809, Abraham Cronk of Sophiasburgh Township purchased a slave from Mrs. Simpson. However, after a period of time "she returned to Mrs. Simpson, with whom she lived till her death."[17]

After surveyor Samuel Wilmot laid out the town plot in 1816, Margaret was among the first to petition the government for title to her land. As required by law, she had a valid claim through her lease arrangements with the Indians and the erection of several buildings, one of which was "a Potashery."[18] This business was located on the water lot in front of her house, beside the Moira, considered one of the best of sites for such a business. The potashery converted ashes obtained from farmers (who burned the forests they cleared for cultivation) into soap and potash.

It is apparent from her correspondence that Margaret had a very limited education. Her written English was poor. However, as Belleville surveyor/historian Tom Ransom pointed out,

"Margaret's spelling and grammar, though considered poor today, were remarkable in her time, when few men and almost no women could read and write."[19]

Her written English was not a handicap when it came to running a successful business. Her tavern was the economic, political, military, social, and political centre for the community. Magistrate William Bell generally held his Court of Requests at the inn. Political meetings and discussions were frequent, and petitions for signatures were available from time to time. The militia trained on the adjacent Wallbridge's Common, and errant militiamen faced court martial in the inn. The Masons held their first local meeting in the tavern in 1801. According to one account, the inn was the meeting site where the settlers decided to name the community after Bella Gore, wife of Lieutenant-Governor Francis Gore. Moreover, Margaret's stables housed horses for travellers. More than once, her generosity was noted in the Kingston press. For example, on April 23, 1819, the *Kingston Gazette,* in reporting the death at Belleville of William King, a shipwright, noted: "Much praise is due to Mrs. Margaret Simpson of Belleville, and her family, for the kindness and attention manifested in this poor man in her house whilst sick, and the decent manner in which the funeral was conducted at her own expense."

Many years later, James Bickford of Oswego reminisced in the *Intelligencer:* "I arrived in Belleville in August 1818, put up at Mother Simpson's Hotel, where I found her two sons, John and George, who soon introduced me into 'society,' not exactly composed of that element I should not seek, but I will say I was always treated kindly by people in Belleville and by John and George in particular."[20] Unfortunately, not all visitors were as pleased.

Hugh Judge, a Quaker missionary, passed through Belleville in 1799 and spent a night at Simpson's Tavern, but was not happy with the accommodation. No doubt his objections were caused "by the horror of the loud sounds of pioneer joviality coming from the tap room as the local settlers enjoyed the inn's celebrated spirits."[21]

Margaret seems to have favoured Canadian and British visitors over American ones. Her grandson, Charles, later recalled that his grandmother had a looking glass with a bird on top of it. She

Margaret Simpson's Tavern, southeast corner of Front and Dundas streets, centre of social life in early Belleville. Courtesy of Hastings County Historical Society, HC-2529.

didn't know what kind of bird it was until one day a visitor asked her why she had the eagle, a symbol of the United States, on the mirror. Immediately, she got up and broke off the eagle. "She was such an awful Britisher, you know."[22]

About 1820, Margaret and her son John built the impressive inn on the northeast corner of Front and Dundas streets. They chose Asa Yeomans as the carpenter to build this hotel in the neo-classical style popular for years in the United States, but just beginning to be accepted in Canada, where it is known as the Loyalist style. Even the most sophisticated traveller must have been impressed by the carpentry skill displayed on the front doors — especially the southern door which led into the inn. The northern door was plainer and, no doubt, was the entrance to the tap room. "The stark white clapboard inn dominated the Moira River from its site on the corner of the Dundas Road. It was ideally situated to catch travellers arriving either by boat or by coach."[23] Only five years later, in 1825, John Simpson sold the inn to William Wallbridge for the modest price of £113. Wallbridge turned it into the private residence that was known as the Wallbridge home throughout most of the nineteenth century. In the twentieth century, the structure was the site of several businesses, including one of the first Canadian Tire stores in the 1930s. The structure finally fell into disrepair and was demolished in 1973.

Towards the end of her life, Margaret sold her tavern and property to her other son, George. The precise dates and facts surrounding her birth and death remain a mystery. "She seems to have simply disappeared into the mists of history. However, these factual details are not as important as the contributions she made to the foundation of the community in which she lived, worked and prospered."[24] Despite the tragedy of losing two husbands within the space of a few years and being forced to look after six children as a single mother, Margaret Simpson had persevered to become "an outstanding and respected businesswoman in the community."[25]

Mrs. Simpson's Inn, northeast corner of Front and Dundas streets, built circa 1820 and later known as the Wallbridge House. Courtesy of Hastings County Historical Society, Mika Collection.

War with the Yankees, 1812

THE COMMUNITY AT the mouth of the Moira began a proud military tradition with the setting up of the Hastings County Militia in 1800. Headquartered at Simpson's Tavern, the volunteers met at Wallbridge's Common every other Saturday for "platoon exercises." Because of limited government aid, the officers had to purchase their own uniforms. The coats were red with blue facings, yellow buttons, and white linings.[26] But with the approach of war, General Isaac Brock advised the officers to forsake their newly purchased uniforms on the field and to dress like the men in order "to avoid the bad consequence of a conspicuous Dress."[27] Brock also appointed three loyal citizens in Thurlow to limit "seditious attempts or designs to disturb the tranquility of the province." They were to keep a sharp eye out for spies and to report the presence of any aliens.[28]

The local militia responded well following the outbreak of war in June 1812. Whole families turned out for service and some local militia members served at Kingston, an important military town and a likely target for American invaders, until March 17, 1813. The following year, a renewed threat of American attack led some two hundred militia members under Captain John McIntosh to return to Kingston's Fort Henry. For the most part, however, the local militia was used to help move supplies to Queenston Heights and other threatened areas.

Unfortunately the prolonged absence from home, strict military discipline, and a loss of interest in the war by the end of 1813 made it difficult to raise forces. There were serious problems. Of the two hundred local men assigned to guard Fort Henry, forty-two deserted in a single month, not a proud record.[29] In addition, there were desertions at other times and several courts martial.

Even Captain John Meyers, one of the king's most loyal subjects, was disturbed by some events. Members of the Commissariat Department were using their powers of confiscation to seize articles at "fair valuation" when the owners held out for market prices or refused to sell produce. Meyers, it was alleged, had refused to sell supplies to the Kingston garrison at a reasonable price. He was also said to have taken his pleasure sleigh apart and hidden the pieces so the army could not requisition it. In addition, instructed to take a wagonload of supplies from Belleville to York (Toronto), he apparently unhitched his team at Brighton and returned to Belleville.[30] Given the condition of the roads, the bone-jarring wagons, and the fact that he was over sixty-eight years of age, it was no wonder he did not fulfill the mission.

The final blow to Meyers' enthusiasm for the war came on April 4, 1814, when he and his wife were billeting four dragoons in their home. The four helped themselves to Meyers' liquor and became troublesome. Two went to the bedroom, where Meyers and his wife lay very ill, and demanded provisions to which they were not entitled. Drawing a pistol, Meyers told them to leave the room, which they did. Meyers bolted the door, but the pair returned, armed with pistols, and broke it down. When Meyers' attempt to scare them off by firing a pistol failed, one soldier attacked Meyers with a sword, swearing that he would cut off Meyers' head. The captain's head was cut, both he and his wife were bruised by clubs, and another occupant of the house suffered a severe head wound. Only the arrival of a sober dragoon corporal saved the trio from further injury, and the drunken dragoons were disarmed and placed in custody.[31]

Throughout the war, Belleville was an important centre on the supply route between Kingston and York. The presence of American naval vessels on Lake Ontario made it necessary for goods to be shipped via the Bay of Quinte and Carrying Place, at the head of the Bay of Quinte, where the boats were hauled across wooden rollers to Brighton Bay on Lake Ontario. No doubt many of the boats stopped at Belleville. In addition, James and Simon McNabb made arrangements for the purchase and shipping of Hastings County products to the government troops at Kingston. These articles included pork, flour, beef, whisky, shingles, and square timber.[32]

The War of 1812 affected the local population. Immediately after the declaration of war, twenty men from the county, including a few from Belleville, moved to the United States.[33] Presumably, many were recent immigrants who sympathized with the Americans. At the end of the war, forty-seven disbanded soldiers from the Glengarry Light Infantry Fencibles received land grants in Thurlow. Prominent among these arrivals were the family names of Bowen, Maybe, Reynolds, and Wellbanks.[34] In these and other ways, the War of 1812 affected the settlers at the mouth of the Moira.

Captain John W. Meyers built one of the earliest brick houses in the province on the hill overlooking his mills. It was in this house that Meyers and his wife were assaulted during the War of 1812. Author Wilma Alexander has used the house and its locale for her children's book Old Coach Road *(1987). The house is shown in a photograph taken after a fire in the 1870s. Courtesy of Hastings County Historical Society.*

Land for a Town

FOR A QUARTER of a century after the first Loyalists arrived in the Belleville area, the land in the heart of the present city was reserved for the Mississauga. They are said to have wintered on this 428-acre reserve, ascending the Moira River to Stoco Lake every spring to hunt and fish. Each year, a canoe from Kingston brought the Mississauga presents of blankets, cloth, guns, and kettles as partial payment for surrendering lands along the Bay of Quinte to the British government.[35] Efforts by Captain John Meyers and others to persuade the government to have the land made available for mills and a town site were unsuccessful, although the Mississauga did allow white settlers to rent land and erect buildings.

The situation changed after the provincial surveyor general advised the lieutenant-governor that the amount of land set aside for the Indian burying ground "was a preposterous quantity for the said purpose" and that the time seemed "to be proper for a Town" at the mouth of the Moira.[36] In September 1811, the surveyor general submitted (in quadruplicate) plans for the purchase of the reserve and for the survey of the proposed town.[37] Unfortunately, the War of 1812 interrupted the process.[38] But the process resumed following the war, and Lieutenant-Governor Francis Gore ordered the purchase of the 428-acre reserve from the Mississauga. This took place on August 5, 1816.[39] Like many other treaties and "surrenders," there have been concerns about the validity of this one. As recently as the early 1990s, Mississauga land researchers carefully examined this treaty, which involved the heart of present-day Belleville. Presumably, the researchers found the treaty had been negotiated properly.

A Surveyor and His Problems, 1816

ONCE THE GOVERNMENT had decided to allow a town at the mouth of the Moira River, the next step was to complete a survey. Accordingly, the surveyor general appointed Surveyor Samuel Street Wilmot to carry out the work. He and his survey team were on site from March 2 to April 28, 1816, and his bill came to £134.12.6.[40] The survey included the entire lot 4 in the first concession of Thurlow Township, however, only the southern section of the lot was divided into town lots. The boundaries of the section for town lots were the Bay of Quinte on the south, the Moira River on the north, Front Street on the west, and Rear Street (of which only the northern section, Hillcrest Avenue, remains) on the east. It is interesting that the land between the west side of Front Street and the Moira was not included in the village; it was part of lot 3 and was already allocated to other early settlers.

Wilmot encountered many problems. His journal records that even before he began the actual survey, his five-man party was plagued by heavy rains and bitter cold on the trip from Oshawa. The men suffered from frozen feet. Bad roads limited progress to twenty miles a day. After his arrival locally, he complained that it was very difficult to get provisions. He had to pay $28 per hundredweight for pork and this price soon rose to $30. Within the month, there was no pork available at any price. Wilmot's party camped on land just east of the area to be surveyed, and when the owner, John Taylor, complained about him trespassing, Wilmot had to rent a house for five shillings per week.

Poor weather continually interrupted his work. Snow and extreme cold caused delays on several days and the men had to spend time cutting firewood to make themselves comfortable.

Moreover, although earlier surveyors such as Louis Kotte had plotted the southern concessions of Thurlow and Sidney townships in 1787, Wilmot's men could find little remaining evidence of their survey stakes. Wilmot was almost convinced that "persons of vile principles" had tampered with the earlier survey markers. He was particularly suspicious of Captain John Meyers' work as an amateur surveyor and thought that Meyers might have altered the boundary markers in order to obtain a better site for his mills.

If Wilmot was unhappy with the work of earlier surveyors — both professional and amateur — it is equally true that not everyone was happy with his work. One of those who approved was Thomas Coleman, an important landholder on the west bank of the river. Wilmot's relocation of the Thurlow-Sidney boundary gave Coleman a good strip of land on the east bank of the river — all of the land west of Front Street. On the other hand, John Taylor, who owned land east of the proposed village, lost a sixty-foot strip and Captain John Meyers was threatened with the loss of his mill dam, fulling mill, and a dwelling because of the altered boundary. These parties complained to the provincial government, and surveyor Henry Smith was sent to Belleville. He was critical of Wilmot's survey, believing that it would be the "source of a great deal of mischief by Litigation." The government dispatched another surveyor, William Chewett, and he recommended that yet a fourth surveyor should look at the site. However, by this point the government wanted the whole matter ended. After Wilmot confirmed his work, the surveyor general accepted his plan and ordered that John Taylor be given the land he believed had been unjustly taken from him and that Captain Meyers be granted the buildings he had erected on the reserve.

Partway through his survey, Wilmot faced a problem that was to remain a serious threat for generations to come. On March 26, he wrote in his journal that the river had overflowed its eastern bank and forced the surveyors to higher ground. This was the first record of the "Mighty Moira" flooding at Belleville. It would not be the last.

Wilmot's Plan, 1816

FEW MUNICIPALITIES IN Canada are fortunate enough to have such a detailed early plan as Wilmot's plan for Belleville, dated April 24, 1816. It showed not only the proposed layout for streets and lots, but also the locations of existing paths and forty-five buildings. Moreover, for each building, an accompanying list indicated its purpose, type of construction, owner's name, and how the owner came to construct the building on land reserved for the exclusive use of the Mississauga. In short, it was a census of the community.[41]

All the buildings had initially been erected with the permission of the Mississauga, and other early records indicate that the settlers made annual rental payments to them for this privilege. The oldest structure standing in 1816 was a frame house belonging to James Harris. It stood on the west side of Rear Street, midway between Dundas and Bridge streets. Martha McIntosh, widow of John McIntosh, owned the largest number of buildings, five in all. Her buildings were the most southerly, at the intersection of Front and Wharf (now St. Paul's) streets, and included a log house (1799), a distillery (1801), a frame house (1806), a storehouse (1808), and a barn (1810). Two of them, the frame house and the storehouse, had been obtained from Israel Ferguson, an earlier trader at the mouth of the Moira, and the newest one, the barn, had been built with "Indian permission." Businesses included Roswell Leavens' store and blacksmith shop, Pennel Selden's hatters shop, Thomas Coleman's blacksmith shop, Allan Taylor's store, and Captain Meyers' distillery. There were four stables and, in at least two of these cases, the accompanying "houses" were actually hotels and/or taverns. For example, Margaret Simpson operated a hotel near the corner of Front and Dundas streets and John Everett had a major hotel at the corner of Front and Hotel streets.

Presumably acting on the advice of local citizens, Wilmot suggested reasonable names for all the streets. Front and Rear streets were the front and back of the town. Dundas took its name from the surveyor who had laid out this road, which ran east from York (Toronto) to the eastern sections of Upper Canada and passed through Belleville. Bridge and Wharf (now St. Paul) streets were named for these structures. Pinnacle Street got its name from the high pinnacle of sand that stretched from behind the present County Administration Building almost to the Moira. Mill Street ran from Front Street to Meyers' mills, just east of the village.

Hotel Street was also aptly named. When the street and lot patterns were laid out, John Everett's large and imposing hotel (1809), apparently the largest building in town, stood in the middle of the new road allowance. However, it also stood at the junction of three existing roads, one of which went in a northeasterly direction and climbed the hill to Captain Meyers' impressive house on what is now Mount Pleasant Road. Rather than move the hotel, Wilmot and the citizens apparently decided to move that section of Hotel Street between Front and Pinnacle streets slightly to the south. This resulted in a jog in Hotel Street. This was not an issue for pedestrians or horses in 1816, but later became a serious problem for cars and trucks. Despite efforts to lessen this jog by several (village, town, and city) councils over the years, it remains an inconvenience and potential hazard, particularly for vehicles travelling east or

Section of Wilmot's 1816 plan showing the problem created by the location of Everett's hotel. The hotel was in the middle of Hotel Street (Victoria Avenue). Everett's brewery and Coleman's grist- and sawmills were on the west side of Front Street and, therefore, outside the town. Wilmot's map reproduced by the Hastings County Historical Society, 1967.

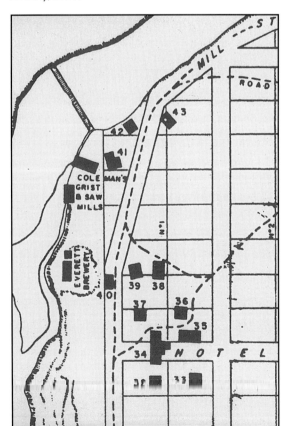

west along Victoria Avenue and attempting to make left turns onto Pinnacle Street.

Fortunately, although a few other buildings were located on street allowances, especially along Front Street south of Dundas Street, most of them did not create major problems for citizens. The exception was Thomas Coleman's log blacksmith shop (1808), which stood on the street allowance near the north end of Front Street, adjacent to his house and mills. Coleman, who had recently purchased the shop from James McNabb, was agreeable to moving it. After all, Coleman was pleased that Wilmot's survey had guaranteed him land on the east bank of the river, and moving the blacksmith shop was a minor inconvenience. Moreover, Wilmot had curved the north end of Front Street in such a way that Thomas Coleman's new house (1815) did not have to be moved.

In addition, Wilmot's plan showed that there were several major businesses just outside the new town's boundaries. To the east, Captain Meyers had his mills and store. To the west, but still on the east bank of the Moira, Thomas Coleman had grist- and sawmills (adjacent to his home) and John Everett, the hotel owner, had a large brewery. Certainly, the residents of the new town were well-supplied with alcoholic beverages by Everett's brewery and distilleries, operated by Martha McIntosh and John Meyers.

Although Wilmot was to survey only lot 4, the former Mississauga Reserve, there was extensive development on the outskirts. The following year, a report identified and described each Thurlow lot along the front. For example, lot 5 (immediately to the east and including the present John, George, William, and Ann streets) was described as having excellent buildings, mills, and orchards owned by John Taylor, James Harris, and John W. Meyers.[42]

Perhaps surprisingly, Wilmot did not estimate the size of the population. However, it may have been about 150, which meant that Belleville was smaller than the Mohawk community near the present town of Deseronto. As late as 1824, Belleville's population was estimated at less than five hundred, whereas in 1829 it had increased to seven hundred, and in 1835 Thomas Rolph placed the population at about eighteen hundred.[43]

What's In a Name?

AN AIR OF uncertainty and mystery surrounds the way in which the new community at the mouth of the Moira River was named in 1816. At least three theories have been advanced. Initially, the editor of the town's closest newspaper, the *Kingston Gazette,* felt that the name was derived from the French *belle ville,* because of the "very pleasant situation of that town."[44] Then, two weeks later, the *Gazette* announced that it had erred and issued a correction. According to the new explanation, the lieutenant-governor-in-council had been pleased to name the town in honour of his wife, Annabella (often known as Bella), "at the request and petition of a great number of the inhabitants of that town, and the township of Thurlow."[45] This explanation was later popularized by the *Intelligencer* and historians William Canniff and W.C. Mikel. According to these sources, Lieutenant-Governor Gore and Bella had stayed a night at Meyers' Creek. Feeling very loyal, the principal men of the village then met at Mrs. Simpson's Tavern and drew up a petition to Gore asking that he honour their request to name the town after his wife. Unfortunately, there are at least three problems with this explanation: There is no record in Gore's journals concerning a visit in 1816. There is no surviving petition.[46] And all the early accounts indicate that James and Simon McNabb, Captain Meyers' chief rivals and the leaders in the movement to have the name changed from Meyers' Creek to "Bellville," were close friends of prominent local teacher and merchant William Bell. In fact, Bell signed the petition asking government to remove Meyers' name from the community.

No doubt the issue of the name change met with opposition, particularly from friends of Captain Meyers, who felt that Meyers deserved to have his name attached to the community. After all, he had established the first mills and other businesses. As a result, two years later, James McNabb, the local member of the Upper Canada Legislative Assembly, announced that he would introduce a bill "to establish and confirm the names of the new towns of Brockville, Belleville, and Toronto."[47] The proposed bill was never introduced, possibly because the government considered Gore's decision in 1816 to be sufficient, even though Gore may have acted on his own and not on the advice of his councillors.

Part of the original communion set purchased by St. Andrew's Presbyterian Church, showing clearly the town's original spelling as "Bellville" and the date 1836. Courtesy of St. Andrew's Presbyterian Church.

Whether Belleville was named after William Bell is uncertain. What is certain is that the original spelling was *Bellville* without the middle *e* and that this *e*-less spelling was accepted for the next twenty years. However, by the late 1830s Belleville had become the accepted spelling. Unfortunately, the reason for dropping the middle *e* remains a mystery.

The Mighty Moira

THE MOIRA RIVER has been a mixed blessing for the residents of Belleville. Certainly, it powered the early saw- and gristmills, provided an economical way to move logs to the lumber mills at its mouth, and offered recreational opportunities. At the same time, the Moira's periodic floods have been a challenge. The earliest written reference to flooding was in the field notes of surveyor Samuel Wilmot. While preparing the original survey for the proposed town at the mouth of the Moira on March 26, 1816, he wrote that the river had overflowed its eastern bank. His surveying party was forced to move to higher ground.

This was the first, but not the last, record of flooding. For the past two centuries, local newspapers have recorded a series of floods, and the archives of the Hastings County Historical Society contain hundreds of flood pictures taken by professional and amateur photographers, all anxious to record the power of nature.

The first detailed study of historical flooding at Belleville is found in the *1950 Moira Valley Conservation Report*.[48] Architectural historian Verschoyle V. Blake conducted extensive research and made use of newspaper files and pictures from the *Intelligencer* as well as flood pictures from city engineer Charles Mott. Blake identified major floods in 1864, 1865, 1868, 1870, 1885, 1886, 1918, and 1936, and lesser floods in many other years. In fact, he found that flooding had occurred on so many occasions that the residents near the mouth of the river had come to expect it on an almost annual basis. Although some people might wonder why there had been so much settlement in the flood plain, he credited it to the fact that "land by the harbour and along the river was too valuable to leave vacant."[49]

Noted Canadian author Susanna Moodie wrote about the floods she witnessed after her arrival in Belleville in 1838. In fact, she devoted almost eight pages to Belleville floods in her 1853 book *Life in the Clearings*.[50] She waxed poetic as she described the actions of the ice and water in the March 1844 flood:

> The river roars and rages like a chafed lion; and frets and foams against its rocky barrier, as if determined to overcome every obstacle that dares to impede its furious course. Great blocks of ice are seen popping up and down in the boiling surges; and unwieldy saw logs perform the most extravagant capers, often starting bolt upright; while their crystal neighbours ... tumble about in the current like mad monsters of the deep.[51]

She then described the efforts to break up the ice jams and the heroic rescue of a blacksmith who had been attempting to cut up the ice blocks threatening the Lower Bridge when the piece he was standing on gave way. He was saved by his brother, also a blacksmith.

The 1852 flood left a lasting impression on Moodie. In humorous fashion, she described a poor cow "who was leisurely pacing over to her shed and supper" when she was suddenly precipitated "into the din of waters." The cow belonged to a poor Irishman, and the crowd was sympathetic. Keeping her head above water, the cow navigated over two dams and finally came ashore at the lower end of Front Street.

Less fortunate was "a little black boy, the only son of a worthy negro who had been a settler for many years in Belleville."[52] A white boy had pushed him, apparently accidentally, from the broken bridge. It was many weeks before his body was found, some miles down the bay. Moodie could empathize with the father, because she too had lost "a fine talented boy of six years — one to whom her soul clave — in those cruel waters."[53] She felt that "this river Moira had caused more tears to flow from the eyes of heart-broken parents than any stream of the like size in the province." The majority of deaths and injuries had come during the log-driving season, when children as young as five or six years old could be seen riding a sawlog down the river.

Many of these floods seriously interfered with the community's business. The first two wooden bridges had been destroyed by ice, and this trouble was chronic until much stronger bridges were built. Even then, there were problems. Blake suggested that it was possible that the building of stronger bridges after 1855 "increased the tendency of the ice to jam and dam back the water. The old wooden bridges were easily carried out by the jams but the newer ones held back the ice even before it was stopped by the Bay ice."[54] Indeed, the 1868 flood entirely swept away the iron Upper (Front Street) Bridge and the piers of the Lower (Bridge Street) Bridge were also destroyed, making it unsafe for traffic, though it still stood.

Belleville's frequent floods received much local press, but even Toronto papers covered the major ones. For example, the *Toronto Leader* of March 16, 1864, provided colourful front-page coverage. The reporter described how the river ice gave way on the night of March 12 after a heavy rainfall and jammed near the Lower Bridge, flooding adjacent buildings and drowning some cattle. The next day, the ice moved on, bending the iron bridge and sweeping away everything in its path. It jammed again near the river's mouth. Water backed up for a quarter of a mile. Buildings in West Belleville were surrounded and cellars of East Bank buildings flooded. Meanwhile, another jam had developed, eight to ten feet high above the water, at the Grand Trunk Railway (now CNR) bridge at the north end of town. Water and ice covered several acres and, when the jam broke in the late afternoon on March 14, the rush carried everything before it:

The remains of Lazier's Dam, just south of the Quinte Sports Centre, is evidence of the early usage of the Moira to power mills. In 2008, just south of this site, work was scheduled to be completed to harness the water to generate electric power. Photo by author, 2006.

> A mass of ice, broken into cakes of from four feet square to twenty feet, came rushing down the rapid river, whose waters had been swollen to twice their extent by the freshet, tumbling over the dams, tearing away sheds and other outbuildings … every moment increasing in velocity and bulk, now and then a huge cake lifted bodily up on its end to the height of fifteen or twenty feet, and then falling on the moving mass, breaking into a hundred pieces. Again a stick of timber shooting its full length and coming down with a crash, the whole mass, ice, timber and the debris of ruined buildings came sweeping on, and as it neared the lower bridge not one in a hundred thought it would withstand it.

Indeed, the ice did damage the Lower Bridge, but it remained in place. When the ice reached the harbour, it piled up to "twenty or thirty feet" high. Unfortunately, the flood the following year (1865), as well as surrounding eighty houses with from two to four feet of water, did carry the iron Lower Bridge with it.

The flood of April 1885 was noteworthy because of the number of factories and businesses that it affected. A blacksmith shoeing a horse was interrupted by the water "pouring in both doors of the shop" and had to wade out.[55] All the low ground south of West Bridge Street was flooded as far as the West Hill (usually known as Murney's Hill because politician Edmund Murney's residence was at its top). Fifty families were driven from their homes.

The following year, nearly 1,000 people were forced to leave their homes for periods of from two to six weeks in bitter weather. City council appropriated $300 for blasting the ice and an equal sum for the relief of flood sufferers. The ice problem began after a thaw in early January and it was not until March 8 that Belleville was completely free from ice and water. For fifty-seven days, Belleville had been more or less flooded. The west side had been particularly hard hit, but even on the east side there was considerable flooding and the water had reached the north side of Market Square.

"The flood of 1886 was probably the most remarkable which has ever occurred on the Moira…."[56] Like most major Moira floods in the nineteenth century, it had been caused by heavy rains in the watershed in the late fall of 1885, followed by cold weather and a thaw with rain in January. The heavy rain had fallen on ground frozen, covered with deep snow, or saturated by recent rain, leading to severe freshets, or river overflows. This problem was made worse by the fact that the Moira flows into a landlocked bay that freezes over to a considerable depth.

The steep fall of the river in northern Belleville further complicated the picture, and contributed to the formation of frazil ice (spongy masses of ice). This produced a fast current that prevented sheet ice from forming. However, very low temperatures caused the formation of frazil ice as the

The flood of 1885 left large blocks of ice on West Bridge Street and elsewhere on the west bank of the Moira River. Courtesy of Hastings County Historical Society, Mika Collection, Neg. B-19.

fast, supercooled water carried ice crystals from the surface, preventing the formation of sheet ice.

Exactly fifty years later, in March 1936, a comparable flood to that of 1886 occurred. Rain began on March 11 and lasted twenty hours. The ice at the Cannifton Dam moved out and took with it the ice from Lazier's Dam and two other dams, until the mass reached the bay, where it was blocked by the bay ice and the CPR Bridge. Blasting at the bridge failed to open a clear channel, and seventy-five acres of the city were flooded. Boats were used in rescue work on the main street, where the water was up to seven feet deep. Electricity was cut off and a milk shortage developed. The late Eugene Lang, whose amazing and vivid memory of historic events has enlivened many discussions, recalled that the 1936 flood dropped the footbridge (at the foot of Catharine Street) to the riverbed. For the convenience of students from the West Hill who attended Belleville Collegiate Institute (BCIVS) on the East Hill, the city built steps at each end of the fallen footbridge so that students (and other residents) could continue to take this shortcut.

The drama and excitement of the 1936 flood formed the basis of an entertaining 1991 book by author Wilma Alexander. A native of Belleville, Alexander wrote *And the Boats Go Up and Down* for children aged eight to twelve.[57] The story centres around a group of modern-day youngsters who are suddenly transported back to Belleville on the eve of the 1936 flood. Will they be able to warn the citizens in time? The reader relives what it would have been like to live through the devastating flood.

Since 1936, there have been occasional floods, but nothing like those of 1885, 1886, and 1936. Nevertheless, on one occasion a few years ago, a blockage at the Lower Bridge caused the river to rise suddenly and left cars bobbing in the South Riverside Parking Lot.

Belleville councils have tried many remedies to deal with flooding. In the early years, workers were hired to attempt to cut channels from the lighthouse to the Lower Bridge.

Blasting was tried on several occasions. In 1886, the city brought in a federal government hydrographical engineer as a consultant. He suggested the closing of the "east channel" at the mouth of the river, which was done later. In addition, flood control measures on the river above Belleville might be of value.

Partly as a result of these floods, the Moira River Conservation Authority (MRCA) was formed on July 31, 1947, and in 1984 the province identified the MRCA as the lead agency in protecting lives and property from flooding in the 3,000-square-kilometre watershed. This responsibility became part of the mandate of Quinte Conservation in 1995 with the amalgamation of three local conservation authorities (Moira River, Prince Edward Region, and Napanee Region) to form Quinte Conservation.

Under the conservation authority's leadership, a series of ice-control dams were constructed at the north end of Belleville late in the twentieth century. Not only have these dams helped to prevent large blocks of ice from coming down the river and amassing at the mouth, but the most southerly one is being modified to provide electric power and raise revenue. Unfortunately, these dams do not prevent frazil ice from forming and, in fact, may help create it as the water goes over the dams, passes through the very cold air, becomes supercooled, and turns into frazil ice.

City council continues to try various methods of dealing with this ice at the mouth of the river. To maintain a channel into the bay, heavy equipment removes the ice and stores it in the adjacent Victoria Park. Most recently, the tugboat *A.L. Killaly* has been based at Belleville during the winter months to help maintain an open channel. In January 2008, a consultant with BMT Fleet Technology, based in Kanata, applauded the city's approach of using dams along the Moira and a tugboat to forge a path for the ice to move out into the bay. He told the *Intelligencer,* "There is no such thing as a 100 percent solution to frazil ice. That's why an ice boom or a dam is your typical solution to frazil ice." Hopefully, these techniques will serve to eliminate, or at least lessen, the likelihood of further floods on the Mighty Moira.

Early Education, 1790–1840

Who was Belleville's first teacher? Was it James Potter, who is said to have taught school near the mouth of the Moira River in 1807 or 1808? Was it a man by the name of Leslie, who may have taught school somewhat earlier? Was it a Presbyterian minister by the name of Wright, who taught school near Mrs. Simpson's Tavern? Was it John Watkins, who taught in

1810 in a little frame schoolhouse just south of the present market? These four suggestions come from Doctor William Canniff (1830–1910), a native of Thurlow Township and a very prominent historian who interviewed Belleville's early settlers in the mid-nineteenth century as background to his monumental history *Settlement of Upper Canada* (1869).[58]

Yet another possibility was William Bell, a sergeant in the 53rd Regiment during the American Revolution who came to Canada shortly after peace was declared and settled near the mouth of the Moira. As early as 1790, Bell had opened a local store before moving in 1796 to Tyendinaga, where he became the second schoolmaster to the Mohawk of the Bay of Quinte. He succeeded John Binninger, who had taught the Mohawk from 1792–95, thereby becoming Hastings County's first schoolteacher. Bell returned to Belleville when the Mohawk school closed due to a lack of students. It has been suggested that he may have taught students at the back of his Belleville store.

Whoever the first teacher at Belleville was, it is certain that he had no teacher training. Occasionally, in larger centres such as Kingston, a minister with a college background might open a school; however, that was not the case in Belleville. Historian William Canniff wrote that the earliest teachers tended to be "such members of the family as were physically incapable of doing hard manual labor, without any regard to their natural or acquired capabilities." One of Canniff's early teachers in Thurlow Township in the late 1830s was a teacher "whose sole qualification to teach consisted in his lameness." This tendency, said to be of "Yankee origin," had the effect of "preventing men of education for a long time, from engaging in the duties of this profession."[59]

What is also certain is that the early local settlers valued education. Canniff interviewed local settlers who recalled receiving basic education from their mothers. One of the principal books used was the Bible. In addition, children of Loyalists who had migrated northward after the American Revolution would learn of the "happy lives people led under British laws and protection previous to the outbreak."[60] For the Loyalists, there was a distrust of American teachers and textbooks, a distrust reinforced by the War of 1812.

Exactly when the first school was built in Belleville is unclear. However, it was prior to April 24, 1816 because a "School House" is clearly marked as one of the forty-five buildings on Samuel Wilmot's original plan of the town. It was located on the west side of Pinnacle Street, halfway between Bridge and Dundas streets. The same year, the government of Upper Canada took steps to encourage education. It became legal for the inhabitants of a community to start "common" or elementary schools. The government would make small grants available to school boards, provided the school section could promise at least twenty pupils and the local residents could obtain and help pay for a teacher, who had to be a British subject.

Accordingly, the inhabitants of Belleville met on October 17, 1816, to select a board. John Hubbard was appointed secretary and Simon McNabb, John Reynolds, and John Taylor were appointed as trustees. The trustees then appointed Henry H. Ansley as teacher.[61] Ansley did not remain long. Within the year, he was replaced by Mrs. Mary Ann Hill, the only female teacher in any of the thirty-two schools in the Midland District.[62] Fees were ten shillings per quarter, said to be the lowest of any area in the province, and somewhat lower than a blacksmith would receive.[63]

This school, with twenty-one students, and one on the first concession of Sidney Township, with thirty-three students, were the only two common schools in Hastings County in 1816–17. Their students studied literature, reading, writing, arithmetic, and English grammar. From Kingston, the Midland District Board of Education kept a watchful eye on the local schools, commenting in 1817 that the "use of Webster's Spelling Book and American Authors will have an injurious effect on the principles of the Pupils." The district board forbade the use of these American books; only British school books could be used. The board also was responsible for distributing the small provincial grants, with the parents picking up most of the education costs in the early years.[64]

What did the students think about education in these early schools? Canniff Haight, who was educated in the Bay of Quinte area in the 1830s, penned one of the most interesting and entertaining accounts. Haight wrote: "I was sent to school early — more, I fancy, to get me out of the way for a good part of the day, than from any expectation that I would learn much. It took a long time to hammer the alphabet into my head. But if I was dull at school, I was noisy and mischievous enough at home, and very fond of tormenting my sisters." As to conduct, the students were expected to sit on hard wooden seats for seven or eight hours a day, behave "as very good children, to make no noise, and to learn our lessons….The Terror of the rod was the only thing that could keep us still, and that often failed."[65]

In the early years, most teachers of common (or elementary) schools were men. More boys than girls attended, because there were fees to be paid and if the parents could not afford to educate all of their children, the boys went to school. However, by the 1830s, as the merchants and district farmers became more prosperous, several small private schools for girls were set up. In 1834, Mrs. Marshall and her sister, Miss Davidson, the latter recently arrived from Scotland, placed

Because of frequent flooding, settlers were slow to build in the area of Front Street immediately north of Dundas Street. The original 1816 plan showed the location of Margaret Simpson's House (13) and stable (14) and the schoolhouse (15) on Pinnacle Street Wilmot's map reproduced by the Hastings County Historical Society, 1967.

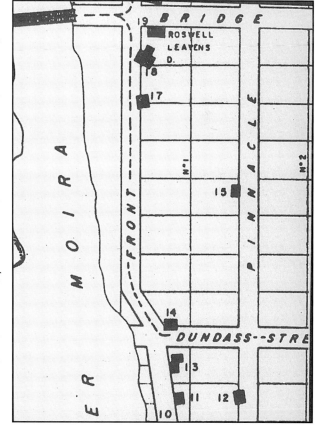

an ad in the Kingston newspaper, then still regarded as Belleville's local paper.[66] The sisters announced that they were prepared "to take under their care and superintendence the education of a few young ladies, the number not to exceed six or eight. They hope by their assiduity and attention to the moral and religious improvement of the youth intrusted [*sic*] to their care, as well as to the useful and ornamental branches of education, to merit a share of the patronage of the parents and guardians of young Females." This was to be a boarding school and an annual payment of £30 would cover "Board, Washing, and the plain branches of Education, namely Reading, Writing, Arithmetic, English Grammar, Geography, History, Plain and Fancy Work." Music, drawing, and French would be available for an additional charge.[67]

Mrs. Marshall's school was not without competition. The same month, Miss Haskins advertised that she was prepared to teach various subjects, including flower drawing, French, and fancy work.[68] These subjects were regarded as particularly appropriate for refined young women. The following year, Mrs. Thomas Campbell, the widow of the late Reverend Thomas Campbell, rector of St. Thomas' Anglican Church, announced that she would open her house to six young ladies.[69]

The success of such private schools and the common schools in educating Belleville's young ladies is questionable. Shortly after his arrival in Belleville from Ireland in 1834, William Hutton, who went on to become district superintendent of education, wrote of "the general uneducated state of the rising generation" and added that "The children's minds here are wildernesses, as uncultivated as those woods around us."[70] He added: "The ladies are princesses in their dress, but I don't think much of their minds from what I have seen."[71] Was he suggesting that boys and girls should be taught separately? More later on the separation of the sexes at the secondary-school level in the 1860s in connection with the section describing the teaching of the classic languages — Latin and Greek — in the Belleville Grammar School.

"Like a Little Heaven Below," 1790–1840

IF EDUCATION WAS very important to Belleville's early settlers, religion was equally, if not more, important. From his school room near the Methodist chapel on Pinnacle Street, Belleville teacher John Holmes described the state of religious enthusiasm in an 1835 letter to his member of Parliament:

> God has by his spirit been at work in Belleville. Oh! How pleasant, how blessed
> to meet with them in the room adjacent my school room and hear them speaking

forth the praises of their Saviour…. It is like a little Heaven below…. It almost seemed at times that Belleville began to rock from centre to circumference as Jesus Christ was riding through in his chariot of Salvation.[72]

Obviously, Holmes was moved by religion and did not hesitate to express his religious fervour in this correspondence. By that date, the Methodists had been active in the community for about forty years. Itinerant Methodist preachers such as Healy and Puffer are said to have preached at Colonel William Bell's home, or possibly his store, at Thurlow in the early years, and the Reverend Darius Dunham probably preached at Meyers' Creek in 1795.[73] "Scolding Dunham," as he was sometimes called, was "plain of speech and very blunt, a man of strong convictions, and possessed of a rich bass voice."[74] A fully ordained elder, he came from the United States in 1795 to assist William Losee, the first Methodist missionary to Canada. Though compatriots in the gospel, the two were competitors in love and Dunham wooed and won Elizabeth Detlor of Fredericksburgh, much to Losee's chagrin and sorrow.

In 1815, a Methodist class was organized under the leadership of John Reynolds, and planning began to build Belleville's first church. Actually, it was to be a chapel, for Methodists were not comfortable using the term "church" for their places of worship. As the Reverend Bill Lamb explained: "In Britain they used the term 'chapel' to refer to non-conformist places of worship. The Yankees used the term 'meeting-house' because the building also served as meeting places for town gatherings."[75]

Unfortunately, until 1828 only the Church of England and the Church of Scotland were allowed to own church property in the province. Accordingly, the Methodists had to find an individual to hold the property in his own name. That person was William Ross, a tanner of hides, a man well-known and trusted by the Mississauga, and a man who followed his wife into Belleville's first Methodist class meeting, organized in 1815.[76] Ross offered a half-acre of his land on the west side of Pinnacle Street. The title remained in his name until he sold it for £200 in 1831, three years after legislation made it legal for the Methodists and other groups to own property.

No doubt a subscription list would have been circulated to raise funds for the building and volunteers would have done much of the work, perhaps through building bees (co-operative work sessions). It would take some years to finish the interior. The only description we have of the first chapel (or church) in Belleville comes from the memory of the aged James H. Meacham, who, as a youngster of seven, sat through many of the early meetings, commencing in 1815:

I remember it well. It didn't look much like a church; It would be considered a poor barn today. A little rough, frame building, its interior uninviting as its exterior, no pews, merely cedar blocks and unplaned planks nailed on them; the bench used by the carpenters while building the church served as the pulpit, and "tallow dips" were used for illuminating purposes. A broad platform led from the street to the three steps up which you ascended to Belleville's first church.[77]

Crude as it might be, this 50 x 30-foot frame building served its purpose well until a second church was commenced in 1831. By that date, the church was almost bursting at its seams. The 118 members and the innumerable adherents made a larger building essential. Moreover, a new building was needed to accommodate the very successful Sunday school. This school originated in the fall of 1822, when the Reverend Thaddeus Osgood, an ordained Congregational minister from Massachusetts, addressed a public meeting in the Pinnacle Street Church. Osgood "outlined the concept of a Sunday afternoon school where children of all denominations and none could be taught to read and learn the scripture."[78] The message won the immediate support of three Presbyterians — John Turnbull, a prominent merchant; Doctor Anthony Marshall, a graduate of the Royal College of Surgeons of London; and Doctor George Cooper, a trained medical doctor who worked as a pharmacist. While waiting for local Presbyterians to receive permission and funding to erect their own church and obtain a minister from Scotland, these three men, together with some Methodists, organized a very successful Sunday school.

At the same time, an important religious change was taking place among the Mississauga of the Bay of Quinte at Belleville, the Natives who had "surrendered" land for the new village. On Sunday morning, February 19, 1826, the Ojibwa language was heard for the first time in the Belleville Chapel as Peter Jones, a Mississauga who had converted to Methodism near Ancaster three years earlier, preached. There was a great revival. Many Mississauga joined the Methodist Church, and membership statistics for the Belleville circuit in 1826 showed 83 Natives, along with 218 whites.[79] This led to the celebrated Grape Island Mission

Early view of the Pinnacle Street Methodist Chapel, parent congregation of Bridge Street Church. In the distance is the school erected circa 1850, just south of the Market Square. The house at left may be that of William Ross, who donated the land for the chapel. Courtesy of Hastings County Historical Society.

Station some five miles southeast of Belleville. The Kingston-area Mississauga soon joined with the Belleville group, remaining on Grape Island until their move to Alderville in 1837. The Reverend John Sunday and several other Grape Island "alumni" played a major role in conversions throughout Canada and the United States.

The arrival of Billa Flint Jr. and his wife, Phoebe Clement, from Brockville on Saturday, July 18, 1829, was an important day for the Sunday school. On their second day in Belleville, they attended church in the morning and returned for Sunday school in the afternoon. They were distressed by what they saw. The children were running around unsupervised, partly because some of the teachers had gone off to a revival service outside the town. The Flints offered to help. The following year, Billa, in search of new scholars, made a personal survey of every home in town. His efforts met with great success, and the school grew from between thirty and sixty children to two hundred. Also contributing to the success of the Sunday school was the "world's first Sunday school picnic" in May 1832. Flint devised this event, with games, races, and refreshments, to "add some fun to faith."[80] The school's officers, teachers, and friends assembled at the church and then marched to the picnic site, a pleasant forest of shade trees referred to as "The Grove." Today, the location is known as Grove Street.

Belleville: Looking East, circa 1830, a watercolour painted by Thomas Burrowes from near the west end of the Bridge Street bridge. At left, he showed the mill as well as the spillway. At the far right was a stone building under construction, with six workers on the top level. Three churches were pictured: St. Michael's Roman Catholic, just to the right of the mill; St. Andrew's Presbyterian, tower visible between the sign posts; and St. Thomas' Anglican, immediately left of the building under construction. The tall sign advertised an inn, the Traveller's Rest. Courtesy of Archives of Ontario, Burrowes Collection, C 1-0-0-0-110.

Faced with increasing attendance in both the regular church services and the Sunday school, the congregation arranged for Benjamin Ketcheson to build a larger church. On Friday, July 22, 1831, local Methodists as well as "the brethren and preachers, both travelling and local, from other Circuits" gathered to celebrate the dedication of "the large and commodious new Church in Bellville."[81] It was a frame building, with a gallery at the east end over the entrance. Unlike all other Methodist churches in Upper or Lower Canada, this church had a steeple and a bell.[82]

The Methodists were not the only religious group to erect a church shortly after the town was surveyed. In 1818, the Anglicans decided to build a church "for the purpose of promoting morality in the County of Hastings and Ameliasburg...."[83] On behalf of many leading citizens (including industrialists Captain John W. Meyers and Captain Thomas Coleman), the local member of the Legislative Assembly, James McNabb, petitioned the government for assistance. The Anglicans sought permission to build the church on land set aside for such a purpose two years earlier. They also asked to be allowed to raise funds for the project at York, Kingston, and Belleville. The government agreed. As a result, construction began in 1819 and was finished the next year. The church was one of the first Anglican ones erected west of Adolphustown.

No longer would a minister from the Kingston area have to visit Belleville to conduct services and perform marriages. In fact, in the first years of local settlement, the closest Anglican minister had been the Reverend John Langhorn of Bath, who insisted that couples wishing to be married do so in his church before eleven in the morning. Late arrival meant the service would not be performed until the following day.[84]

The Reverend Thomas Campbell was the first minister at St. Thomas' Anglican Church, and continued in charge until his death in 1835. While the church was under construction, Campbell was said to have entered the building and climbed up a ladder to the elevated pulpit. Immediately, a workman named Smith removed the ladder, leaving the minister a prisoner. He was released only after he agreed to send a messenger to his rectory to obtain "a certain beverage" for the workers.[85]

The story of the imprisoned rector is not the only unusual feature of St. Thomas' Church's early years. Allan Taylor, who had been contracted to build the church for £700, died before the church was completed and was buried in the centre of the unfinished structure. Once the church was operational, his mother sat in a pew directly above her son's grave.[86] In her history of the congregation, Ina Bellstedt described a meeting held on February 20, 1819, at which Thomas Coleman was asked to name the church. He named it "St. Thomas'." This led to a "rumour that Mr. Coleman did not really have the apostle's name in mind when he named the church, but only his own."[87] There was certainly some unhappiness among the other trustees. Two months later, when Coleman disagreed with the other trustees concerning a resolution, it was resolved unanimously that he be dismissed as a trustee and that the secretary "erase his name from the list of trustees."

The Roman Catholics were the next denomination to erect a church. They were encouraged in their activities by the Reverend Alexander Macdonell, pastor of St. Raphael's, Glengarry, and later the first Roman Catholic Bishop of Upper Canada. Macdonell travelled through the Quinte area, probably on at least an annual basis, ministering to the growing flock. Belleville was one of Macdonell's favourite sites to visit because his relatives, the Macdonells and the Chisholms, had settled here. In a report, dated November 4, 1819, on the state of religion in Upper Canada, Macdonell wrote: "Around the Bay of Quinty [*sic*] there are several hundred Catholics, besides many respectable Protestants who are offering very liberal assistance towards the erection of a Catholic church at the village of Belleville, a very central location."[88]

Macdonell was correct in stating that both Roman Catholics and Protestants wanted a Roman Catholic church in Belleville. In 1821, more than sixty inhabitants of the Belleville area, many of whom had no connection with the parish whatsoever, petitioned the government. They asked for "religious toleration extended to all denominations" and to have a grant of land "as will suffice for the erection of a chapel."[89] The government's response was to grant two lots — land upon which the present St. Michael's Church stands. A small frame building, the origins of which are somewhat obscure, was built or moved to the site for the use of visiting ministers.[90] Finally, on August 28, 1829, Macdonell, now a bishop, ordained the Reverend Michael Brennan to take charge of the mission at the "Bay of Quinty" and, on October 13, Brennan conducted his first baptism at Belleville.

The Presbyterians were also active early. After 1804, the Reverend Robert McDowall of Fredericksburgh (west of Kingston on the Bay of Quinte) brought the word of God to communities in this area. Sometimes referred to as "the Father of Presbyterianism on the Bay of Quinte," McDowall's theology was Presbyterian, although he had been sent as a missionary by the Dutch Reformed Church of the United States. He had a powerful voice and when he was excited, it was said, he could be heard a mile off. To quote a young girl near Belleville, "All who were inclined to marry he spliced, with many a kind word to the young folks to be sure to be prosperous by industry and perseverance … When the other girls would smirk and look pleasant at him, thinking he was a great benefactor to the race, he would chuck them under the chin and say, 'It will soon be your turn. I am going to Clarke, a long way off, through the woods, with very few settlements on the way, and when I come back, mind and be ready.'"[91]

After 1806, McDowall's failing health made his visits less frequent. However, he continued to make the occasional stop at Belleville, where he found a growing number of Presbyterians. In June 1821, almost one hundred Presbyterians petitioned the government for land for a church and burying grounds. While waiting for a response, they met in private homes, with the more learned trustees conducting the services. When the answer did come, it granted a single lot on the east side of Church Street. Although pleased with the response, the trustees sent the government several further requests in which they pointed out that the Roman Catholics had received two lots. Why, they wondered, should the Presbyterians settle for anything less? Finally, government saw it their way and granted a second lot.

Despite this positive answer for a second lot, which came in February 1823, the Presbyterians did not construct a church for several years. In the interim, they continued to meet in private homes, to plan for a church and minister, and to encourage good works within the community, For example, as noted earlier, three Presbyterians helped the Methodists establish the first Sunday school at Belleville.

By 1829, a few Presbyterians — mostly of recent American origin — suggested that the trustees approach the American Home Missionary Society to send out a missionary from the United States. Spurred to action by the threat of intervention by American Presbyterians, the Church of Scotland responded to requests for assistance. The requests from the church trustees were forwarded by local MLAs, James Samson of Belleville and William Morris of Perth. Upon hearing that the congregation had entered into a contract for the erection of a church, and would guarantee to pay from £90 to £100 per annum to the clergyman, the Glasgow Colonial Society agreed to send the Reverend James Ketchan to Belleville. By mid-September 1831, Ketchan had arrived in Kingston. But when he heard of the unfinished state of the Belleville church, he decided to remain in Kingston for a time and then, rather surprisingly, went to York and Niagara Falls to do some sightseeing. Only when the church was completed did he return to Belleville and, on November 6, 1831, the building welcomed the congregation and its first minister for the first time. It was described as being "a handsome, frame edifice painted white, large enough to seat 300, although a gallery could be added." The seats were rough — planks on blocks of wood — and tallow candles were used for lighting. As was the case with other early local churches, St. Andrew's Presbyterian Church was built by subscription and assistance came from Christians of other denominations, since the Presbyterians made up no more than one twenty-fourth of the village's population.[92]

St. Andrew's was associated with a tragic accident in 1834. The Reverend Matthew Miller, the Presbyterian minister at Cobourg and Colborne for less than a year, was travelling to Cobourg from Ramsay in Lanark County by horse and cutter in late February. The sleighing had been good on the trip east from Cobourg, but on the return trip a thaw set in and the snow began to rapidly disappear. The roads were bare in many places, making sleighing by land tedious and difficult. Accordingly, at Kingston, Miller decided to complete the journey home by travelling on the ice of the Bay of Quinte. Near Adolphustown, the horse and cutter went through the ice.

Miller drowned. Later, searchers found a box floating near the scene that had been kept afloat by an air pocket. The box contained the communion pieces from St. Andrew's (Kingston), which Miller was taking on loan to the Belleville congregation. Immediately thereafter, St. Andrew's (Belleville) returned the set to Kingston and arranged to obtain its own set.[93]

Although the Methodists, Anglicans, Roman Catholics, and Presbyterians were the largest denominations in Belleville, they were not the only ones. A number of Baptists settled near Foxboro, in what is now part of Belleville. The minister was Elder Turner, who, before the building of a small frame church, is said to have preached at Captain McIntosh's at Meyers' Creek and Colonel Bell's in Thurlow.[94] The Baptist church was reported to have been near Fairfield's Bridge, just north of Corbyville. In addition, Joseph Leavens, a Quaker preacher, "had a place for preaching in a loft of his brother's store in Belleville."[95] With the passage of time, other denominations would enter the community, including the Salvation Army.

From time to time, there were examples of co-operation among the Protestant denominations. One notable example was the formation on February 10, 1819, of the Belleville Branch of the Upper Canada Bible Society. James McNabb, an Anglican, was chairman of the meeting, while the Reverend William Case, a Methodist, was the speaker and Methodist John Reynolds was elected president. A further example of co-operation took place on September 7, 1837, when the cornerstone of the new Roman Catholic church was laid. The procession through the downtown streets was joined by "a large number of respectable inhabitants of the town," apparently representing several denominations.[96]

Unfortunately, there were more examples of rivalry than of co-operation. On occasion, denominations bitterly quarrelled with each other, and even amongst themselves. In 1826, the Kingston press reported a fierce controversy between the Presbyterians and the Anglicans in Belleville. A Presbyterian declared that the Anglican clergyman preached on Good Friday to a congregation of only nine persons, three of whom were Presbyterians.[97] The Anglican minister replied that his congregation averaged close to a hundred and that, in fine weather, it was almost double that figure.[98]

The Anglicans and Methodists then launched a battle in print. The Methodists were upset that the Anglicans had chosen to establish "a weekly Ball on the same evening as near to the Methodist chapel as possible for the professed purpose of enticing the people away from the place appointed for the worship of God."[99] The Anglicans replied by labelling the attack's writer, the Reverend Gilbert Miller, as a man possessed of an "envious and malignant mind." After all, the balls were organized without the minister's knowledge and it was mere coincidence that they were held near the Methodist chapel on prayer meeting nights.

Reflecting on his experiences in Canada during the Rebellion of 1837, British military leader Sir Richard Henry Bonnycastle referred to the Methodists as "the peddling preachers from the go-ahead people." He noted: "The worst feature about Belleville in 1837 was that it was the focus of American saddle-bag preachers, teachers, and rebelliously disposed folk; but I am told that many of these uneasy loafers have left it, and that its character has improved wonderfully.... It is surprising with what facility, in England, as well as in Canada, a saddle-bag doctor of divinity takes his degree...."[100]

Internal rifts weakened some denominations, including the Methodists. After 1833, a bitter struggle between the Wesleyan and Episcopalian Methodists developed over the question of church union and the ownership of the Pinnacle Street Chapel. A complicated and costly legal battle took place. The Wesleyan Methodists ultimately won, but John Reynolds and several others withdrew to establish a separate church.[101] For their part, the Presbyterians were also divided into two groups. The larger group, associated with the Church of Scotland, had established St. Andrew's. A smaller group, many of whom had American roots, supported the Free Church, which felt that it should be independent of government influence and patronage.

In 1840, the 3,908 local residents were asked to indicate their denominations. Fortunately, the results of that religious census survive:[102]

Church of England	690
Episcopal Methodist	689
Wesleyan Methodist	654
[Roman] Catholic	528
Church of Scotland	496
Baptist	208
Quaker	137
Presbyterian	116
Lutheran	7
Other	282

Although occasional external and even internal religious disputes interrupted the churches' work, the fact remains that they made a very positive contribution to the life of the community in pioneer times. Certainly, they ministered to more than the spiritual needs of the citizens. They were community, social, welfare, and educational centres that improved the lot of the individual. They undertook a wide range of activities often carried out today by governments or registered charities. Their efforts helped to make Belleville a better community in which to live.

3
LAW AND ORDER

Government by the People, May 15, 1790

ON MAY 15, 1790, a few of Belleville's earliest settlers probably participated in a history-making event in neighbouring Sidney Township. On that day, several citizens of Sidney and one or more from Thurlow Township held a town meeting to elect officials to administer their affairs.[1] This was the second such meeting in what is now Ontario, taking place a month after a similar meeting in Grimsby Township. However, Grimsby Township was soon divided, leaving Sidney with Ontario's oldest continuous local government, a record that continued until Sidney became part of the City of Quinte West on January 1, 1998.

Initially, the Sidney landholders (and those in Thurlow) included a few Loyalists and the sons and daughters of Loyalists who had originally settled near Kingston. Their tickets of location authorized them "to settle and improve" their lands, for which they would receive a patent, grant, or deed of concession after twelve months. The quantity of land depended on their Loyalist credentials and their rank during the American Revolution. The earliest tickets of location were issued at "Bay de Quinte" on behalf of the government of the "Province of Quebec" in 1787, and were for lots in "Seigneurie No. 8" (Sidney Township) or "Seigneurie No. 9" (Thurlow). This wording indicated that there was a single government for what are now Ontario and Quebec, that French civil law and landholding systems were used throughout the colony, and that the ten seigneuries above Cataraqui on the Bay of Quinte were as yet unnamed. Shortly thereafter, the British government did assign names: Sidney was named in honour of Thomas Townshend (Viscount Sydney), a veteran British politician who helped make preparations for the Loyalists to settle in the Quinte area. Thurlow was named after Edward A. Thurlow, first Baron of Thurlow, an outstanding British statesman who strongly supported George III's policies during the American Revolution.

British names for the townships did not ease local concerns about the continuation of French landholding and civil-law systems, as well as the distance from the seat of government in Quebec. Nor did the creation in 1788 of four administrative districts in the province, whereby the southern townships of Hastings County were assigned to the Mecklenburg District, which was soon renamed the Midland District. The district magistrates and justices of the peace, who controlled the administration and legal functions, met only at Kingston and Adolphustown.[2] Although the settlers appreciated the creation of a district land board to process land-grant applications, they wanted to have *local* authorities to whom they could present their concerns. After all, most Loyalists had been accustomed to participating in town meetings prior to the revolution.

When the government at Quebec refused requests for locally elected officials, the inhabitants of Sidney Township took matters into their own hands and called a meeting for May 15, 1790. This meeting, if not exactly illegal, was certainly extra-legal, or outside the law. Nevertheless, the settlers chose seven residents to serve as moderator (chair), town clerk, constable, path masters, and fence viewers. The moderator was Captain John W. Meyers, a resident of Sidney who was in the process of establishing mills upstream from the mouth of the Moira River in Thurlow Township.

Following the division of Quebec into Upper and Lower Canada, the Legislative Assembly for Upper Canada acted to satisfy the Loyalist settlers. English civil law was introduced, the court system included juries, and the freehold system of landholding replaced the seigneurial system. Unfortunately, the legislature delayed the legalization of town meetings until 1793, when legislation provided for the election of "Parish and Town Officers" in any parish or township with at least thirty resident landholders. This minimum number meant that Thurlow landowners had to attend the Sidney town meetings until 1798, when there were more than thirty in Thurlow and they could hold their own meetings.

Possibly, the white settlers on the Mississauga Reserve did not have the right to attend because they leased their land from the Indians. Similarly, it is unclear if some other regulations affected these settlers. Did they pay taxes or perform statute labour to maintain the roads? To what extent were they affected by the 1798 legislation that set up a class society? Class was determined by the amount of real or personal property a person had. A first-class citizen held property worth between £50 and £100, while an eighth-class citizen (the highest category) was worth over £400.

Nevertheless, after the Mississauga Reserve was "surrendered" to the government, the Belleville settlers were under the same regulations as other settlers in Upper Canada.

A Legal Light — Belleville's First Lawyer

JAMES HUNTER SAMSON holds the distinction of being Belleville's first resident lawyer. Born in Ireland, the son of an officer in the British Army, Samson came to Canada in 1813 when his father's regiment began a tour of duty here. After he was unsuccessful in seeking an ensigncy in the regiment in 1816, he studied at York (Toronto), where he became a close friend of Robert Baldwin, who would become an outstanding political leader. In 1819, as a law student in Kingston, he began a regular correspondence with Baldwin, much of which is preserved in the Baldwin Room of the Toronto Reference Library. His letters reveal Samson to have been "articulate, sensitive, fond of poetry, hardworking, and ambitious, but also insecure, subject to fits of depression, and extremely jealous of anyone who threatened to come between himself and Baldwin."[3] Samson and Baldwin shared their innermost thoughts, often in poetry, which they exchanged and critiqued for each other.

Samson moved to Belleville, then a town of fewer than five-hundred people, after he was called to the bar in 1823. Life in Belleville was not easy for Samson. He experienced "many battles and storms" with one judge and was financially embarrassed on more than one occasion. Still, he enjoyed a reputation as a "Barrister of no ordinary talent" and championed several important causes. He was a strong supporter of St. Andrew's Presbyterian Church, serving as a trustee, encouraging the Glasgow Colonial Society to send a minister, and putting up the Reverend James Ketchan after his arrival from Scotland. He also acted on the local board of health, served as a village councillor and, perhaps most importantly, was largely responsible for the construction of Belleville's first hospital.

From 1828 until his death in 1836, he represented the riding of Hastings in the House of Assembly. Although initially claiming to be a moderate, supporting the "principles of Whiggism," he soon revealed himself to be a Tory and a supporter of the Family Compact. In fact, he was one of the most conservative members of the assembly, a political outlook that was influenced by his military background, aristocratic connections through marriage, and a basic distrust of republicanism. William Lyon Mackenzie, the noted Reformer, described Samson as "a selfish illiberal creature" and put him on his "Black List" for 1830. In response, Samson played a leading role in the libel and breach-of-privilege charges against Mackenzie in December 1831. He described articles in Mackenzie's *Colonial Advocate* as "gross, scandalous, and malicious libels." The assembly found Mackenzie guilty of this libel and supported Samson's resolutions that Mackenzie's defence tactics made him "guilty of a high breach of the privilege of this house," that Mackenzie should be expelled from the house, and that a new election should be held in the district Mackenzie represented.

Samson then spoke out against the protest rallies held by Mackenzie's supporters. At the Belleville rally, Samson put forward a resolution of loyalty recognizing that Upper Canada's institutions were imperfect, but maintaining that "we have less cause of complaint, than any people on earth; and the means of redress are in our own power."

Samson continued to play a role in the assembly, chairing several committees and pressing for the creation of more banks and the need for improved navigation on the St. Lawrence River. Unfortunately, by early 1836 his health and state of mind became topics for local editorial comments when he was unable to attend sessions of the House. He had been affected by the death of his father in 1832, and serious political differences with Baldwin, whose moderate reform views greatly differed from Samson's conservative politics. Their once-vital friendship was gone. Samson sought comfort in alcohol, and this contributed to his death in March 1836 at the youthful age of thirty-six. Nevertheless, Samson should be remembered as a Belleville lawyer who played an active role in local and provincial matters.

Belleville: "The Friendly City"?

THIS SLOGAN HAS been associated with Belleville for many years, but it probably wouldn't have been considered appropriate by immigrants to the town in 1832. That year, a cholera epidemic struck many parts of the province. It claimed a dozen lives at Picton and a much larger number at Kingston.[4] Fearing that the epidemic would arrive in Belleville, James Hunter Samson, one of two Hastings County representatives in the provincial legislature, requested financial assistance from the government to build a hospital. The sum of £200 was granted and a 28 x 44-foot hospital was built on the north side of Hotel Street, on lands set aside for such a purpose in 1816.

Fortunately, the epidemic did not visit Belleville. This was because the local magistrates had placed armed guards on all roads leading into town in order to keep out strangers who might be ill. Also, no steam- or sailboat was allowed to land goods or passengers.[5] As a result, the two-storey wooden hospital building sat empty for a time, until it was pressed into use, first as a temporary shelter for immigrants and then as an elementary school. By 1860, it was described as being in a "ruinous condition."[6] So much for the slogan!

Erected in 1832 by a provincial grant and photographed circa 1865, this building (at left) on the "Hospital Lot" (now the site of St. Michael's Academy) was never used as a hospital. The boys were standing in front of the cemetery and fence that surrounded St. Andrew's Presbyterian Church, erected in 1831. Courtesy of Hastings County Historical Society, Boyce Collection, Neg. B-90.

The Press and the Politicians, 1831–34

IN THE DAYS before telephone, radio, television, the Internet, and other communication devices, the local newspaper was one of the main sources of information about life in Belleville and elsewhere. From 1810 until 1833, Belleville's local papers were the Kingston weeklies. They contained much news about the Belleville area. The first local item appeared in the *Kingston Gazette* on November 3, 1810, when F. Thomson offered "books and tracts for children and a variety of useful pamphlets" in exchange for rags. Fortunately, an index of the Kingston newspapers from 1810 to 1848 was compiled several years ago by the Kingston Public Library and is now available online at the Digital Kingston website.

After 1830, a series of newspapers dared to publish at Belleville.[7] The first was the *Anglo-Canadian* in February 1831. Edited by Doctor Alexander Johnston Williamson, former publisher of the *Anglo-Canadian* at Niagara, it was well-received. The *Kingston Chronicle* described it as "ably edited" and wished Williamson all manner of success.[8] Good wishes were not enough, however, and the *Anglo-Canadian* lasted less than a year. Early in July 1831, T. Slicer launched the *Phoenix* to compete with the *Anglo-Canadian*. One year later, the editor of the *Hallowell Free Press* of Picton wrote: "Is the Belleville *Phoenix*, which I understand is about to expire, expected to disappear in a flame, as is the custom of its ancestors; if so, I think it would not be amiss to inform the public when its exit will take place, as it would be a great curiosity in our day, to witness a sight so pleasing."[9] The Picton editor did not witness this curiosity, since the final issue of the *Phoenix* had already come off the press. *The Hastings Times and Farmers' Journal* and *The Standard of Moira* followed in quick succession and were also short-lived.

When the editor of the *Kingston Chronicle and Gazette* received the prospectus for yet another paper to be launched at Belleville, he was not impressed and wrote that if the paper "should have the good fortune to live six months, we will speak further of it."[10] Not only did the new paper last six months, but it is still in business. The *Belleville Intelligencer and Hastings General Advertiser* has undergone several name and ownership changes and now is known simply as the *Intelligencer*. It ranks as one of the oldest newspapers in Ontario. Toronto's oldest newspaper, the *Globe,* was not founded until ten years after the *Intelligencer*.

George Benjamin (1799–1864), founder of the Intelligencer, *1834; warden of the Victoria District, 1846–49 and Hastings County 1851–56 and 1859–61; prominent Orangeman; and MLA for North Hastings, 1856–61.* Courtesy of Library and Archives Canada, C-9556.

The *Intelligencer*'s early survival, at a time when many other papers were unsuccessful, can be attributed to sound management. The founder, publisher, and editor was George Benjamin, a short, stout, bespectacled man with a ringing laugh and a "gentleman of more than ordinary ability," according to historian William Canniff.[11] Within a few months, other provincial papers were quoting Benjamin's editorials on such matters as the Canadian and American banking systems, and voting by ballot.[12] On the latter issue, the paper was strongly opposed, citing as its main reason the failure of the American system of government. Benjamin wrote, "We hope, never to see it introduced … if it is, then there is the first blow of a total subversion of our principles of government."[13]

Benjamin was a man with an intriguing past. Born in England to a family of strong Jewish commitment, his name at birth was Moses Cohen. Many of his relatives would be recognized on three continents "for uncommon achievements in the fields of journalism and politics."[14] Apparently well-educated, Benjamin travelled extensively prior to arriving in Belleville in 1834 with his fourteen-year-old Jewish wife and their infant son. The first prominent Jew in the community, he would become the subject in 1991 of an exciting biography by Sheldon and Judith Godfrey, *Burn This Gossip*. The book includes the sad incident in which an effigy of Benjamin was burned outside the newspaper's office and the subsequent poem in Kingston's *British Whig* entitled, "Elegy on the Execution of the Belleville Jew."[15]

Despite such attacks, Benjamin was as successful as a journalist as he was later in politics. In 1836, he was elected clerk of Thurlow (which included Belleville), the first recorded instance of a Jew being elected to municipal office in British North America.[16] Later, he served as warden of Hastings County, Belleville's first superintendent of common schools, and as a member of Parliament (1857–63) for the Province of Canada. In fact, he was the first Jewish member of a Canadian Parliament permitted to be seated in a legislature.[17] What amazed the editor of the rival *Hastings Chronicle* about Benjamin's election to Parliament in 1856 was that he won the seat by "some extraordinary means," securing "the combined Orange and Catholic vote."[18] Not an easy task!

Benjamin was an astute businessman and judge of character. Shortly after commencing the *Intelligencer* in 1834, he hired a recent immigrant as an apprentice. By 1848, when Benjamin stepped down as editor and publisher of the paper, this protege, the twenty-five-year-old Mackenzie Bowell, replaced him. The two men shared a dream of improving Canada by encouraging a strong, independent press in Belleville; by supporting the Loyal Orange Lodge; and by entering politics. However, while Benjamin entered the Legislature of the United Canada and achieved considerable success, though not all the results he had hoped for, Bowell, his protege would later enter Parliament and become prime minister.

Soon after Benjamin established the *Intelligencer,* there was a new addition to Belleville's publishing world — a church magazine with an unusual publication site. The Reverend James Gardiner, a young man with newspaper experience in Cobourg and a class leadership role in the Methodist Episcopal Church, became a co-owner with the Reverend G.D. Greenleaf of the assets of the *Plain Speaker,* the paper that had been wrecked by the super-loyalists in the Rebellion of 1837. Greenleaf and Gardiner set about publishing a magazine "in the interests of the Methodist Episcopal Church in Canada." The site was the hotel that had given its name to Hotel Street and resulted in the jog at the corner of Pinnacle. The ballroom was used for preaching, other rooms as a parsonage, and the barroom was the printing office. The magazine was entitled the *Repository.* When it was determined that the magazine could only support one person, Gardiner sold his share to Greenleaf and turned to teaching and then full-time ministry.[19]

The next decades — the 1840s and 1850s — would see further achievements in the literary world, highlighted by the writings of Susanna Moodie and William Hutton.

Changes and More Changes in the Twenties and Thirties

EARLY NEWSPAPERS PERFORMED many functions. They kept citizens up-to-date on current events in Belleville and abroad. They provided information about what goods could be purchased and where. And they called attention to community needs.

In Belleville, one of these needs was improved policing. Crime was a recurring problem. Possibly the most publicized crime of the period occurred in 1832. The *Hallowell Free Press* (Picton) of April 17 described an incident in Belleville as "a most serious and terrible affray … in the course of which the lives of one of the leading Magistrates and one or two of the most respectable inhabitants were very near being sacrificed." The incident involved an attack by ten journeymen tailors "of notoriously bad character" on their employer late one evening. Armed with billets of wood, they assaulted the tailor in his shop. His cries brought the neighbours to his aid, and the journeymen vented their anger on these intruders. One of those assaulted was James McNabb, described as a very powerful young man. With every blow, he knocked one of the assailants down, until he was felled by "one of the villain's clubs." While McNabb was lying on the ground, the group kicked him "and beat him dreadfully with both sticks, and stones" until he lay perfectly still. Magistrate Thomas Parker and Doctor Ridley arrived to aid McNabb, but they were assaulted as well. Fortunately, all of the victims recovered and three of the attackers were jailed. This riot, unchecked robber bands said to be operating in the district, and the occasional violent political rally led the *Intelligencer* to

Unrest and Rebellion: Counting the Dead, 1837

ASK THE AVERAGE Belleville resident what he or she knows about the Rebellion of 1837, and you will find a few who can recall the name of William Lyon Mackenzie. Less likely, some will recall the name of Montgomery's Tavern or the result of the rebels' march down Yonge Street. Ask a resident about the effects of the rebellion on Belleville, and you will probably get a blank stare. Yet the Rebellion of 1837 saw the arrest of many area citizens, the calling out of the local militia, and the death of one of our principal citizens and military leaders.

Fortunately, some original rebellion documents have survived. For more than a century, Hastings County officials preserved the county's Rebellion Losses Claims, and Clerk Erle Denyes turned this collection over to the Hastings County Historical Society in 1961.[29] Prompted by reading the claims for compensation submitted several years after the rebellion, local historian Betsy Boyce decided to research and write the history of the event.[30] Her fascinating book, *The Rebels of Hastings,* sheds much light on this little-known but important chapter in our history.[31]

Causes of the local unrest were similar to those elsewhere in the province. They included a government — dominated by a group sometimes referred to as the Family Compact — that was not always responsive to the wishes of the majority of the people. Although the propertied male citizens elected members of the Legislative Assembly (the lower house), the governor and his advisors appointed members of the Legislative Council (the upper house). Other causes of discontent were the privileged position of the Church of England and a lack of funds for roads, schools, and other projects. Moreover, there was an economic depression in the late 1830s, and the harvest of 1837 was only adequate. In short, there was a growing demand for change and reform.

Probably, the birth of a reform movement in the Belleville-Quinte area took place before 1820, after the arrival of Robert Gourlay from Scotland. Described by one historian as "a congenital dissident, an inveterate scribbler, a stiff-necked individualist who sooner or later fell out with nearly everyone he knew, whether friend or foe," Gourlay was dismayed by the slow progress of his new country.[32] He circulated a questionnaire throughout Upper Canada to find out the reasons for this slow growth, and then held a series of township meetings, including one for Thurlow Township on February 6, 1818. James McNabb, Simon McNabb, John W. Meyers, John Canniff, and other loyal subjects drew up a statistical report that concluded the township's improvement was retarded by a lack of an adequate yeoman population and insufficient investment in agriculture.[33] The gathering selected Thomas Coleman as the township's representative to meet with those of other townships to protest directly to the British government.

Arrested in Kingston, Gourlay was forced to leave the province the following year. Nevertheless, his influence remained and Thomas Coleman was the chief local supporter. A leading Belleville merchant, Coleman, like Gourlay, had been charged with seditious libel. The charge followed angry words in Nelson's Tavern between Coleman and James McNabb, a government supporter in the Legislative Assembly representing Hastings County and Ameliasburgh Township. Apparently McNabb, described as a "mean malignant man," had treated Coleman to several drinks in order to loosen his tongue and make him say something seditious. Coleman obliged. He damned Lieutenant-Governor Gore and accused government supporters of filling their own pockets with £3,000 at the expense of the public. However, Coleman denied calling the Crown ministers "a damned set of perjured villains."[34] McNabb ended the discussion, much of which was reported in the Kingston newspaper, stating that he had no objection to meeting "this scurrilous and most turbulent person … in further warfare by paper," however, as a member of the Legislative Assembly (MLA), he had more important things to do for "his worthy constituents."[35] No doubt the political wrangling continued privately, since the two owned adjacent properties on the west bank of the Moira River.

The local reform movement continued to grow, challenging the existing order. More than one political meeting broke into two hostile camps. For example, on March 10, 1832, a meeting was held in the court room to discuss reform leader William Lyon Mackenzie's criticisms of the system of government. About eight-hundred citizens attended. No sooner had the local MLA, James H. Samson, begun to expose the "falsehood, absurdity, and inconsistency" of Mackenzie's position than some of the reformers interrupted repeatedly. When it appeared that violence might break out, Samson jumped from the platform, was immediately raised on the shoulders of his friends, and carried into Nelson's Tavern. About half of the gathering followed. The other half remained in the court room and approved an address of loyalty to king and country.[36]

The election that followed Samson's death in March 1836 further illustrated the friction between the constitutionalists (supporters of the status quo) and the reformers. Reporting the election victory of James McNabb, the constitutional candidate, the *Kingston Chronicle and Gazette* showed a high degree of political bias. Its bold headline read: THE RADICALS DEFEATED — AND TOTALLY VANQUISHED BY THE GLORIOUS RE-ACTION AT HASTINGS. The margin of victory? A scant eleven votes!

Sensing the growing unrest, the government prepared for any eventuality, even armed rebellion. In 1835, the First Hastings Yeomanry Cavalry under Captain D. Perry was formed. On the eve of the rebellion, this volunteer corps numbered about fifty men, and Perry offered the service of his force on a permanent basis in November 1837. In a letter to the *Kingston Chronicle and Gazette*, he wrote of the spirit of loyalty "that is bursting forth in all well disposed men in this neighbourhood," notwithstanding the "Terrible Meeting at Hayden's."[37] This was a reference to a reform meeting at Doctor Anson Hayden's (now Corbyville).

It was at this point that Captain James McNabb of the First Hastings Rifles lost his life.[38] This was the same McNabb who had been elected to the Legislative Assembly the previous year and resided in the still-standing Riverboat House on West Bridge Street. McNabb and his men were guarding prisoners in a Front Street inn. Early one morning, the town fire bell rang to summon the volunteer firemen. Misinterpreting the bell and thinking that Reformers were trying to free some prisoners, the soldiers dressed hurriedly. In moving quickly through a darkened passage, McNabb ran upon the bayonet of one of his men. He died within a day and was buried with full military honours in St. Thomas' Church Cemetery, where his gravestone is now fastened to the church's exterior wall.

McNabb's death was the only Belleville fatality associated with the rebellion. The only other Hastings County fatality occurred in a "melancholy manner" at a tavern in Shannonville, some eleven miles east of Belleville. William Church of that village, a dragoon guard escorting the mail through the Indian Woods, had stopped for refreshment. Unfortunately another dragoon, while loosening his cloak, let his pistol drop. The pistol struck the stove and discharged, fatally wounding Church.[39] Meanwhile, across Upper Canada (as Ontario was then known), there were a number of other deaths, and the hangings of more than twenty men suspected of being disloyal to the government.

Not all of the local militia were well-prepared to deal with the unrest. For example, in mid-October, after Colonel Coleman gave the required eight days of notice for the Belleville Company of the First Hastings Regiment to parade, only 25 of 120 men turned out.[40] When the militia was prepared to act in December, there were insufficient arms and ammunition. A deputation sought help at Kingston, and, on the evening of December 8, the steamer *Kingston* set out for Belleville with 1,500 weapons, ammunition, a protective guard of Kingston militia, and members of the Belleville deputation headed by Lieutenant Colonel Anthony Manahan of the Second Hastings Regiment.[41] When ice stopped the *Kingston* near Deseronto, the boat landed at John Culbertson's wharf and the call went out for help. Within a few hours, the weapons were transferred into a dozen wagons and the party started off for Belleville. Tyendinaga Mohawk warriors in battle dress led the way. Their arrival in Belleville impressed the loyalty of the Mohawk and the strength of the Crown's forces upon the town's citizens.

Within a short time, the local militia arrested a large number of suspected rebels and escorted them to Kingston to be secured in the Midland District Gaol or Fort Henry. Those arrested included some very prominent citizens. As a result, when Thurlow Township held a town meeting on January 1, 1838, it did so without its clerk, Doctor Anson Hayden of Hayden's Corners.

Sir Richard Henry Bonnycastle, British commander in the Kingston-Belleville area. Courtesy of Archives of Ontario, Acc. F887, MU281, Acc. 4909

Similarly, Sidney Township Clerk Gideon Turner was not available for civic service. Both men were behind bars because of suspected disloyalty. Turner returned to the area after spending three months in jail, and Hayden left the country quickly and took up residence in the United States. Even former members of Parliament, such as Joseph Lockwood (1828–30), were not exempt from arrest. However, of the large number sent to Kingston, most were never tried for treason and there was not enough evidence to convict any.

Notwithstanding the large number of arrests, fear remained that there might be enough rebels in the Belleville area to help carry out an attack on Kingston. To guard against this possibility, the government ordered members of the local militia to Kingston. In late February 1838, fifty officers and men of the Belleville Rifle Company under Captain Wellington Murney and two companies of the Second Hastings Militia under Captains McKenzie and McAnnany went to Kingston. They were joined by Captain Portt with about seventy Mohawk warriors.[42] Fearing an attack on Kingston on February 22, 1838, the commander of the militia at Kingston, Lieutenant Colonel R.H. Bonnycastle, sent "proper persons to Belleville to watch the disaffected there." He also sent the Mohawk warriors, "under the guise of deer hunting parties" out along the approaches to Kingston.[43] On the night of February 21, Bonnycastle was awakened by a militia rider who had quickly ridden from Belleville. The rider brought news that the rebels from the Belleville area were marching on Kingston.[44] Although the land attack failed to materialize, several prisoners were taken near Napanee. One was an American gunsmith from Belleville who was armed with a bowie knife and other "murderous" weapons, including special bullets designed "to render a wound as painful and as difficult to cure as possible."[45] Soon after, to protect Kingston's eastern flank, members of the Belleville Rifle Company and "a strong force of Indian warriors" (actually only eleven Indians) were sent to reinforce Gananoque.[46]

By the summer of 1838, most of the Belleville prisoners who had been imprisoned at Kingston, on suspicion of treason, were released. Only Nelson Reynolds remained to be tried and he, like the others before him, was soon released.[47] The freeing of the prisoners and the activities of Bill Johnson, "the Pirate of the St. Lawrence," led to the county and the town being in "a most excited state." An intercepted letter warned that the pirates and their rebel-minded friends in Hastings County "would set fire to Belleville and plunder it."[48] Accordingly, the magistrates asked that a permanent military force be stationed at Belleville, together with a pair of cannon. In the interim, the magistrates would continue to post a nightly guard.[49]

In the fall of 1838, the threat from the Reformers and their American allies, the Hunter Lodges who were determined to "liberate Canada" from Britain, loomed larger.

A report on October 26, 1838, by Major Warren, who commanded the local militia forces, showed something of the citizens' loyalties: "It appears that the population of the two frontier townships of Sidney and Thurlow including the town of Belleville are inclined to rise against the government, and I believe they frequently hold meetings and carry a correspondence with the States for the purpose of arranging plans in that effect."[50] Warren felt that the residents of the townships north of the front were more trustworthy.

Major Warren's estimates of local loyalties generally coincided with those of Clifton McCollom. A Belleville merchant who had fled to the United States during the rebellion, he wrote that 482 Hastings residents "had pledged themselves upon oath, to embark their lives, Honour and fortunes in the cause of liberty."[51] Of these "pledged Patriots," 165 were in Sidney Township, 93 were in Thurlow Township, and 41 were in Belleville. All were said to be in possession of arms, and would have joined Mackenzie on his march to Kingston had Mackenzie's Toronto attack in December 1837 been successful.

Upon learning of this unrest, Lieutenant-Governor Sir George Arthur dispatched one of his staff to Belleville. Captain George, de Rottenburg, found that there was "great discontent and great excitement." Subsequently, Arthur himself visited Belleville to meet with the magistrates. They told him about "frequent communication with the States" and several meetings that "had recently taken place among known disaffected people." Even the magistrates were unhappy, because many accounts incurred in turning out the militia the previous winter had not been paid.[52]

The government took action as a result of these findings, stationing a permanent militia guard of one-hundred men at Belleville. "Better late than never," commented the Kingston press.[53] The First Hastings Cavalry under Benjamin Dougall, as well as troops raised the preceding year, were placed on active service at Belleville. In addition, Arthur appointed Baron de Rottenburg to replace Warren as commanding officer. De Rottenburg's reports from October 1838 to December 1839 told the government of the landing of arms near Point Anne, secret meetings in Sidney, "threats of vengeance and retaliation," and outrages in Sidney and Thurlow.[54]

In reality, some actual acts of violence that occurred were generated by the "super-loyal" and not by the reformers. The offices of a Belleville newspaper, the *Plain Speaker*, were wrecked and much of the type was thrown into the street. Although no copy of the offending issue has survived, the action followed an apparent publishing error in which the queen's coat of arms, at the head of a proclamation, appeared upside down.[55] Certainly the publisher, Samuel

Hart was anti-government. In fact, the government had instructed de Rottenburg to place him under arrest, but de Rottenburg had not done so, since he felt the paper "was fast sinking into the insignificance it so justly merits" and that Hart's influence in the country was "slowly declining."[56] De Rottenburg was somewhat embarrassed by the fact that no attempt was made to stop the attack, since two companies of soldiers were stationed nearby. Immediately thereafter, militia guards were placed on the premises and the magistrates posted a reward of one-hundred dollars for the apprehension of the guilty parties. Local legend has it that the paper's foreman was also dragged through the slush and mud. However, the foreman himself, James Gardiner, later denied this story. Gardiner would go on to become a Methodist minister.[57] Samuel Hart had been absent the day of the raid, but was later involved in the "Cobourg Conspiracy."

John O'Carroll, a local merchant, received a similar punishment. The windows in his store and inn were smashed on nineteen occasions, and he was imprisoned for eight weeks at Fort Henry. Armed militiamen intimidated his customers so much that they were "in dread of their lives." Finally, he was obliged to sell his property and was reduced to a debtor. All this happened because O'Carroll was suspected of being a rebel sympathizer. He had been an active letter writer, raising funds for a new Roman Catholic church, and his many letters made him suspect in the eyes of some militiamen.[58] Several years later, his heirs received some compensation.

The militia forces at Belleville remained from November 1838 to mid-May 1839. They were quartered near West Bridge and Coleman streets in a building rented for £75 a year. Then they were "suffered to depart to their homes, where their presences were required in the cultivation of their farms."[59] Before disbanding, the officers gave Baron de Rottenburg a public banquet at Belleville.

The years of the rebellion were an exciting and colourful period in Belleville's history. Historian Betsy Boyce noted that any description of those years must be enhanced by Baron de Rottenburg's arrival in Belleville in 1838 and by his marriage here the following year. As well, the rebellion was responsible for the town's first contact with one of its outstanding families — the John Wedderburn Dunbar and Susanna Moodie family. John Moodie arrived in December 1838 as paymaster for the militia. After this service, he returned as first sheriff of the Victoria District. On her arrival, Susanna Moodie was struck by the state of society — "everything but friendly or agreeable." She found the town divided into "two fierce political factions."[60] The Tories regarded any person who desired change as a traitor. Despite her intense loyalty to the British Crown and its institutions, she was later sympathetic toward Mackenzie and actively supported moderate Reform leader Robert Baldwin, after whom she christened a son in 1843.[61]

As Susanna Moodie correctly observed, the town was politically divided. This division would continue, although some steps were taken to ease the bitterness. In 1839, in the last session of the old Upper Canada Assembly, members passed a Rebellion Losses Bill to be enacted by the new union legislature (combining Upper and Lower Canada). The bill's purpose was to ascertain and provide for payment of all just claims arising from the rebellion. However, it was only in 1845 that the allottment of money required to carry out this order was voted upon. Locally, six commissioners were appointed. They included Benjamin Dougall, William McAnnany, and William Ketcheson — all distinguished, respected, and conservative gentlemen. In December, the commissioners held two three-day sittings at Fanning's Hotel in Belleville and at Jonas

The McNabb-Yeomans House on West Bridge Street, also known as the Riverboat House, home of Captain James McNabb during the 1830s. The veranda was added later. Courtesy of Hastings County Historical Society, Building Research Committee, circa 1978.

Canniff's Tavern in Thurlow. They rendered judgment on January 23, 1846. Fortunately, with few exceptions, the written claims have survived, as has the commissioners' report.

From reading these claims, it is apparent the commissioners "were not in sympathy with Reformers…. No compensation was awarded to anyone who put in a claim for loss due to imprisonment, however unjust it may seem…." Some of those imprisoned had spent more than a hundred days jailed in Kingston and suffered serious financial losses, but there was no compensation. For example, Joseph Canniff, a successful mill operator in Thurlow, where he held the office of assessor and tax collector, was arrested in the early days of the rebellion, and again after the threatened raid on Gananoque, when he was held for eighty days. In addition, he listed a pair of gloves and a pistol that were taken from him and not returned. He claimed £505.5s. He received nothing. "Those who were in any way associated with disloyalty, even to the extent of appearing as witnesses at the trial of a neighbour charged with 'a treasonable offence,' had their claims refused."[62]

On the other hand, the commissioners usually paid claims for military services or supplies, at least in part and usually in full. Belleville jailer and constable Zenas Dafoe claimed £9.2s. for serving subpoenas on thirty-four people and the mileage involved. He received the total payment. What was remarkable was that he had not been paid for seven years. Prominent Belleville magistrate and merchant Billa Flint claimed more than £52 for providing food and other supplies for men and horses. He was also out of pocket for accounts and rents because the debtors ran away. Flint received the entire amount. Several Belleville residents received partial compensation for damage done to their buildings by billeted militia. One received payment for providing black crepe and blank ammunition for Captain McNabb's funeral. The largest award was £420, which went to William and George Portt, of Tyendinaga Township, farmers and respected justices of the peace. They claimed, and witnesses supported them, that their barn full of wheat had been burned by arsonists, because one man was a militia leader and the other served as "Captain and leader of the Mohawks."[63]

The Rebellion of 1837 certainly affected the citizens of Belleville and the surrounding area. Political differences had divided families. Many had been jailed, some for more than a hundred days, only to be released without trial. "Super-loyal" residents had caused more property damage in Belleville than the rebels. The local Rebellion Losses Claims process had not resolved the political differences. Fortunately, Lord Durham's celebrated mission to Canada in 1838 would lead to greater provincial control over purely Canadian matters and improved municipal government by 1850. However, the healing process would take time.

noted writer Susanna Moodie) was the first sheriff. Edmund Murney was first clerk of the peace and county crown attorney. Among the promising young lawyers was John A. Macdonald, later to become prime minister of Canada. He represented the Commercial Bank of Kingston in the early 1840s, and his signature can be found on some of the court documents housed in the Hastings Heritage Centre in Cannifton. With Belleville residents no longer having to travel to Kingston or Adolphustown to attend important criminal and civil law cases, the local courthouse soon became busier. A magnificent structure, similar to other courthouses built in that era, it would continue to serve the citizens of Belleville and Hastings County until 1961.

Municipal Government, 1836–40

AS MENTIONED EARLIER, Belleville could be a lawless place in its early years. This lawlessness, coupled with citizens' growing desire to have more control over their own affairs, led them to request incorporation as a police village. As early as 1823, the Legislative Council refused such a request.[69] A second petition in 1826 stated that the urban residents wanted the authority to keep the streets in repairs, prevent "Nuisances and racing of Horses in the streets," and regulate animals running at large.[70] They felt that their interests were not identical to those of the rural residents of Thurlow Township.

This urban-rural conflict was showing up more and more, as illustrated by the disputed election of a township clerk at the annual township meeting in 1836. George Benjamin of Belleville defeated Doctor Anson Hayden of Hayden's Corners (Corbyville) by a 69–68 count. Hayden's supporters demanded a written ballot, and each candidate rounded up more supporters. The ballot confirmed Benjamin by a 144–122 count. Immediately thereafter, Belleville won over Hayden's Corners as the location for the next meeting — by a 31–20 count.[71]

Before the next annual meeting could be held, however, the government of Upper Canada had separated Belleville from the township and incorporated it as a police village. This status had originally been granted on March 6, 1834, but a faulty description of the village's boundaries required a new act in 1836. For the first time, Belleville had lands to the west of the Moira River, thus ending the hopes of Billa Flint, Thomas Coleman, and others that the small settlement to the west of the Moira could be set up as a separate village of "Moira."

Once elected by the principal male householders and leaseholders, the president and the members of the Board of Police (comparable to today's council) had the power to control local roads, slaughterhouses, fire regulations, market hours, and many other aspects of village life. It was to ensure that new streets were at least sixty-six feet in width to prevent indecent writing and pictures in public places, and "generally to prevent vice and preserve good order."[72]

The surviving police regulations of 1840 reflect a much different time and lifestyle from twenty-first century Belleville.[73] After repealing all existing bylaws, the Board of Police approved a one-page summary of replacement bylaws and ordered Clerk George Benjamin to have them printed for posting. The first dealt with "Immoderate Riding or Driving" and provided for a fine from five to thirty shillings for driving or riding in any street at an immoderate speed or for riding and driving "faster than a walk" upon any bridge across the Moira River. The second provided for any person who set off any gun or played ball on any street to be liable for a fine up to twenty shillings. A fine of up to thirty shillings was provided for any person found guilty of shooting or using firearms, fishing, or skating on the Sabbath. Obviously, the Sabbath was to be protected, since another regulation prohibited any vessel from loading or unloading goods on the Sabbath, unless permission had been received from a member of the board.

Youthful morality was to be encouraged by prohibiting young lads (under the age of twenty-one) from being harboured in grocery stores in late evening. They were prohibited from visiting grocery stores after nine o'clock, "unless they have been sent on business, doing it in a reasonable time and departing immediately." Moreover, the doors of all public houses and groceries were "to be closed for the night, immediately after ten o'clock p.m. except for the admission of travellers, not inhabitants of the town." Grocers also were prohibited from allowing "any game at cards or dice or any other game of hazard." Any person found guilty of challenging another to a fight was liable to a ten-shilling fine.

Fire regulations occupied a large part of the one-page sheet. Every dwelling or store was to have at least "one good painted leather bucket with the initials of the owners names printed thereon." Building owners were to have chimneys swept by a public chimney sweeper (appointed by the town) on a regular basis — once per month in winter. Such regulations reflected the serious threat fire posed to the town's very existence. Nowhere is the threat identified more clearly than in the writings of Susanna Moodie. In December 1840, she had "the misfortune to be burnt out, and lost a great part of our furniture, clothing, and winter stores." Moreover, her two-month-old son went missing at the time and, fortunately, was found "by a kind neighbour in the kitchen of the burning building, whither he had crept from among the crowds, and was scarcely rescued before the roof fell in."[74]

4
THE 1840S AND 1850S

The Imported Authors: Willie, John, and Susie

By 1840, THERE were several people living in the Belleville area who would distinguish themselves in the literary world. In addition to journalist George Benjamin and historian William Canniff, they included William Hutton and the Moodies — Susanna and John Wedderburn Dunbar.

A native of Ireland, William Hutton left his homeland in 1834 because of terrible farming conditions. Although Hutton's original plan had been to settle in the Simcoe District of Upper Canada, he first toured other areas of the province and New York State. He rejected settling among the Yankees because he found them to be "filthy in their habits as far as the use of tobacco is concerned, eternally chewing, smoking and spitting and their manners are exceedingly disagreeable." He admitted that they were educated and "very industrious and enterprising" and would "go through thick and thin to make money," but this money-making appeared to be "their sole pursuit."[1] Obviously an opinionated individual, Hutton found much to dislike about many parts of Upper Canada. "In Peterborough," he was "sorry to say that *drinking,* cursing and swearing are indulged in by the young men to a frightening extent."[2]

Fortunately for his career plans in Canada, Hutton generally restricted such comments to the private letters he sent to his mother in Ireland. Fortunately for historians, his mother saved his letters, and excerpts were published in 1972. They reveal the trials and tribulations of an educated, articulate immigrant who sought to provide a comfortable living for his family and to serve the needs of his new country.

After a prolonged search, he decided that a farm immediately west of Belleville, but now within the city limits, was the ideal place. Accordingly, he brought his wife and children to Sidney

Cottage (now demolished) on the Trent Road. A man of many talents, Hutton tried his hand at scientific farming, teaching, municipal government, public administration, and writing. He was the first warden of the Victoria District (as Hastings County was known in the 1840s), the first superintendent of schools for the district, and the first secretary (deputy minister) of agriculture for the United Province of Canada.

Throughout his career, his letters home contained fascinating comments on life in the colony. The following apparently contradictory lines would make today's environmentalist shudder: "Manure is given away. The innkeepers thank you to have it drawn away for them and at this Inn, where there are a number of horses, *they have a door overhanging the river and throw it out* to the stream. The River Moira on which Belleville stands is a beautiful river."[3] Today's woman must be concerned when she reads Hutton's comment on the fair sex: "The women are princesses in their dress, but I don't think much of their minds from what I have seen."[4]

In addition to his candid private letters, Hutton wrote letters encouraging emigration from Great Britain to Canada, and particularly to the Quinte district. For two essays on agriculture, he won a gold medal at the Provincial Exhibition of Upper Canada held at Brockville in 1851 and a prize of £15 the following year for a *Report on the State of Agriculture in Hastings County*.[5] His most significant books were *Canada: Its Present Condition, Prospects, and Resources*, published in London in 1854 as one of Stanford's emigrant guides, and (commencing in 1857), a series of government pamphlets intended to attract immigrants to Canada.

Two of Hutton's closest neighbours in what is now the west end of Belleville were John W. D. Moodie and his wife, Susanna Moodie. As emigrants from England in 1832, they arrived in Canada, after a difficult eight-week voyage, only to find a widespread cholera epidemic. They tried farming in Hamilton Township, near Port Hope, and then at Lakefield, near Peterborough. Unfortunately, they were not well-suited to the rigours of pioneer farm life.

The Rebellion of 1837 offered the Moodies a way to escape from the bush. Susanna's recently composed patriotic poems attracted favourable attention from the newly appointed lieutenant-governor, Sir George Arthur, and John was appointed paymaster to the militia at Belleville. At the conclusion of hostilities, he was appointed sheriff of the newly formed Hastings County, and Susanna

William Hutton, first superintendent of schools for the Victoria District (as Hastings County was known in the 1840s), first district warden, and first secretary (deputy minister) of the Bureau of Agriculture for the United Province of Canada. Courtesy of Hastings County Historical Society, HC-5696.

and the family joined him here at the end of 1839. His term as sheriff would not be easy. He was "well aware that his appointment had stirred up a hornet's nest of controversy and anger, especially among Tory supports and office-seekers in the Belleville and Kingston area ... he was seen as an outsider and, even worse, a Reform sympathizer."[6]

Always aware of the political enemies who plotted against him, Moodie conscientiously devoted himself to his duties as sheriff. Unfortunately, he did take some actions that left him open to court action, and his opponents pressed him at every turn, launching nuisance court suits and attempting to limit his income. On one occasion, while serving as returning officer in a provincial election, the threat of violence led him to call in government troops and close the polls early. At that point the Reform candidate, Robert Baldwin of Toronto, was leading Belleville Tory Edmund Murney, a distinguished and socially prominent lawyer. The Tories were suspicious of Moodie's handling of

John Wedderburn Dunbar Moodie, Susanna Moodie, and niece in front of Moodie Cottage, circa 1860. Courtesy of Hastings County Historical Society.

the election, because Baldwin was known to be a friend of the Moodies, who, in fact, soon named a son after him. Tory protests led the government to award the election to Murney and dismiss Moodie as returning officer. For his part, Baldwin remained in the legislature, having won a seat in Toronto and another in Ramous in Canada East (Quebec).[7]

Although Susanna has always been recognized as the more successful author of the couple, John helped her on several occasions, and also wrote two books on his eleven years as a soldier in the Cape Colony in South Africa. With his wife, he was a contributor to *The Literary Garland*, a new magazine published by John Lovell in Montreal. The Moodies, in particular Susanna, found the magazine to be a significant source of income. In fact, Susanna was the magazine's most prolific writer between 1840 and 1849 and provided "a serialized novel or memoirs — along with numerous stories and poems — nearly every year."[8] She had been well-trained for this type

Literary figures from the past returned on September 10, 2001, when the Hastings County Historical Society officially opened the Hastings Heritage Centre in the former Thurlow Town Hall in Cannifton. Although not on particularly good terms during their lifetimes, George Benjamin (founder of the Intelligencer *in 1834) and Susanna Moodie (noted author) agreed to assist in the festive occasion. In real life, they are Lee and Eleanor Jourard. Photo by author.*

of work during her early years in England, where she had been a successful author of children's literature, and of two books on the evils of Negro slavery as seen through the eyes of former slave Mary Prince of Antigua and slave Ashton Warner of St. Vincent.[9]

It was in Belleville during the 1850s that Susanna wrote the six books that led to her becoming one of the best-known literary figures in the colony. The first was the legendary *Roughing it in the Bush,* in which she described the tragedies and occasional lighter moments of her early years in the backwoods. It soon was followed by *Life in the Clearings*, in which she stressed conditions in the developing towns of Canada West, especially Belleville. Unfortunately, local readers had to import copies of *Life in the Clearings* from England or the United States, since it was not printed in Canada until 1959, more than a century after its original publication.[10]

Those Belleville readers who did have access to copies of *Life in the Clearings* in the 1850s must

have enjoyed its rich description of local life, covering all aspects, from markets and firefighting to weather and floods. As well as positive features of Belleville life, Susanna offered the occasional negative comment. Members of St. Thomas' Anglican Church might have been taken aback by her description of St. Thomas' Church as "but a homely structure … a great eyesore." No doubt Roman Catholics were upset when they read about their "enslavement … with a thousand superstitious observances which to us appear absurd." And few devout Presbyterians would have agreed when they read of "the soul-fettering doctrines of John Calvin," who was described as "stern, uncompromising, unlovable and unloved, an object of fear, rather than of affection."[11] Given these views on mainstream denominations, it is no wonder that the Moodies helped to establish a small Congregational church in Belleville in 1844. It is also not surprising that they were excommunicated from that church's fellowship and privileges within a year for what was described as "disorderly walk."[12]

If Susanna Moodie and her Strickland relatives were an important "cottage industry" of writers in the nineteenth century, it is also true that the study of their work has generated a healthy cottage industry in modern times. The discovery of correspondence and writings by the Moodies in an attic in New York State a few years ago, as well as other discoveries, has resulted in an overfilled library shelf in my den. The leader in this industry is Michael Peterman of Trent University. He is ably abetted by others, including Carl Ballstadt, Margaret Hopkins, Charlotte Gray, John Thurston, Audrey Morris, Marian Fowler, William New, Hugh Brewster, and even Margaret Atwood. The Moodies and their Strickland relatives, including the Catharine Parr Traill family, are in no danger of being forgotten.

Spiritualism and Séances

AT LEAST TWO of the new literary figures in Belleville were actively involved in séances and spiritualism. Susanna and John Moodie certainly dabbled in the occult and were, at times, strong believers. Their interest in the occult and the fact that Moodie Cottage had been the site of supernatural events, though this was strongly denied by some later owners, was long suspected.

The proof came after the National Library of Canada purchased a collection of family letters and journals found in the attic of a Moodie descendant in New York State. Known as the Patrick Henry Ewing Collection, this documentary treasure trove described the Moodies' strong interest in the supernatural. Fortunately, Michael Peterman and his associates have printed many of the letters in two books.

For example, in the autumn of 1855, Susanna wrote to Richard Bentley, her publisher in London, England, and described how Miss Kate Fox, the celebrated spirit rapper, had visited Moodie Cottage on several occasions at the invitation of John Moodie. As a spirit rapper, Fox was supposed to be able to communicate with the dead by tapping questions and awaiting responses by listening to tapping on tables or other objects. Susanna wrote: "She is certainly a witch, for you cannot help looking into the dreamy depths of those sweet violet eyes till you feel magnitized [*sic*] by them. . . . I do not believe that the raps are produced by spirits that have been of this world, but I cannot believe that she, with her pure spiritual face is capable of deceiving."

Susanna went on to describe how Fox apparently communicated with one of Susanna's deceased childhood friends, about whom "perhaps no one but myself on the whole American continent knew that such a person had ever existed." At the front door, Susanna heard raps and the door shook and vibrated. In the garden, the raps sounded from the ground. Susanna felt that the sounds were coming from Fox's spirit and not from the dead.[13]

Two days later, while the two women were standing by the piano, each with a hand resting on it, Susanna heard the strings of the piano accompany her husband on the flute. With Fox serving as a spirit medium, the answers to certain questions about Susanna's father (including the date, the place, and the cause of his death) were rapped out. Amazed, Susanna wrote, "The question being mental could not have been guessed by any person of common powers. But she may be Clairvoyant, and able to read unwritten thoughts."[14]

Certainly, Susanna could not fully fathom what she had witnessed. Nor could her husband, who wrote a letter two years later in which he described some of the same events. In addition, he described an unusual séance. Apparently, while walking in the street, he had met the town's mayor, Benjamin F. Davy. Knowing John's "curiosity on the subject of Spiritualism," the mayor told Moodie that Mrs. Davy had become "a tipping medium." He then invited Moodie to stop by for a demonstration. Having associated with Mrs. Davy for almost twenty years, Moodie knew that she was "a very intelligent and sincere woman … incapable of deception of any kind." On his first visit to the Davy house, with the mayor and one of their daughters also present, Moodie asked for information about his father. However, the messages that followed came not from Moodie's father, but from his eldest sister, about whom the spirit medium could not have had any information. Moodie found most of the answers highly credible, although not all were correct. He went on to describe other séances in Belleville and Toronto, and even developed a "spiritscope," an improved spirit machine based on a Ouija board, to facilitate communication with the spirit world, including his deceased son.

Moodie Cottage and the Davy House (still standing immediately east of the former Belleville Public Library) were not the only sites for unusual activities. Number 11 Charlotte Street, the residence of J. W. Tait, a civil engineer with the Grand Trunk Railway, was a centre for séances and strange appearances. Mary, a young Scottish servant, reported seeing a pale light spreading from the corner of a room, in the midst of which stood a man — later identified as John Reid, the former owner. Heavy furniture and various other objects moved and were thrown about the house and taps followed Mary wherever she went, convincing John Moodie that she was a spirit medium.[15] A

The Moodie tombstone at the Belleville Cemetery. The base was rebuilt a few years ago by Campbell Monument Co. Limited. Photo by author, 1991.

meticulous recorder of supernormal phenomena, he noted each séance in his Spiritualist diary and wrote several long articles for the *Spiritual Telegraph*, the movement's newspaper.

Prominent Brockville businessman A.N. Buell also left detailed records of séances. When he visited his daughter and her family at 231 John Street in January 1855, he attended several and left a word-by-word account of each.[16] In addition, before purchasing a house for his daughter and her husband, John O'Hare, Belleville's first Roman Catholic mayor, he consulted his wife. Although it was not unusual for a man to consult his wife about providing a home for their daughter's family, this case was unusual — his wife had been dead for three years.

In a recently published book, Stan McMullin of Carleton University credited the Fox sisters of New York State (and originally from Consecon), with introducing spiritualism to central Canada as a result of Kate's sessions with the Moodies. He explained that "Spirit communication, both as a religious exercise and as a scientific endeavour, grew out of the nineteenth century dialogue between science and religion."[17]

Although the 1850s were a high point in spiritualism locally, there have been numerous examples of its manifestations over the years. Currently, this writer has identified some forty local buildings and sites where unusual occurrences have been reported. They range from ghostly sightings in two Charles Street residences to UFO sightings over Elmwood Cemetery and Elizabeth Crescent.

Life and Culture in Mid-Century

ANYONE WISHING TO know what life was like in mid-nineteenth century Belleville must read the personal letters of Susanna Moodie and William Hutton. Their private descriptions are revealing and often entertaining. Moodie's public comments in *Life in the Clearings* were also frank, as seen in her criticism of *Intelligencer* founder George Benjamin and this description of the town in the early 1840s: "In spite of the great beauty of the locality, it was but an insignificant, dirty-looking place. The main street of the town (Front Street, as it is called) was only partially paved with rough slabs of limestone.... The few streets it then possessed were chiefly composed of frame houses, put up in the most unartistic and irregular fashion, their gable ends or fronts turned to the street, as it suited the whim or convenience of the owner, without the least regard to taste or neatness."[18] Fortunately, she later noted some improvements.

Other residents and visitors also commented. One apparently good-humoured merchant put the following notice in the newspaper: "The mudhole in front of our store is not without a bottom. Drive up, gentlemen, the town is good for damages if you lose your team...."[19] Visitors commented on the quality of the hotels. Although Munro's Mansion House at the Four Corners could advertise itself as "the largest, most comfortable, and most conveniently, and pleasantly situated Hotel in Belleville," it was apparent that Sir James Alexander was not impressed when he stayed at a rival hotel in 1848. He wrote: "... put up at the George Inn, where for one night they charged the same as for a whole day, that is, one dollar each. Our sleeping accommodation was not worth this, for we were put into a room six feet square, the bed occupying about four, and there was no chair to put one's clothes on."[20]

Visitors were particularly impressed with the churches, the courthouse, and the citizens' respect for law and order. In 1840, the editor of the *British Whig* wrote that the buildings that stood atop Taylor's Hill (the East Hill) "have a magnificent appearance and give Belleville the air of being a much larger town than it really is."[21] Susanna Moodie noted that there was not one execution at Belleville in the 1840s, and that "the thought of thieves and housebreakers never for a moment disturbs our rest." The editor of the *British Whig* agreed, noting that "but few criminals were convicted."[22] Reports in the Montreal press of a riot in 1846 between three-hundred Orangemen and Roman Catholics were branded as false. Drink, not religion, inspired the fracas in Harper's Bar during the Kingston Fire Companies' visit to Belleville.[23]

Certainly, there were more than enough taverns in the town, leading to the rise of Temperance organizations. There were hotels run on Temperance principles, where *temperance* meant temperance, not abstinence. Liquor was also a problem beyond Belleville's borders. An 1855 visitor complained that stagecoach travel was slow because the driver stopped at "every tavern between Belleville and Trenton."[24]

There were major changes in education. By 1845, the Victoria District's first grammar school was opened in rented quarters on the southwest corner of the courthouse lot. Alexander Burdon, recently arrived from Scotland, was the first teacher. The students used to play tricks on him. If he left the school to go downtown for a few minutes, the students would leave by a rear window that opened onto the side of the hill. When they saw him returning, they would quickly re-enter.

After 1850, when the Victoria District again became Hastings County, county council decided to build a grammar school on a lot set apart for that purpose in 1816. Accordingly, the grammar school trustees asked the Roman Catholics to remove their small, frame elementary school that had occupied part of the lot for a few years. The Roman Catholics were reluctant to move the school, which had served the congregation as its church until it was moved south in 1838. The dispute only ended when fire destroyed the building.[25] Accordingly, the grammar school became the second school on the site. It would be followed by the Belleville High School and then the Belleville Collegiate Institute and Vocational School.

Another important development was the opening of the Belleville Seminary in 1857 by the Methodist Episcopal Church. The school was intended for imparting "a sound mental and moral as well as a religious education to the children of our numerous friends, and especially to those young men who are desirous of qualifying themselves more fully for the ministry of our church." Rejecting possible government grants, church members raised enough funds to open the seminary to students on July 16, 1857, despite a business depression in both the United States and Canada. The school experienced serious problems in its early years. For example, in a letter home in the school's first year, a female student wrote that the boys were rowdy, that they would throw their washing water into the halls, and once threw a large rock at the principal's door, splitting the panel from top to bottom. While the board was holding a meeting to discuss the principal's disciplining of the students, the boys provided some light relief by hoisting a bedstead up to the top of the roof.[26]

Notwithstanding the "constant battle to meet the scarcity of money," the efforts of Albert Carman, newly appointed as principal in 1858, helped save the school. On August 15, 1866, the seminary received its university charter and became Albert University, with power to give degrees in arts. Alexandra College was established as the women's college, also with power to grant degrees, such as Mistress of Arts. Distinguished faculty members included the Reverend Joseph Wild, a noted orator, and John Macoun, professor of natural history and botany, whose surveys for the government helped determine the route for the transcontinental railway. After Methodist Union in 1884, Albert College lost most of its university powers to Victoria College, Cobourg,

Albert College, when it was located on College Street prior to the fire. The street was named for the college. Courtesy of Hastings County Historical Society.

and became largely a secondary school. In recent years, it has extended its successful program to include elementary grades. Today, Albert College attracts students from around the world.

Another significant development was the opening of the area's first library. Although most people assume that the Mechanics' Institute established the first public library, the first one, in fact, was the Thurlow Circulating Library, established just north of Belleville in Cannifton, a community that became part of Belleville in 1998. W.R. Bigg, a teacher, helped set up the library, which printed a *Report of the*

Board of Management of the Thurlow Circulating Library to its Members, Thurlow, Jan. 4, 1848.[27] Annual membership fees were five shillings, and no one could borrow more than one book at a time from the collection of 120 volumes. Although the library was not in Belleville, several donations of cash or books came from such prominent Belleville residents as Edmund Murney, Francis McAnnany, and John Moodie.

There were many other activities for those not interested in using the library. Cricket was arguably the leading sport. Cricket teams were formed at least as early as the 1830s, and the boast of the Belleville teams in the 1840s was "Belleville against Toronto — Cobourg — Kingston — the whole world." The editor of a Kingston newspaper once referred to team members as "singed cats — ugly to look at but very devils to go."[28] Horse racing was another popular sport. The Victoria Turf Club was set up in August 1850, and races were held at the end of September "over the Course on Lot No. 6, first concession of Thurlow."[29] Circuses, gambling and lotteries, and the Belleville fair (revived in 1848 after a period of dormancy) were also very popular.

Susanna Moodie, who approved of entertainment designed to elevate rather than degrade, was a strong supporter of the Victoria Brass Band, formed in the 1840s. Its repertoire in 1847 included a new song, "O Can You Leave Your Native Land," with words by Susanna and music by her husband.[30] Some concerts were fundraisers. In 1855, there was a concert to aid the orphans and widows of the Crimean War, and in 1857 a concert in the Town Hall helped to raise funds for Belleville's poor.

There were a few theatrical performances, usually by local amateurs. One of the few professionals to appear was Horton Rhys, an English performer who described his stay in 1860 in unflattering terms. Not only was Mr. Lester's theatre new, consisting simply of lath and plaster, but it was cold, so cold that the actors regretted having come to Belleville at US$50 a night.[31]

Despite the international depression of the 1850s, there were encouraging economic developments. Thanks in part to the Crimean War (1854–56), which increased British demand for Belleville's products, the Port of Belleville continued to export large quantities of timber, other wood products, flour, and grain to Britain and the United States. Furs, high wines, and whiskies also went to the States, as well as a number of oxen, which were sent across the ice in winter. Belleville's imports were largely manufactured goods, three-quarters of which came from the United States.

The local government assumed additional responsibilities when Belleville was incorporated as a town, effective January 1, 1850. The wooden market building, destroyed by fire, was soon replaced by a brick building that housed town offices and a police court, as well as a market. In 1854, the gas works were set up to provide gas for lighting and other purposes. The same year, the provincial government began intensive efforts to open the land north of Madoc for settlement. The Hastings Colonization Road moved settlers into the area — settlers who came through Belleville and purchased supplies from local merchants. Unfortunately, the inhospitable landscape led to the failure of most farms.

The economy received a further boost after November 30, 1859, when county council voted to make all toll roads free. The decision followed a vote of county ratepayers, including those in Belleville. Among the roads where tolls had been charged for some twenty years was the Belleville to Frankford road. Toll roads had served their purpose by encouraging private companies to construct them, but by 1859 they were creating problems. In 1863, all toll houses were sold. This action was one of the last county council took on behalf of Belleville. On June 27, 1860, council agreed to Belleville's separation from the county for municipal purposes. Belleville was now independent, although there was a continuing need for co-operation between the two municipalities. Today the City of Belleville, the County of Hastings, and the City of Quinte West work together in a large number of areas.

Education: Equality and Segregation

The 1850s and 1860s saw three major developments that affected the education of girls in Belleville. The first, which benefited girls more than boys, was the removal of fees and the provision of free education for students in the common schools (comparable to today's elementary schools). The second, which affected boys and girls equally, was the decision to build four new schools. The third, which was far more controversial, was the transfer of girls from the Belleville Grammar School to their own secondary school.

In 1850, the Police Village of Belleville became the Town of Belleville. In accordance with the School Act of 1850, the newly created Board of School Trustees (composed of very prominent citizens, including three medical doctors), appointed the Reverend William Gregg of John Street Presbyterian Church as school superintendent and declared that four common schools should be built, one in each of the town's four wards. The board applied to town council for a tax levy to build these schoolhouses. It also asked the town to remove its "Hook and Ladder house" from the common school lot.[32]

Prior to this time, the schools had been located in rented facilities, usually in buildings provided by the teachers themselves. Until the four schools could be built, the board agreed to pay the teachers for the use of their schoolhouses. For example, the board minutes of January 27, 1851 indicated that it would pay popular teacher John Steele "for the Rent of his school house and the use of his stove." Annual teachers' salaries were set at a £100.

On January 17, 1851, the school board unanimously agreed that the schools should be free for the ensuing year, and that the funds for supporting them be levied by assessment.[33] This development, made possible by the new legislation and encouraged by the chief superintendent of education (Egerton Ryerson), and the Council of Public Instruction for Upper Canada, was a major change in policy. Its effects would be dramatic. Whereas parents had previously sent most of their sons and some of their daughters to school, they were now sending almost all of their children. In 1852, average attendance at Steele's school climbed from 67 in January to 94 in June.[34] The following year, it reached 100 for the first quarter of the year and 120 for the second quarter. Given this rapid increase, the board approved the employment of assistant teachers in schools where attendance warranted it, commencing in September 1852. After further consideration, the board adopted "a system of classification," whereby it employed female assistant teachers to instruct the younger scholars."[35] The board also resolved that the teachers "have the privilege of Teaching night school

The Pinnacle Street School, just south of Market Square, erected in 1851 as one of several schools built during the early 1850s. Courtesy of Topley Studio/ Library and Archives Canada, PA-12561.

in their respective School Houses."[36] This would provide the teachers with added revenue.

August 18, 1852 was a "red letter" day for education. The board held "a Public Jubilee" to celebrate the opening of its new schoolhouses. The pupils assembled at the schoolhouse just south of the Market Square and marched north along Pinnacle and North Front streets to the grove, where speeches "are to be delivered and refreshments served in the usual manner of a Picnic."[37] Notices were placed in both the *Intelligencer* and the *Chronicle* and handbills were posted up about the town announcing the program. At the last minute, a special invitation was extended to the Orangemen and Masons. Like many events of its type — both then and now — this celebration included addresses by members of the board and numerous other dignitaries, among them seven local ministers. No doubt the young students were somewhat bored and fidgety while they waited for the refreshments. However, they were well-supervised by their teachers, under the direction of Doctor G.V.N. Relyea, described as "the resident dentist of Belleville for twenty years," who had been named "Marshall of the Day."

Life was not easy for the school trustees. They faced various challenges, some of them similar to those faced by trustees in the modern era. Because of the rapidly expanding cost of education (caused in large part by the increased numbers of students and teachers), town council refused to levy the funds the school board requested in 1853.[38] As a result, the board hired its own tax collector. In addition, the board instructed its superintendent to ensure that he strictly enforce the board's policy of excluding the children of Roman Catholic separate school supporters, since their education taxes went to that board.[39] In 1856, the public board went so far as to petition the legislature to protest the proposed extension of the powers of the separate school system and to ask for the "repeal of the law altogether."[40] Further, there was a problem concerning the disappearance of a "sheet containing the Ten Commandments" from Mr. Lynch's schoolhouse. Following an investigation, the board ruled that panels listing the Ten Commandments be posted behind each teacher's desk. Also, selections from the Holy Scriptures were to be read "without note or comment" twice in each week — Monday and Saturday mornings at the opening of school.[41]

Another occasional problem the board faced was the question of staff relations. Although there was no teachers' association or union in the 1850s, increasing workloads and other concerns led the male teachers to approach the board collectively. On August 15, 1854, the board considered an application from these teachers for an increase in salary. The issue was referred to a committee for study. Possibly upset by the lack of a positive response, John Steele submitted his resignation, allegedly caused by "his failing health." Two months later, he was re-engaged at a salary of £125, an increase of 25 per cent over his previous salary.[42] His health must have improved quickly, since he taught for several more years.

Steele must have wondered whether the extra payment was worth the effort. So popular a teacher was he that students in his school who should have transferred to the grammar school tried to remain with him. The board normally ruled against such requests, although it did allow William Kerr's children to remain with Steele because of "the inability of little girls to attend at a long distance during the inclement season."[43] Moreover, parents from other school districts tried to transfer their students to his school. These requests were generally denied because the school's attendance had reached 150. No wonder frequent staff changes remained a problem throughout the 1850s.

Among the most active trustees was Mackenzie Bowell, publisher of the *Intelligencer*. Bowell chaired the board for several years and made an impassioned plea for parents to help the school system. He called on them:

1. to encourage rather than hinder the teachers' attempts to encourage punctuality,
2. to support, rather than criticize teachers,
3. to attend the quarterly exams, thus encouraging the students and the teachers, and
4. to supply the children with paper, books and slates.[44]

Women's role in education took a step forward in 1853, when the board allowed a female teacher to be in charge of a new school, known as Number 5. Located in the former hospital on Hotel Street (Victoria Avenue), it was opened to help relieve crowding in Steele's school.[45] Further, by 1858, the four other common schools all had female assistants.[46] Some of these teachers (for example, Miss Tapson), had previously operated private schools.

The situation in the local Roman Catholic schools was similar in several ways. Enrolment continued to increase. There were more boys than girls (223 compared to 173 in 1860). Male teachers received higher salaries than female teachers, although all teachers' salaries were reduced by 10 percent in 1860, because of financial problems. To provide a practical and aesthetic option for girls, needlework became part of the curriculum in 1862 and 50 girls took the subject.[47]

Meanwhile, there were changes taking place in the grammar, or secondary, schools. By 1850, about half of the grammar schools in the province were admitting girls, although these schools, based on the English model, were intended for boys only. Similarly, some grammar schools were rivals to the common schools, since they received pupils who were unable to write. The Belleville board tried to deal with this problem by examining its students and recommending those it felt should be admitted to the grammar school. The provincial grammar school inspector reported on such problems following a one-day visit to the Belleville school on November 5, 1855. He found that 20 of the 110 registered students were girls and that attendance "as in most large towns is not regular." Only 77 students were present. More important, there were only 23 students taking Latin and no students taking Greek. Yet these classical languages were supposed to be key components of the grammar school curriculum.[48]

In an attempt to stress the classical languages, Egerton Ryerson persuaded the legislature to pass the Grammar School Act of 1865. Effective January 1, 1866, no school was to receive any portion of the Grammar School Fund unless it had an average daily attendance of at least 10 pupils learning Greek or Latin.[49] Moreover, the board had to raise an amount (exclusive of student fees) equal to at least half of the provincial grants and only students taking the classics would count for grant purposes. This was a change from the previous year, when counties received funding in proportion to their populations. Ryerson felt that the many girls entering the classics "impaired the efficiency and standing of the Grammar Schools."[50] Nevertheless, in 1865, the grammar school grants were apportioned "without distinction to sex." The following year, grants for girls in grammar schools were cut in half, causing much concern since it cost as much to educate a girl as a boy. Finally, in 1867, grants for girls were discontinued entirely. These actions followed biting comments by former Grammar School Inspector Professor Young: "Boys and Girls alike, with the merest smattering of English Grammar, — every child supposed to have any chance of wriggling through the meshes of the Inspector's examining net, — driven like sheep into the Grammar School, and put into Latin in order to swell the roll of the Grammar School pupils, and to entitle the School to a larger share of the Grammar School Fund."[51]

Following a tour of neighbouring states in the United States and several European countries in 1867, Ryerson brought in a report for government consideration. Confessing to be concerned with the need for the "superior education of girls," he suggested the possibility of high schools for girls.[52] The Belleville board jumped at this possibility, especially after receiving legal advice that it did not have "the power to permit the continued attendance of Girls at the County Grammar School."[53] On July 7, 1868, the board set up a committee to make arrangements for "renting a School Room in the building known as the Bull Building for the Education of the Girls now leaving the Grammar School and such others as may be of advanced age and acquirements."[54] This school, known as School Number 6, was to be "taught and conducted by females … on the principal [sic] of the Girls' Model school of Toronto." The board anticipated up to a hundred scholars and arranged for entrance exams on Monday mornings.

During the 1868–69 academic year, the girls had their school in the Bull Block on Dundas Street, and the Belleville Grammar School was an all-boys school. When Grammar School Inspector Mackenzie made a visit to the school at the end of the school year, he found only 52 students — all boys — in attendance. He reported that Alexander Burdon, the principal teacher, was "full of energy, and seemed to be ten years younger." The clear implication was that Burdon found it much easier to administer and teach in an all-boys school. At the same time, the inspector was sorry to see the "extreme youthfulness of many of the Entrance Pupils; it does not promise well for the vigor [*sic*] of the school."[55]

Undoubtedly, these younger students were admitted to swell the government grant, which was much larger for grammar school scholars than for those in the common schools.

After only one year, the government relented and girls were recognized as regular grammar school pupils. Nevertheless, the school board continued to operate the girls' school, with some changes. The school's Junior Department was abolished and the Senior Department was to accommodate all the senior girls in the town, to a maximum of fifty. Presumably, if there were more than fifty, the regular board policy would apply. Although the teacher would not dismiss any student already admitted, if any student was absent without satisfactory cause, that student would forfeit the seat. She could be readmitted when a vacancy occurred.[56]

Students at the girls' school did something that few boys in the grammar school had ever done. They submitted a petition to the board. It asked for a week's holidays at Easter, 1870. The request was not granted, "inasmuch as the Common School Law does not permit of such holidays to be given. Good Friday was the only holiday allowed."[57] Later that year, the board discontinued the girls' school.[58]

In the course of twenty years, female education in Belleville had witnessed some major changes. Girls could attend common schools without paying fees. They could attend grammar school and not be required to take Latin and/or Greek. They could be the principal teacher in a Belleville school. Moreover, they could go on to the Ladies College (part of Albert College) where they could earn a Mistress in English Literature (MEL) without taking the classics, or a Mistress in Liberal Arts (ML.A). Still, they had a long way to go to attain full equality with boys if you believe that the Reverend Septimus Jones, M.A., first rector of Christ Church and

The Belleville Grammar School with senior elementary and high school students under headmaster Alexander Burdon and assistant William Tilley, circa 1860. Courtesy of Hastings County Historical Society.

Belleville Superintendent of Schools, was serious when he included this statement in an 1869 article on logic: "Many (especially it is said, of the gentler sex) seem to leap to their conclusions, some run, some walk, some hobble, and some even seem to crawl."[59]

The Belleville Abolitionist[60]

THE NAME OF Alexander Milton Ross is largely unknown in Belleville. Yet, he is remembered elsewhere as a Belleville native who was part of the Underground Railroad and helped free slaves in the United States prior to the Civil War. A man of "diverse interests and accomplishments," he was also a physician, author, naturalist, and reformer.

Ross (1832–97), the child of William Ross and Frederika Grant, was "born into a family with a tradition of public activity." From his mother, he gained his idealism and "love of nature and freedom." From his father, who died when Alexander was only eleven, he gained a sense of independence, since he had to leave home when he was sixteen. Employed in the New York newspaper office of William Cullen Bryant, he soon devoted himself to the study of medicine (1851–55) and then became active in the abolition movement. Wandering through the southern states, he posed as an ornithologist while secretly meeting with slaves and giving them information and supplies to help them reach Canada.

Dr. Alexander Milton Ross, "The Abolitionist," a lithograph in the Canadian Illustrated News, *March 19, 1881.* Courtesy of Library and Archives Canada, C-76543.

He described his southern activities — highlighted by meetings with many abolitionists, including the legendary John Brown — in two books — *Recollections and Experiences of an Abolitionist, from 1855 to 1865* (1875) and *Memoirs of a Reformer, 1832–1892* (1893). The books also described his acquaintanceship with such famous people as Abraham Lincoln, for whom he acted as a secret agent to uncover Confederate activities in Canada, Giuseppe Garibaldi, the unifier of Italy, and such authors as Ralph Waldo Emerson and Henry Wadsworth Longfellow.

Ross also championed other causes. In 1865, he criticized British and Canadian politicians for stirring up groundless anti-Americanism and urged Canadians to free themselves from the monarchy. In his travels he collected and classified Canadian flora and fauna and published several related books, complete with pencil sketches. From 1875 to 1882 he led a crusade for moral and physical reform. He formed the Canadian Society for the Diffusion of Physiological Knowledge and published a tract entitled *The evils arising from unphysiological habits in youth* (presumably masturbation). In the early 1880s, he joined the campaign against compulsory vaccination and, with associates in the Canadian Anti-Vaccination League, successfully challenged the imposition of compulsory vaccination in the Quebec courts. He argued that the uneven quality of the vaccine rendered vaccination "a risky and unpredictable operation," and that compulsory vaccination was an abuse of human rights and "a physical crime" that "tramples down parental authority in relation to children."

Ross was ahead of his time in some ways. He emphasized prevention instead of cure, and crusaded for municipalities to provide improved water and sewage systems. He also wanted public education to stress personal and domestic cleanliness and a healthy diet.

Biographer Carl Ballstadt described Ross as an enigmatic figure, in that "most of what is known about him seems to have come from his own accounts of his career." Supporting documentation is needed from other sources to confirm his roles in various activities, especially his role in freeing American slaves. Nevertheless, Ross could be described as "a nineteenth-century crusader for individual freedom" whose major concerns were abolition, natural history, and the evils of vaccination.

It is unknown if any of the slaves Ross helped ended up settling in Belleville. However, we do know that William Hutton employed former slaves on his local farm. On August 20, 1852, he wrote: "We have had three coloured men working for us this harvest, escaped slaves; very excellent workmen and very intelligent men."[61] Also, church records indicate the burial of "mulattoes" (persons with one white and one black parent) in at least one cemetery.

The Arrival of the Railway, October 27, 1856

MONDAY, OCTOBER 27, 1856, was one of the most important days in Belleville's history. On that day, dignitaries and citizens gathered to welcome the arrival of the first railway train. No doubt there were some children present, since children generally love trains, although there is no evidence to suggest that this was an official school holiday.

The celebration had been anticipated for a long time. Almost twenty years earlier, George Benjamin's *Intelligencer* had come out strongly in favour of railways, especially one linking Belleville to Madoc and Marmora and their mining resources.[62] However, this "Moira Valley Route" would have to wait until after the construction of a line linking the communities along the shores of Lake Ontario.

As early as 1845, a meeting to consider constructing a Toronto to Kingston railway was held at Belleville, described by the Kingston press as "the most central Town on the intended line." Edmund Murney, MLA, chaired the "GREAT RAILWAY MEETING," at which Francis McAnnany, Henry Corby, and other leading businessmen spoke in favour of the railway. Some speakers also wanted a branch line to Marmora, where convict labour might be used to work the mines, with the iron then taken to Belleville for manufacturing. The Kingston press concluded its account: "Let every one think of the Railway, speak of the Railway, and all who can write of the Railway. Agitate! Agitate! Agitate![63]

Soon the concept of a Toronto to Kingston railway expanded to Prescott and then Montreal. The result was the Grand Trunk Railway, chartered in 1852 and largely financed by British capital. Construction was done in sections, and the company soon advertised for two-hundred men to work on the track and bridges at Belleville. Inasmuch as Sandford Fleming had not yet introduced the concept of standard time zones — that would be done in 1884 — the trains ran on Montreal time, which was 14½ minutes faster than Belleville time.

These early trains were quite unlike today's trains. The coaches were open-platform and hand-braked. A stove at each end of the coach provided warmth, and kerosene lamps provided some light. Toilet facilities were primitive. The maximum speed of thirty-five miles an hour was slow by modern standards, but fast compared to stagecoaches, which only travelled about seventy-five miles a day. Writing to her London publisher a month after the railway opened, Susanna Moodie marvelled at the locomotive engine: "The sight filled me with awe. The spirit of man seemed at work in the wondrous machine, as the spirit of God works in us. What will not mind accomplish, when it can perform wonders like this." Although she had not yet ventured as a passenger, she noted that traffic upon the railway in its first month was "immense." She hoped that it would pay its shareholders handsomely "as it will be of immense importance to the colony."[64]

The Grand Trunk railway station, shortly after its erection in 1856. A second storey was later added to the station, which continues to serve VIA passengers today. Courtesy of Hastings County Historical Society, HC-6101.

Susanna was correct in her prediction. The Grand Trunk, now part of the Canadian National (CNR) system, was vitally important to Canada and to Belleville. Local lawyer John Bell was the company's first solicitor. Belleville was an original surveying and contracting centre, and then a divisional point. One of the railway's first locomotive shops was located here. By 1864, there were a hundred people employed at the shops and yards, and employment would later pass the 1,000 mark, making the railway the city's largest employer for many years. Prior to the First World War, the roundhouse in Belleville was described as one of the largest in North America. For several years after the Second World War, until railway restructuring, the city served as the headquarters of the CNR Rideau District.

Other railways served Belleville in addition to the Grand Trunk Railway. The earliest was the Grand Junction Railway. Incorporated first in 1852, it was intended to

Actors in period costume watched the 1956 ceremonial re-enactment of the driving of the last spike to complete the Grand Trunk Railway line between Toronto and Montreal in 1856. Courtesy of Hastings County Historical Society, Mika Collection, CN Photograph 52504-7.

run through Peterborough to Toronto and serve as a loop line for the Grand Trunk. Unfortunately, despite offers of substantial assistance from the councils of both Belleville and Hastings County, little was accomplished. However, in 1870, the charter was revived by a Belleville group that received about $500,000 worth of municipal and provincial aid. Although little money was raised through the sale of stocks, and construction was held up by legal disputes and the bankruptcy of the Brockville contractor, work did proceed. On June 28, 1877, the Toronto *Globe* reported that the first carload of freight had passed over the road from Stirling to Belleville. Two years later, the line reached Peterborough, a distance of about 145 kilometres.

The Grand Junction Railway's southern terminal was at the Belleville waterfront, the site

of a small switching yard. The passenger station was in the former Pinnacle Street Methodist Chapel. Rolling stock included several "diamond stack" wood-burning locomotives that pulled carloads of lumber and other products to Belleville. By 1880, the Grand Junction Railway also controlled the Belleville and North Hastings Railway, which ran north from Madoc Junction to Madoc, Eldorado, and the nearby iron works. The following year, the Midland Railway, which was essentially a branch of the Grand Trunk, absorbed both railways. The Pinnacle Street track continued to be used until 1964, when it was officially closed as part of Railway Week.

Unfortunately, other changes had taken place that resulted in less traffic for the Belleville-based northern rail system. By 1884 the Central Ontario Railway, an expansion of the Prince Edward Railway Company line between Picton and Trenton Junction, had reached Coe Hill and, on November 7, 1907, the citizens of Bancroft welcomed this rail link to Trenton and Picton. Likewise, the Canadian Pacific Railway line through Tweed and the Bay of Quinte Railway line linking Deseronto, Napanee, and Central Hastings drew rail traffic away from Belleville.

Nevertheless, Belleville remains an important rail centre. It has large freight yards and excellent passenger train service to Toronto, Montreal, and Ottawa. The waterfront is the site of an important railway monument, largely financed by railroaders and their friends. The locomotive that stood on Zwick's Park as a memorial to our railway history is gone; however it is preserved at Memory Junction, located in the former Grand Trunk/CNR station in Brighton, within sight of the dozen or more passenger trains that pass daily. There have been several celebrations to remember Belleville's historic railway past, including events in 2006 to commemorate the 150th anniversary of the arrival of the first train on October 27, 1856. Certainly, many present and former railroaders, as well as their families, are proud to call Belleville home.

A Capital Idea

There was a time in the mid-1850s when Belleville residents thought their town might become the capital of the United Province of Canada (as Ontario and Quebec were then known). Arguably, the seat-of-government issue was "the most contentious matter" to be faced by the province's politicians.[65] From 1841 to 1859, there were 218 votes directly related to the issue and several cities were considered — notably Quebec, Montreal, Ottawa (known as Bytown until 1855), Kingston, and Toronto.[66]

Belleville residents submitted a petition suggesting their town as the logical choice. After all, it had 6,000 residents, expanding industry (including bustling lumber mills), and several foundries and similar businesses. It was the centre of an important agricultural district whose products went to markets in the United Kingdom and the United States. The Grand Trunk Railway had selected Belleville as one of two divisional points on the railway line being built between Montreal and Toronto. There were boat connections with Kingston and Toronto, and the Bay of Quinte offered shelter for vessels. In addition, the government was opening the Hastings Colonization Road north from Madoc, and there were mineral deposits in the area. The town was also a cultural centre. There was a new district grammar school, Albert College was about to open at the town's north end, author Susanna Moodie had lived in Belleville for some fifteen years, and churches were prospering. Residents were sure that Belleville offered greater advantages than other centres such as Toronto (too far west), Quebec City (too far east), Ottawa (too remote), and Kingston (too gentrified and too close to the United States). Unfortunately, the local parties responsible for seeing that the petition reached Queen Victoria were either not aware of the prescribed route for petitioning the queen or simply failed to follow it. Accordingly, when the government received the petition, officials refused to forward it because it had not gone through the proper channels.[67]

Finally, when it was decided in 1857 to refer the issue to Queen Victoria, the mayors of the five principal contending cities were invited to send memorials to the queen for a decision. For its part, the Town of Belleville also sent a memorial in another attempt to influence the capital choice. On behalf of the town council and its citizens, Mayor Francis McAnnany signed and submitted a petition supporting Kingston's candidacy.[68] It stressed that Kingston was "situated at the entrance of the beautiful Bay of Quinte, the natural outlet of the fertile country that borders its waters." Moreover, Kingston was accessible to all areas of the provinces and had good defences. The petition concluded with a prayer "for your Majesty's continued prosperity."

Canadian Governor General Sir Edmund Head was the leading figure in the decision-making process. In a confidential memorandum, he wrote that "the least objectionable place is the city of Ottawa. Every city is jealous of every other city except Ottawa…. The whole matter is a choice of evils."[69]

Did Queen Victoria read or even see Belleville's petition in support of Kingston? Probably not. However, she could not help but be aware of the next incident involving the royal family and Belleville, namely the ill-fated attempt by her eldest son, the Prince of Wales, to walk the streets of the town and meet its citizens on September 6, 1860.

5
THE CONFEDERATION ERA

A Royal Problem, September 6, 1860[1]

SINCE THE UNITED Empire Loyalists arrived in the area following the American Revolution, the citizens of Belleville have had positive feelings about the British monarchy. Nowhere in our history was this more evident than when the Prince of Wales (the future King Edward VII), eldest son of Queen Victoria and heir apparent to the throne, came to North America in 1860 and planned an overnight stay in the town as part of his itinerary. Officially, he was in Canada (at the invitation of the Canadian government) to open Montreal's Victoria Bridge (the railway-connecting link between the Atlantic colonies and Canada West, now called Ontario), and lay the cornerstone for the new Parliament Buildings at Ottawa. Unofficially, he was in the British colonies to reassure the colonists that British imperialists valued them, to express the queen's appreciation for Canadian assistance during the Crimean War (1854–56), and to promote a positive image of the monarchy. In addition, the prince would make an unofficial whirlwind tour of a dozen major cities in the eastern United States in an effort to improve relations between Great Britain and her former colonies.

Certainly, Albert Edward (or "Bertie" as he was commonly known), the eighteen-year-old Prince of Wales, was an excellent choice to make this inaugural visit by a British royal to Canada. Handsome, intelligent, and the son of a beloved queen, he was the oldest of the queen's nine children, and was heir to the world's most powerful nation and empire.

Belleville and Hastings County citizens were excited about the proposed visit. Town and county governments took the lead in making preparations. County council set up a committee to draft an address of loyalty and set aside $500 to help provide an elaborate reception. Belleville

The Prince of Wales, 1859, engraving by A.W. Graham based on a painting by Franz Xavier Winterhalter, from frontispiece in The Tour of H.R.H. The Prince of Wales through British America and the United States by a British Canadian *(Montreal: John Lovell, 1860).*

council took similar steps, but a dispute between the mayor, Doctor William Hope, and the majority of councillors marred the planning. Councillors had refused to accept an address drawn up at a public meeting and, in retaliation, the mayor refused to sign the council's congratulatory address to the prince. Accordingly, council instructed the Belleville reeve to sign the address on behalf of council and the citizens. Council also declared September 6 a public holiday and placed large posters throughout the district. Farmers were advised that the market would be closed and that "Disappointment and loss will ensue from bringing any produce to the town … except full loads of Canada's best produce, her MEN, WOMEN, AND CHILDREN."

Businesses, organizations, and citizens had gone all-out with decorations. They had erected nine great arches across the prince's procession route. Evergreens decorated many of these arches, and the one constructed by Brown's Foundry had pillars made of potash kettles stacked one above the other. There were no Loyal Orange Lodge emblems or flags visible on any arch. This was in keeping with instructions from the British colonial secretary, the Duke of Newcastle, who accompanied the prince. Newcastle had decreed that the prince must not associate with any partisan "banners or other badges of distinction which are known to be offensive to any portion of Her Majesty's subjects," since a display of such emblems might "lead to religious feud and breach of the peace." In other words, Newcastle did not want to offend Canadian Roman Catholics. In Kingston, when the Orangemen had displayed their emblems on September 4, the duke had instructed the prince not to leave his boat. The aborted visit disappointed Kingstonians, who were eager to receive the prince.

When the *Kingston*, an Upper Canada mail steamer that had been refitted and decorated for carrying the prince and his party, arrived at Belleville at nine o'clock on the evening of September 5, the church bells rang out to welcome the distinguished visitor. The militia fired three guns on the Court House Hill as a welcome. Meanwhile, Colonel Thomas Wily, a young officer in the Canadian militia who had helped make advance arrangements for the tour, was already on the scene. Governor General Sir Edmund Head had sent Wily ahead to Belleville, by train, to check for possible problems. He learned from Belleville mayor, Doctor Hope, that no difficulties were expected from the local Orangemen. Dressed in their regalia, they would remain by their arch. The prince could then enter the town by another route and avoid them.

Unfortunately the situation changed overnight. There are conflicting versions as to what actually happened. A newspaper account indicated that at 12:30 a.m. the steamer *Bay of Quinte* sailed into Belleville's harbour and Orange demonstrators from Kingston streamed ashore. Colonel Wily recalled that the group arrived "first thing the next morning" by train.[2] Perhaps the Kingston Orangemen came both by land and by water. In any event, they convinced local Orangemen to join them in showing their great loyalty to the Crown by prominently displaying more Orange flags and emblems. At daybreak, they mustered "in full numbers, in full regalia, with their bands of music, paraded the street, determined to receive the Prince." Alerted to these developments by Wily, Governor General Head's face "turned as black as thunder" and the Duke of Newcastle prepared to give orders to leave Belleville. But first, his staff invited Mayor Hope to come to the ship at 7:30 a.m. "to smooth the way for the landing." The mayor was rowed out to the *Kingston,* but failed to negotiate a solution. The prince and his party sailed on to Cobourg aboard the steamer.

Thousands of disappointed people remained on shore. They included 1,500 town and county schoolchildren, dressed alike in black and white, who were to have sung the national anthem. According to one account, "It was perfectly touching to witness the sorrowful countenances of the people … all their exertions, all their toil destroyed." Particularly upset were a number of young women who had expected to provide a mounted escort for the prince. Colonel Wily described the "sad looks on their pretty faces." Shortly, Mayor Hope addressed the crowd and hoped that those who came from a distance would "spend a pleasant day." The crowd gave three cheers for the queen, three for the prince, and three for Mayor Hope.

An hour later, two-hundred Orangemen gathered in front of the Dafoe House. They reaffirmed their loyalty to the queen, the Kingston Orangemen, and Giuseppe Garibaldi (an Italian patriot trying to unify his country). They gave three groans for the Duke of Newcastle, and then paraded the streets with bands playing and banners flying.

In addition, about two-hundred "Phisiogs" in outlandish costumes paraded. Formally known as the Phisiocarnivalogicalists, these men mocked the fraternal orders that were prominent in the official civic processions. They billed themselves as "belonging to the 'tribes of the Illustrious Order of the Chloronophthelossossulphuricosso'" and added a humorous touch to the day.[3] That evening, despite the absence of the guests of honour, the town illuminated. There were coloured lamps, bonfires, and fireworks.

Edmund Murney and his family were among the many disappointed citizens. There is a long-standing belief that the Murneys had redecorated their already attractive residence on Murney's Hill in anticipation of the Prince of Wales spending part of his visit there, perhaps for a formal dinner or even an overnight stay. However, there is no record of such a planned stay in Colonel Wily's reminiscences.

Town officials and leading citizens refused to give up. Mayor Hope, his council, and three-hundred citizens were waiting for the prince when he reached Toronto two days later. They expressed their apologies and loyalty to him, and asked him to return to Belleville. Mackenzie Bowell and other leading local Orangemen promised that lodge members would not display any emblems or flags. The Prince of Wales replied that this display of loyalty had removed "all painful feelings occasioned by the proceedings." However, his itinerary could not be changed.

No official representatives from Hastings County Council went to Toronto with the Belleville delegation. In fact, county council felt that the prince's advisors should be the ones to apologize. Warden George Benjamin, founder of the *Intelligencer,* felt that he had been slighted. The prince's advisors had contacted Mayor Hope about the problem the Orangemen had created, but had made no attempt to contact the warden. When Doctor Hope wrote privately, asking Benjamin to accompany him in the rowboat to speak to the Duke of Newcastle and the Prince of Wales, Benjamin refused, noting, "The same effort which discovered your residence would enable his Grace to discover mine if he desired to see me." Accordingly, by an overwhelming majority, county council approved a resolution concerning the "want of courtesy" shown by the prince's advisors.

So ended one of the most unusual events in our history. The events of September 6 illustrated such positive attributes as the importance of the monarchy to local residents and their pride in their community. Yet it also shed light on some underlying problem areas, including relations between Protestants and Roman Catholics, and between town and county governments.

History would record that the local events had an impact on the rest of the prince's tour. Aware that the prince had not met with the citizens of Kingston and Belleville because of the Orange/Catholic issue, Orangemen in other Ontario centres kept their flags furled, their emblems hidden, and their slogans out of sight. They wanted to meet the prince and demonstrate their loyalty. If that meant keeping their Orange agenda out of sight for a brief time, so be it.

The Aylwards Must Hang

THE HASTINGS COUNTY Court House in Belleville was the site of several important trials in the nineteenth century. Arguably, the most significant was the Aylward trial on October 20, 1862. Not only did it result in a double hanging that was attended by thousands of area residents, but it also revealed the bitter local rivalry between Roman Catholics and Protestants, and subsequently reached the Parliament of Canada. In addition, a full report of the facts of the case, complete with the testimony of all witnesses, was published in Quebec.[4]

The trial involved Richard and Mary Aylward of Monteagle Township, about 125 kilometres north of Belleville in North Hastings. They were charged with murdering William Munro, a neighbouring farmer in Wicklow Township, on May 16, 1862, following a dispute over Munro's hens trespassing in the Aylwards' wheat field. The two families lived on opposite side of the road separating the two townships. The Aylwards were alleged to have killed Munro with a blow from a scythe, which penetrated his brain. Munro had not died immediately, but lived for about ten days. Witnesses testified that Mary Aylward was not apologetic about Munro's death. In fact, she was quoted as saying that she was glad "Old Baldie was dead; that if he was alive she would cut the head off him again, or any persons who would do anything to her."

The judge in the case was Chief Justice William Henry Draper, a former attorney general who had been virtually prime minister of Canada from 1844–47. The crown attorney was Adam Wilson, solicitor general for Upper Canada. Belleville lawyers James O'Reilly and John Finn represented the Aylwards. Together, Draper and Wilson were a formidable pair, since Draper, through his comments, helped weaken the case for the defence.

Following the testimony of ten witnesses and a two-hour deliberation, the jury found the Aylwards guilty and strongly recommended mercy. Nevertheless, Chief Justice Draper sentenced them to be executed on December 8. Immediately, many Belleville and county residents sent petitions to the government asking that the sentenced be commuted. Belleville merchant James Kennedy stated that they were signed by "gentlemen of the greatest intelligence and highest standing in this county, all of which were present at the criminal trial, and are acquainted with the facts." Some witnesses who had testified against the Aylwards suggested "transportation to some distant land," presumably Australia. Even the deceased's widow and son pleaded for mercy and asked that the sentence be commuted to life imprisonment.

A petition from the Honourable Robert Read suggested that the jury had found the Aylwards guilty because of local reaction to a preceding case in which an accused had been acquitted "contrary to all expectations." In addition, the Aylwards had "three young children, including a child at the breast." Furthermore, the Reverend Michael Brennan of St. Michael's Parish in Belleville described them as "not being spiritually prepared."

The Reverend Edmund B. Lawlor, the Roman Catholic priest at Stoco, and 150 petitioners questioned the trial evidence, surmised that Munro might have lived had he not been treated by a "quack doctor," and suggested that Mary was pregnant. On the basis of a medical exam by the jail surgeon, supported by an examination by the jailer's wife, County Sheriff John Moodie quickly ruled out

View of East Hill from West Hill with the Belleville Court House in the distance, the Bridge Street bridge across Moira River (centre right), and newly planted trees along West Bridge Street, circa 1860. Courtesy of Hastings County Historical Society, Neg. B-33.

pregnancy. Meeting in Quebec on December 3, the Executive Council considered Moodie's report, the petitions, and the evidence, and ruled that the execution should proceed.

Locally, this decision must have pleased at least a few people. On December 3, an editorial in the *Hastings Chronicle* objected to local citizens attempting to interfere with the ways of justice: "Murder of a fellow being is a crime so enormous and so dangerous to the life of every member of society that the law has wisely attached the highest punishment to its commission — If they are to be reprieved, then capital punishment would become a farce."

Meanwhile, with the support of Belleville's Roman Catholic clergy, Mary Aylward was preparing to meet her maker. She wrote a letter to her eldest daughter, Ellen, in which she explained what had happened, how Munro had come to the home and threatened her, and how she had struck the blow with the scythe to protect her husband, who was under attack. She told Ellen to look after the two younger daughters and concluded:

> Mary Aylward is my name
> Belleville gaol is my station
> And on the trap I lose my life
> In Heaven I expect salvation.[5]

The morning of the execution (December 8) was bitterly cold. The thermometer had dropped to minus five degrees that night. Nonetheless business was brisk, for thousands of outsiders were bustling into town. Large sleighloads of people made their way to the place of execution, no doubt near the court house, although the exact location remains unknown. Perhaps 5,000 people made up "the gallows mob," a quarter of them women. Many had travelled through the night from up to sixty or more miles away. According to the *Chronicle* reporter:

> In the immense crowd we saw numerous instances of young men drunk and unable to stand without assistance. And quarrelling, hooting and yelling combined to make it one of the most terrible and heart-rending scenes we ever witnessed. And we cannot but pause and ask what good effects arise from these disgusting public executions. Do they not pander more to the vitiated taste of low morals, than act as warnings to others?[6]

The Aylwards had been kept in separate cells since the trial and had not seen each other since. An eyewitness described their final parting before the gallows as "affecting in extreme." Accompanied by

Reverends E.B. Lawlor and John Brennan, they were conducted to the scaffold, where they joined in the responses of the Catholic Liturgy to the Dying and in the recitation of the Lord's Prayer. The trap was then sprung. Mary died within ninety seconds and Richard lived another full minute.

The bodies remained suspended for almost thirty-five minutes before they were taken down and delivered into the care of friends. They were taken to St. Michael's Church and placed in the centre aisle, where Father Brennan conducted the service. He deviated from the usual course on such occasions by stating, "The two whose corpses are before you, I have reason implicitly to believe, were never guilty of the crime for which they died…. That I believe as I believe I am living." The priest then lamented that some local citizens were heard to boast publicly that "Aylward and his wife are doomed" even before the trial began.

The burials took place in Mount St. Patrick's Catholic Cemetery in east-end Belleville later that afternoon. Shortly thereafter, a public meeting of the Roman Catholics of Belleville took place in the vestry of St. Michael's Church, and it was unanimously resolved that, "owing to the Unjust Execution of Richard and Mary Aylward," a fund would be set up for the three orphans. The organizers invited "every class and creed" to aid the fund.

The fund for the orphans helped keep the issue of religious friction alive in the Belleville area. The Aylward case "became a weapon in the battle between English and French Canada and developed into a national issue."[7] The Aylwards became martyrs. Reverend Lawler toured the pioneer churches, speaking out against the injustices of the Protestants and the Orangemen, in particular. The *Hastings Chronicle* blamed the *Intelligencer* for arousing all the controversy because it had published the "Ill judged and very inflammatory address by the Reverend Priest who attended the condemned culprits in their last moments,"[8] On March 6, 1863, the *Intelligencer* noted that the case was producing "extraordinary excitement throughout the country" with newspapers and members of Parliament entering into "elaborate discussions of the details of the unfortunate affair." Indeed, the case became a political issue, with the Catholic priests in the 1860s actively campaigning against Billa Flint, a strong Methodist supporter. Then, in the spring of 1886, the issue again loomed up in Parliament in connection with the execution of Metis leader Louis Riel. Several generations later, a reporter for the *Bancroft Times* noted that the hanging remained a painful issue, especially in North Hastings.[9]

Certainly, this double hanging in Belleville focused attention on the religious and cultural divisions within Canada, as well as the disgusting nature of public hangings. Nonetheless, it would be a few years before public hangings would be banned in Canada.[10]

Gateway to the Golden North

GOLD IS ONE of the world's most sought-after commodities. Its discovery has led to gold rushes around the world, including California, British Columbia, Australia, and Alaska. Contrary to popular belief, Ontario's first gold rush did not take place in the province's north, although that is where gold is produced today. Rather, Ontario's first gold rush took place in Hastings County, some fifty kilometres north of Belleville.[11]

The discovery led to the site becoming known as Eldorado (or El Dorado), and Belleville being dubbed "The Gateway to the Golden North."

Marcus Herbert Powell of Malone, in Marmora Township, made the first discovery. A clerk of the division court and a part-time prospector, Powell made his find while prospecting for copper on August 15, 1866. He had entered into an agreement with John Richardson to be allowed to prospect on Richardson's farm on lot 18 of the fifth concession of Madoc Township. Working with an older miner, Nicholas Schneider, Powell stumbled upon a considerable quantity of free or easily extracted gold in two pockets about sixteen feet below the surface. One assay indicated this free gold to be remarkably pure, between 22 and 23 carats fine.

Word of the gold discovery was kept quiet for a time, but it was soon common knowledge. The *Weekly Intelligencer* of November 9, 1866, noted that the discovery was "causing great excitement to extend beyond the boundaries of central Canada." Geologists, professors, practical miners, and capitalists from Canada and the United States were said to have visited the new gold region.

From the beginning, Belleville residents played a major role in the gold rush because of the town's proximity to the gold field and the fact that the only decent access to the area was by stagecoach, wagon, or carriage from Belleville. Perhaps the first Belleville participant was Fred Murchall, a drummer with mining experience in Australia. One source reported that it was Murchall who determined that Powell had, in fact, found gold.[12] Whereas the editor of the *Madoc Mercury* initially questioned whether there would be enough gold to make extracting it worthwhile, Belleville newspapers harboured no such reservation. The *Intelligencer* claimed the discovery "Rich not only in the ordinary use of the term, but very rich." It compared the quality of gold favourably to that of Australia and California.[13]

The Dafoe House, on the site of the present Clarion Inn and Suites in downtown Belleville, was the centre of many of the negotiations surrounding the gold discovery. It was there that Joseph F. Carr, a Bostonian who was prospecting for oil in neighbouring Sidney Township, overheard a conversation between Lyman Moon, one of the first persons to learn of the find, and several Belleville businessmen.[14] They were forming a company to purchase and develop the

Richardson property. Carr struck up a conversation with Moon, discovered the nature of the discovery, and, before the Belleville businessmen could act, quickly visited the site and negotiated agreements with Richardson and the discoverers. Unfortunately, this action led to a series of court cases that would see mining rights to the property divided into several blocks claimed by various groups and individuals.

Meanwhile, hundreds of people were beginning to arrive in the Madoc-Eldorado area. The editor of the *Madoc Mercury* was delighted to see that many professional and business people from Belleville had "condescended to show

Home of the Richardson Family at Eldorado where the gold discovery was made. Courtesy of Library and Archives Canada, C-35918.

the light of their countenances" in the area they had once described as "the most God-forsaken place in the world."[15] Amazingly, the mine operators allowed many of the visitors to take ore samples away. One visitor, Jacob Yeomans of Belleville, while examining rock thrown from the mine, picked up "an exceedingly rich specimen of quartz, full of gold."[16]

Such newspaper publicity encouraged the gold fever. By early December, nearly every farm in Madoc Township was being prospected for gold, often by the landholders themselves.[17] Potential prospectors — and they included people of all occupations — were looking for information on geology and mineralogy. In response, the Reverend Joseph Wild spoke on "Geology" in Neilson's Hall in Belleville. Wild, the recently appointed minister of the Methodist Episcopal Church and the teacher of Hebrew at Albert College, had a splendid reputation for his brilliant creative thinking and outstanding oratory. More than six-hundred people paid the 10 cent admission charge, hoping to hear of his visit to the gold area and pick up a "few hints." Many were forced to stand and more than a hundred could not get in.[18] More than a few attendees were disappointed when his lecture largely dealt with the biblical account of creation and geologists' theories about the formation of the earth's surface. The next evening, Thomas Campbell Wallbridge, a prominent Belleville lawyer and the member of Parliament for North Hastings, lectured on the county's geology at Madoc.

By early 1867, Belleville citizens spoke of their town as sure to become the "Gateway to the Golden North" and plans were announced to double the size of the principal hotel, the Dafoe House.[19] The Crown Lands Department appointed an agent at Belleville to deal with the mining claims. Belleville grocer R.D. Conger used the heading "Gold Discovered in Belleville" to announce the reopening of his family grocery stand; he even advertised "Golden Syrup."[20] The New Year's night carnival at the Victoria Skating Rink had a mining theme.[21]

Meanwhile, because of a series of disputes, the entrance to the Richardson mine shaft was under "treble lock and key," and operations ceased. The first lock protected Richardson's interests; the second, the discoverers' interests; and the third, the purchasers' interests. The disputing purchasers included Joseph Carr and his Boston associates, Chicago bankers Benjamin Lombard and Seth Hardin, and a "Belleville Company of Citizens." Unfortunately, there were suspicions that the Richardson site had been "salted" or enriched with pieces of gold-bearing quartz from other locations, in an attempt to encourage investors and promote the site. Sir William Logan, director of the Geological Survey of Canada, sent Montreal geologist A. Michel to check on this and other sites. Michel spent more than two weeks visiting the locations where Belleville newspapers had reported gold finds. Although his examinations were generally "superficial and slight," he confirmed the presence of gold in several locations.[22] Further, he described the Richardson gold deposit as "an established fact … of extraordinary richness" and noted that it "could hardly be exceptional in the region."

The American press gave wide publicity to the discovery, and in the spring of 1867 the gold rush began in earnest. John Moore's farm adjoining the Richardson property became the site of a planned community to be known as "Eldorado" or "El Dorado," commemorating the Spaniards' sixteenth-century search for the fabled Golden Man and the Golden City of South America. Belleville business interests were quick to take advantage of the influx of prospectors and speculators. Demand for products of all kinds led to dramatic price increases. Delia O'Hare, the wife of a former Belleville mayor, cut short a letter to her father in Brockville, noting that she "had better get a barrel of flour before it raises."[23] By early February, a Picton businessman introduced the first four-horse line of stagecoaches from Belleville to Madoc and Eldorado. Carrying up to a dozen people, they were like omnibuses on runners, fitted up inside "as a New York street railway car."[24] Soon there were eight stagecoaches, each loaded inside and out with up to twenty passengers, leaving Belleville hotels at 7:30 a.m. and arriving at Madoc at noon. Return stagecoaches left the principal Madoc hotels at 1:30 p.m., reaching Belleville in time to connect with the evening trains.[25]

Newspaper reports speculated that thousands of people would pass through Belleville on their way to the gold fields that summer — perhaps as many as 2,000 from Prince Edward County alone, and 8,000 Chinese from the California gold fields.[26] Fearful for their safety, Belleville residents sought to increase the size of the five-man police force.[27]

Literally dozens of small mining companies were set up throughout the gold region and beyond. Even the employees of the Grand Trunk Railway station at Belleville organized a gold-mining venture, with Locomotive Superintendent S. Phipps serving as president.[28] Other companies included The Provincial Mining Company, headed by Thomas Kelso, president of the Belleville Board of Trade; J.J.B. Flint and Alexander Robertson; and Kingston business interests. With planned capital of $500,000, it was by far the most ambitious local company.

The most important Belleville company was the Richardson Gold Mining Company, which was jointly controlled by Chicago banking interests (under Lombard and Hardin), and the Belleville investors who had set up the earlier Citizens Company. After the resolution of a major court battle concerning the ownership of the Richardson mine site, the company was reorganized on June 13, 1867. Its directors included three prominent local citizens — Francis McAnnany, Thomas Kelso, and James Glass. Although he owned only one share, McAnnany was elected president because he was extremely well-known and respected. Glass, the owner of 1,398 shares, was elected secretary.[29] Six weeks later, the company officially opened the Richardson Mine, with Hardin as superintendent. Within a few months, a large and solidly built stone mill and crushing house was in operation. Unfortunately, this mining venture and other legitimate ones were negatively affected by a number of scams and other dishonest measures. Such factors led Mark Twain to describe a gold mine as "a hole in the ground with a liar standing over it."

Despite these problems, the gold rush continued to buoy Belleville's economy. By the summer of 1867, Belleville engineers and surveyors Henry Macleod and a Mr. Carre were selling a series of township maps showing valuable resources — including known gold locations. There was so much news of the gold rush, and so many advertisers anxious to promote their services and wares that, as of March 25, 1867, newspaper proprietor Mackenzie Bowell added a daily edition to his *Weekly Intelligencer*. James Thompson Bell, a student of natural history and an assayer, began a weekly series on mineralogy in the May 13 edition. In layman's terms, the column explained how to recognize gold and prospect for it. Bell became *the* local expert on gold, and, in January 1869, Hastings County Council established a chair of mining at Albert College, with Bell as professor of mines and agriculture.[30]

The gold rush greatly benefited Belleville's manufacturing industries. The Brown Foundry and Machine Shop constructed a gold-crushing mill for Eldorado, leading the *Daily Intelligencer* of April 23, 1868 to state that there was no longer a need to import such mills from Montreal, New York, or elsewhere. The theme was "Buy Belleville," according to this nineteenth-century predecessor of the current Belleville "Buy Locally Owned Group."[31]

Sadly, by the summer of 1868, many mines and mills were shutting down. The nature of the ore was a major problem. The crushers were unable to recover the gold from the local ore, and it would be several years before a suitable process would be developed in Australia.

Throughout the entire process, the Belleville *Intelligencer* remained a strong supporter of mining ventures in Centre and North Hastings. This could be explained by the potential advertising revenues, the fact that Mackenzie Bowell represented North Hastings in the first Parliament of the Dominion of Canada, and the strong support that Bowell and the community's business leaders were giving to the development of a railway reaching into North Hastings.

Although the gold rush of 1866–68 was short-lived, there have been recurring gold and mineral rushes since. Very few years elapse between announcements in the press of yet "Another Great Gold Discovery." The soaring price of gold in the late 1970s — it peaked at a high of US$850 per ounce in 1980 — caused mining engineers and geologists to carefully review work done in the previous century. Changes to the Income Tax Act in 1983 gave substantial tax breaks to individual investors. As a result, Mono Gold Mines Inc. of Vancouver spent more than $4,000,000 on a high-grade gold mineralization operation near Bannockburn, and the Noranda Exploration Company investigated the large low-grade Dingman prospect near Malone. A substantial drop in gold-exploration activity occurred in 1990. However, recent increased demand and high prices have led to new developments on old sites. Opawica Explorations Inc. drilled 19 test holes in the fall of 2007 on the Dingman site at Malone, near where Marcus Powell, the original discoverer of gold in 1866, lived. A junior exploration company listed on the Toronto Stock Exchange, the long-established Opawica anticipates further drilling.[32] Could such mineral exploration result in Belleville once again becoming known as "The Gateway to the Golden North"?

Canada's First Mounted Police Force

MOST HISTORIANS, EVEN those most knowledgeable about the Royal Canadian Mounted Police, have overlooked Belleville's role in the beginnings of a mounted police force in Canada. But the fact is that a mounted police force was recruited and trained at Belleville in 1867.

The force was organized as the result of the Madoc Gold Rush. Thousands of prospectors, speculators, and perhaps some ne'er-do-wells were expected to arrive in the Madoc-Eldorado gold fields in the summer of 1867. As a result, there had been growing local support for improved policing. For example, Dora O'Hare of Belleville had written her grandfather that "so many rowdies [were] in town just now on account of the Gold excitement."[33] The Honourable

Alexander Campbell, the crown lands commissioner, shared this sentiment and noted that a considerable number of the new arrivals "would probably be men of violent character and habits."[34] To prepare for any problems and to enforce new regulations governing miners, speculators, and tavern operators in an expanding gold region, the Canadian government created the Quinte Gold Mining Division on March 21, 1867. This division came under the jurisdiction of Alexander Campbell, and he appointed his brother, Colonel Alfred A. Campbell, Crown lands agent at Belleville, to supervise the division and set up a police force.

An active member of the local militia and the rifle association, Colonel Campbell was a good choice for this supervisory role. His first decision was to appoint Sergeant Major Foxton, a Kingston police officer, as head of the force. Foxton was described as a hero of the Crimean War and an "efficient cavalryman."[35] In late March, recruiting posters went up in the Belleville area and a force of twenty-five men was quickly raised. Each man supplied his own horse, and the government provided uniforms, saddles, bridles, weapons, and daily pay ranging from 75¢ to $2.50. Also, there were daily allowances of 50¢ for rations and 50¢ for the use of each horse. The government accepted no responsibility for the loss of a horse "unless killed on duty."

Certainly the mounted police would have made an impressive sight, with their blue uniforms with gold buttons and facings. Each man also carried a long sword.[36] They were described as looking "like a troop of cavalry," no doubt reflecting Foxton's military training. The majority were said to be "old soldiers, and of the right stamp to deal effectively with the desperate classes who generally inhabit gold-digging regions."[37]

After drilling for two weeks at Belleville, the mounted police force (less two members who had been arrested and jailed at Belleville for robbery) arrived at Madoc. One squad soon was assigned to Eldorado. Despite an almost complete lack of major crime, the police were kept busy with, among other tasks, ensuring that miners and tavern-keepers had the necessary licences. On May 31, Sergeant Dunbar and twelve men left Belleville on the steamer *Empress*; they had been ordered to the Chaudiere gold fields in Canada East because of a disturbance among miners there.[38]

The Gold Rush Police Force, recruited at Belleville by Sergeant Major Foxton in 1867. The uniforms were blue with gold facing. The "x" indicated John S. Marsh, an ancestor of Mrs. J.E. Marsh who allowed the picture to be copied. Courtesy of Hastings County Historical Society, Marsh Collection, Neg. Military 6.

On the eve of the celebration of Canada's Confederation, the government notified the remaining policemen that their services would no longer be required because control of Crown lands was passing to the provinces.[39] Local public pressure twice forced the government to allow the force to continue, however it was finally disbanded on September 30, 1867, by order of the Ontario cabinet. Thus ended the Quinte Gold Mining Division's mounted police force, a force raised and trained at Belleville and, arguably, an important predecessor to the present Royal Canadian Mounted Police.

Approaching and Celebrating Confederation

BELLEVILLE NEWSPAPERS FROM the early 1860s did not allot much news or editorial space to the approaching union of several of Britain's North American colonies to form the Dominion of Canada. There were other seemingly more important stories to be covered. Locally, these stories included the formation of the Belleville Board of Trade (later renamed the Belleville & District Chamber of Commerce) in 1865, the need for more industrial development, and the continued success of the lumber trade. The Belleville mills of Flint and Yeomans, H.B. Rathbun, and William Bleecker were described as "some of the largest west of Ottawa." The area's agriculture participated in the boom as, thanks to the healthy American market, local barley growers expanded their acreage. The cheese industry was also expanding, and some cheese factories were marketing a finished product capable of taking honours at provincial fairs.

Manufacturing continued to thrive. Local companies won prizes at provincial exhibitions and at least one invention, the celebrated family sewing machine patented by Charles Irwin and Company, made the manufacturer's name a "household word." At the 1867 Kingston exhibition, the machine was said to be superior for all kinds of work over every other American and Canadian machine, including that of the I.M. Singer Company.

A number of prominent visitors came to town. Even the governor general, Charles Stanley Monck, took time out from preparing the colonies for union to visit the Belleville Fair in October 1862. Monck professed his "surprise at the quality and quantity of Stock" shown at the fair. Although he had arrived by steamer, he had to leave by special train; the *Bay of Quinte* had run aground at the Belleville wharf. It was no wonder that Mayor James Brown, in his inaugural speech to council the next January, gave high priority to dredging the harbour.[40]

Belleville council was also busy with many other matters. For example, in 1864, council allowed the Board of Health to use the town hall to vaccinate against the dreaded disease smallpox. Doctors would "receive and vaccinate gratis, all poor wishing to the have the operation performed." Two years later, council took action to build a new engine house and police station next to the Upper Bridge. There was concern about increasing lawlessness, with a Front Street tavern being described as "one about the greatest hell-holes in Canada, wherein more liquor is sold, more crime committed, than in the lowest slums of New York, in which place no less than four deaths occurred from delirium tremens inside of one year."

Pollution was another concern. Meeting on August 19, 1866, council agreed to notify the lumbermen and tanners that the dumping of rubbish into the river would result in prosecution; a reward of $10 was offered to informants. Despite such action, pollution on the Moira River would remain a problem. In fact, a consultant's report to council in the 1990s suggested that the excrement of as few as thirteen gulls roosting under the Highway 401 bridge could contaminate the waters at both Riverside Park beaches.

Several Bellevillians were in the news as Confederation approached. William Hutton, who had helped to arrange the Canadian censuses of 1851 and 1861, had died in 1861. Billa Flint, one of the area's most famous businessmen, continued to extend his operations and help to establish such communities as Bridgewater (Actinolite) and Flinton and, later, Bancroft. In 1863, *Intelligencer* editor Mackenzie Bowell lost his bid to win the North Hastings seat in the Canadian Parliament. It would be his last such election loss. Following Confederation, he would represent that riding until his appointment to the Senate in 1892. A largely unnoticed event took place on February 26, 1866: Joseph and Sarah Dow, American citizens who were temporary Belleville residents living on John Street, had a son — Herbert Henry Dow. The family returned to the United States when he was two months old. The son later founded and became president of one of the world's most famous businesses — the Dow Chemical Company.

Unfortunately, not all connections with the United States were as cordial. In fact, there was fear of an attack from American soil in the mid–1860s, and this was a factor in encouraging the British colonies to draw closer together. The threat came from the Fenians, a group of Irish-Americans who hoped to capture Canada and exchange it for Ireland's independence. Armed Irish-Americans openly drilled in several American cities, and there were attacks across the border.[41] The American government seemed reluctant to stop the Fenian activities, perhaps because there was a feeling that Britain had seemed to favour the South against the North in the American Civil War. In 1865, the First Hastings Rifles and the recently formed 15th Battalion of the Argyll Light Infantry were called out to defend the country. Fenian attacks were anticipated at Niagara, Cobourg, and Kingston. For five months, local militia stood on guard at Amherstburg.

Shortly after the militia returned to Belleville, the Fenians crossed the border and captured Fort Erie, which they briefly held. News of the invasion of June 2, 1866, was circulated that day in a special edition of the *Intelligencer*. In the evening, vast crowds paraded the streets, singing patriotic songs and cheering for Queen Victoria, the Empire, and Canada. At two o'clock the next morning, the call to arms came and, eight hours later, local militiamen were on their way to Prescott and Cornwall. On June 8, the Fenian attack came, but further east, in Quebec, and the Hochelaga Voltigeurs drove the 2,000 invaders back across the border.

Nevertheless, the Fenian threat remained for another five years, and the Belleville militia remained on alert. In addition, for several years Belleville served as the base for a company of the Grand Trunk Railway Brigade. The men, all railway employees, were assigned to guard bridges, shops, and the roundhouse.[42] A letter recommending the granting of a medal to one participant stated: "Applicant was in charge of an engine, which was kept constantly ready and steamed up and down the track with himself and comrades detailed for that duty during the time when attacks were anticipated. The order was given after a mixed train had been fired into by some miscreants and the car penetrated by several bullets." While on duty, the soldiers arrested "several suspicious characters as Fenian spies, who were afterwards released."[43]

While the militia was standing on guard locally, Belleville was also preparing to welcome a detachment of British regulars. On September 3, 1867, town council set up a special committee to see what buildings might "be suitable for the reception of troops" and the quartering of officers, and where a powder magazine might be safely located.[44] Subsequently, council decided that it would move to the second storey of the engine house (then nearing completion near the Upper Bridge) to free up room in the former town council room over the market so that the 15th Battalion could move in. This would allow the British garrison to move into the 15th's armoury on Church Street. Although the Canadian government spent $12,000 to renovate several buildings and entered into contracts with bakers, butchers, and others, the British troops did not establish a garrison here, much to the chagrin of the town's businessmen and young women of marriageable age.

With so much excitement and a somewhat depressed economy, it was no wonder that the citizens did not pay very much attention to Confederation. Only a week before the celebration, council set aside $250 "for the purpose of celebrating, the commencement of a new era in our nationality." The money was to provide the inhabitants of the Belleville area with "the largest amount of amusement and entertainment on that day."[45] Council also agreed to pay the town's labourers "on Dominion Day as if they were at work on that day" and to allot "$40 for small gifts for citizens on relief."

July 1st celebrations began at midnight with the firing of the cannon on the Court House Hill. At 9:00 a.m., the Moira Company Band played on the courthouse steps, followed by a parade from the Pinnacle Street armouries to the courthouse. Mayor Henry Corby read the proclamation creating the Dominion of Canada from the Provinces of Canada, Nova Scotia, and New Brunswick. A military volley followed, and the band of the 15th Battalion played "God Save the Queen." Various games and amusements occupied the afternoon, and the *Intelligencer* reporter noted that "the remainder of the day passed off very quietly, there being no display of fireworks in the evening." The paper's next-day account of the event lamented that "The birthday of our new Dominion was not celebrated in Belleville with the spirit which should have been shown on the occasion."

Court House Hill, pictured shortly after Confederation by George Ackermann. Buildings include (left to right): Grammar School, Court House, St. Thomas' Church, B.F. Davy residence on Campbell Street, Bridge Street Church, the Merchants Bank (later the library) and the Dafoe House (site of the Clarion Inn). Courtesy of Belleville Public Library and John M. Parrott Art Gallery.

Mayor Henry Corby, who read the official proclamation on the courthouse steps on July 1, 1867. Courtesy of Hastings County Historical Society, Mika Collection.

Later celebrations were often more spectacular, although there have been occasions when they have been quite small. Most recently, The Belleville Buy Locally Owned Group has sponsored the July 1st celebrations and attracted thousands of area residents to the many family activities on Zwick's Island.

Dominion Day 1867 was followed shortly by elections for the first Parliament. Mackenzie Bowell was elected in Hastings North, James Brown in Hastings West, and Robert Read in Hastings East. All were supporters of John A. Macdonald, and all had strong Belleville connections. Mackenzie Bowell edited the *Intelligencer*, had chaired the school board, and was a founder of the Board of Trade; James Brown was a successful agricultural implement manufacturer at Belleville; and Robert Read was a tanner, distiller, and farmer near Belleville. On Read's appointment to the Senate in 1876, the voters of Hastings East elected John White, a machinist and foundry proprietor at Roslin, who had served as Tyendinaga Township reeve. Perhaps the most interesting local member, White was the subject of a fascinating biographical fiction by Don Akenson.[46] Akenson proposed that White may have been more than a trustworthy Tory backbencher with a notable understanding of the political situation of women and indigenous minorities. He may have been the same person as his sister, Eliza McCormack White, a transvestite prostitute and, therefore, Canada's first female-male MP. After White's death in 1894, the *Intelligencer* commented that White's funeral "was remarkable for the number of ladies present ... How often has he been heard to say 'give me the ladies on my side and I don't care much for the men' and he could even count on them as his staunchest friends and greatest admirers."[47] Readers have found White's story to be absorbing, entertaining, and certainly non-traditional. Who says history is dull?

6
THE EARLY DOMINION

Arrival of the Minstrels

MINSTREL SHOWS WERE among the leading entertainments of the mid-nineteenth century. Some were produced by local musicians who donned blackface (by using burnt cork), and parodied the songs of the Deep South. Travelling minstrels, who went from town to town, performed other minstrel shows. One travelling group, which left an amazing hidden souvenir for Belleville residents living a century later, was headed by Hugh Hamall of Montreal.[1] Hamall organized Hamall's Serenaders, and the group opened in Montreal on December 3, 1867.

The following year the group, which had since changed its name to Hamall's Minstrels, went on tour. Their advance agent pasted large, multi-coloured posters on the blank south wall of Philip Hambly's bakery, confectionery, and saloon at 258 Front Street. The wall was blank because the neighbouring two-storey stone building, which occupied the 256 Front Street site until April 21, 1868, had been destroyed by a major fire. In fact, the fire had been stopped by the stone walls of Hambly's business and "the strenuous exertions of the neighbours, who with pails of water and blankets prevented the roof of this building from taking fire."

Almost immediately, the posters went up and covered a 17 x 6-foot section of wall. Produced by Joseph Warren and Company Engravers and printed by a Buffalo (New York) printer, they identified some of the members of the company and indicated that this would be more than a minstrel show. In addition to Hugh Hamall (described as being a balladist of the Academy of Music of New Orleans), his Minstrels, and Skiff and Gaylord's Minstrels from the United States, there was a brass band, Johnny Howard (the King of Comedians), gymnasts, cloggers, and other acts. They were to perform at Neilson's Hall, located in an upstairs location

Bill and Ruth Greenley with the posters advertising Hamall's Minstrel Show on June 22 and 23, 1868. Photo by author, 1993.

on the west side of Front Street, on Monday, June 22 and Tuesday, June 23, 1868. Unfortunately, there was no review of the performances in the local newspapers. The posters were visible for only a short time, since the building at 256 Front Street was repaired and reoccupied by September.

In the summer of 1993, fire again destroyed 256 Front Street. This time, the fire uncovered the posters, which had been hidden for 125 years. Most of the printing was legible, and the colours were still reasonably bright. Unfortunately, many of the faces had been vandalized in 1868. In addition, exposure to weather after the 1993 fire caused fading and peeling. The posters could not be preserved. However, small samples were saved, framed, and mounted in the stairway leading to Greenley's Bargain Basement.

Sports, Schools, and Other Successes

Most Bellevillians entered the new nation with optimism. The economy was progressing reasonably well, and there were some exciting developments in sports, education, and other areas.

In sports, Belleville was among the first communities in Ontario to have a recognized lacrosse team. Inspired by the aboriginal inhabitants, whose lacrosse games could involve 2,000 warriors, George Beers laid down the basic rules for a professional game in 1860, and the sport was designated our national game in 1867.[2] That September, less than a month after a convention at Kingston established the National Lacrosse Association, a Belleville team was formed and the first match was held between "the volunteers and civilians," probably a reference to the militia, then preparing for possible Fenian attacks.[3] Known as the OKAS, the team was described as "the greatest team that ever represented Belleville." They were the central Ontario champions for many years, and several members were counted "among the best Canadian players of their day."[4] After the glory days of the 1870s and 1880s, the game lost some of its appeal and this note appeared in the *Intelligencer* in 1904: "This is about the time of year when the average Belleville lacrosse player comes out and looks for the sun. If he sees his shadow he crawls back under cover."[5] In the early 1960s, the game caught on at some local high schools, but ultimately suffered from a shortage of coaches and officials, and a lack of discipline on the part of some female participants who were unruly and took delight in tripping and whacking opposing players with their sticks.

Baseball (sometimes referred to as "Bass Ball" in the early years) was growing in popularity. Although it had been played locally since the 1850s — there is a record of Smithville (Foxboro) defeating Cannifton by 23 runs to 10 in 1858 — the first formal clubs were not formed until 1869.[6] At a meeting in Hambly's Saloon, a number of "gentlemen" formed the Hastings Base Ball Club, with Frank Flynn as president. The club was to practise "the second Monday in every month." This was hardly enough time to develop skilled players; however, Belleville teams did amazingly well.

At times, baseball could be a dangerous sport — for the fans. Consider the little boy who was knocked down by the first baseman as he ran into the crowd after a foul ball. The boy's arm was broken — again; the lad already had his arm in a sling because it had been broken in a similar collision the previous week. Likewise, several reporters sitting on the scorer's bench were knocked down at the same game when Keenan, the pitcher, ran for a foul ball and collided with them. The crowd laughed at the reporters.[7]

The early years of the Dominion were exciting ones in education. In 1868, Samuel G. Beatty and George Wallbridge opened the Ontario Business College. It was one of the province's outstanding business schools for more than a century, and earned an international reputation. Students from the West Indies and elsewhere attended. Unfortunately, competition from community colleges and other schools, combined with overexpansion, brought about its closure after more than a hundred successful years.

A major event in the province's educational history took place on October 20, 1870, when the provincial government opened its first permanent school for deaf students. Known by various names over its long history, the Sir James Whitney School for the Deaf would become a community landmark. Also in the 1870s, the Belleville High School was built adjacent to the grammar school. Sometimes referred to as the Union School, the building housed elementary classes in Queen Victoria School on the ground floor, while high-school classes were held

The Marchmont Home, a splendid example of co-operation between local residents and those in the British Isles. Like many other Ontario communities, Belleville readily accepted orphans and other children in need of assistance. Courtesy of Belleville Public Library and John M. Parrott Art Gallery.

on the second floor. The old two-roomed stone grammar school was used for home economics and other classes. Meanwhile, the foundation of a public library system had been laid on November 21, 1876, with the reorganization of the Mechanics' Institute, which had conducted a public library from 1851 to 1859, in addition to other public functions.

Some Belleville's citizens were interested in helping children from the British Isles come to Canada and experience a better life. Commencing in the spring of 1870, British children began to arrive in Belleville. They became known as the "home children," and the temporary home in Belleville for these "little immigrants" or "waifs and strays" was called Marchmont. Unfortunately, both the first and second Marchmont homes were destroyed by fire and a young boy, Robbie Gray, died in the first fire when he went back into the building after he had escaped. The third building, near the intersection of West Moira and Yeomans streets, still stands, though much altered. All three homes were the results of the efforts of Annie Macpherson (operator of the Home of Industry in London, England), her friends, and the residents of the Belleville area. County government was very supportive and provided the first building (a former Highland Avenue residence for invalid soldiers) rent-free. As well, Senator Billa Flint played a major role in supporting the venture, rallying the people to raise the necessary funds to rebuild. From 1870 to 1925, thousands of girls and boys, along with some widows, passed through Marchmont. Jim Gilchrist related the emotional stories of some of them in his captivating book, *Marchmont*.[8] Some Marchmont children experienced problems in their new homes. Many more benefited from their move to Belleville.

The face of Belleville was changing in other ways. Effective 1870, the town could collect harbour dues, which helped to fund more dredging of the too-shallow harbour. In 1872, a horticultural society was formed in a meeting in the Town Hall, leading to the beautification of the town. Yet another change in the landscape followed a county council decision that affected prisoners in the jail. Effective November 15, 1875, prisoners who worked on the lawns and gardens outside the courthouse and jail were required to wear balls and chains.

In 1874, following the expansion of its boundaries, a publishing company marketed a *Bird's Eye View* of the town. Council purchased a hundred copies for distribution and others were offered for sale. The drawing was amazingly accurate, and perhaps only one building, Shire Hall on Church Street, was omitted. Unfortunately, the view was published just before a major addition to the streetscape — rails down Front Street. In 1876, council authorized a charter for a horse-drawn street railway from the harbour to the railway station.

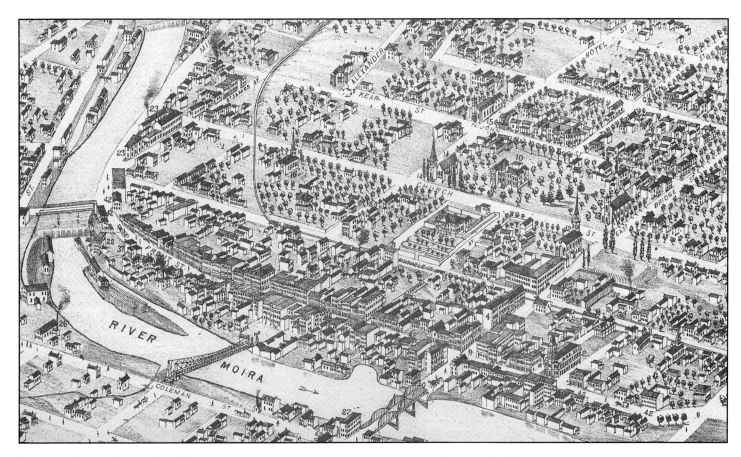

Bird's Eye View of Belleville, *1874, an amazingly accurate depiction of the town. Numbered buildings east of the river include: Public Buildings: (1) Court House and Gaol, (2) City Hall and Market, (4) Post Office, (8) Grand Junction Railway Station; Schools: (10) Grammar and High School (1) Public Schools; Churches: (12) Wesleyan Methodist, (13) St. Thomas' English, (14) St. Andrew's Presbyterian, (15) Canada Presbyterian, (16) St. Michael's Roman Catholic, (17) Methodist Episcopal, (18) Congregational; Industries: J.M. Walker & Co., Foundry and Machine Shops, (23) J.&G. Brown, (32) Planing Mills; Hotels: (34) Dafoe House, (36) Anglo-American House, (37 Albion Hotel, (40) Eureka House, (42) Other hotels. On the west of the river, the view showed (25) Irvin Diamond Flouring Mill, (26) A.N. Pringle Planing Mill, (27) W.H. Vermilyea, Carriage Factory and (42) hotels.* Courtesy of Hastings County Historical Society.

The Peddler and the Wheelbarrow[9]

E.J. CASTREE WAS a middle-aged Englishman, a seller of wire toasters, who was in Belleville attempting to sell his wares. Late Saturday afternoon, September 20, 1873, he dropped in to Philip Hambly's tavern (formerly Henry Corby's bakeshop, and, presently the site of Greenley's Book Store). Castree made his way to a room in the rear of the bar, where he eased his stout frame into one of Hambly's more comfortable chairs. Soon relaxing over a glass of whisky, his thoughts probably turned to what his wife and three children were doing at home in England. Thinking that another drink might revive him before going to his lodgings for the night, he ordered a second whisky, and then a glass of ginger beer.

When the closing hour arrived — 7:00 p.m. was dictated by the observance of the Sabbath — Castree remained at his table, slumped in his chair. Neither Hambly nor his assistant Neal could rouse him. They found this surprising, since both men would later recall that Castree appeared perfectly sober when he entered the saloon. Thinking it amazing what two whiskies and a ginger beer could do, they nevertheless decided that Castree was drunk and needed to sleep it off. Accordingly, they carefully placed the portly wire-toaster peddler in a wheelbarrow and wheeled him into the backyard. They then arranged his hands so as to make him as comfortable as possible. Hambly intended to check on him in an hour or so, but busied himself cleaning up the saloon and forgot.

The next morning, Hambly emerged from the saloon's rear door, near the Moira River, and looked at the wheelbarrow. Castree was still in it, and had not moved during the night. Castree was dead.

Two days later, an inquest was held in the Town Hall, over the fire hall near the Upper Bridge. Doctors Tracy and Curlett, who had conducted a detailed autopsy, testified before a coroner's jury. They concluded that death had resulted from loss of blood caused by the rupture of the main artery. The doctors wondered if alcohol had played a role. Doctor Tracy told the jury that "Overstimulation by drinking would predispose to such an effect." However, "a man might die from a ruptured artery or aneurism without ever drinking a drop of liquor." The jury found that the deceased came to his death "from internal haemorrhage, cause unknown." Neal was convinced that Castree must have been dead when wheeled from the saloon, because he had not moved. The doctors could neither confirm nor deny this.

Castree was buried in the St. Thomas' Church Cemetery, but no stone marks his burial site.

Our First Regatta[10]

THE SHELTERED BAY of Quinte has always played an important role in Belleville's history. That role took on new life on September 21, 1873 (the same day that E.J. Castree's body was discovered), when local sailors sponsored Belleville's first regatta. In August, a group of sailors, headed by businessmen Morgan Jellett and Thomas Holden and barrister Frederick Ridley, formed the Bay of Quinte Regatta Club. Invitations went out to other boating centres, and there was a good response. In fact, a race scheduled from Toronto to Niagara on the same day was postponed, at the suggestion of *The Toronto Mail,* so as not to compete with the Belleville event.[11]

September 22 was a beautiful day with a slight southeasterly breeze. The "splendid yachts *Ina, Coral,* and *Lady Stanley*" were on hand from the Toronto area for the first-class race, and were joined by a local yacht, the *Rivet.* The race course was from Massassaga Point in Prince Edward County to the mouth of the Salmon River, then to Big Island, and then back to the starting point. The circuit was fifteen miles and had to be completed twice, making it thirty miles in total.[12] Imagine the spectators' delight as the local yacht *Rivet* took an early lead. Then there was a reality check as the Toronto sailors and their boats gradually asserted their superiority. The *Lady Stanley* crossed the finish line first, about a mile ahead of the *Ina.* However, having received a seven-and-a-half-minute tonnage allowance, the *Ina* was declared the winner by nearly two minutes. The *Ina* received $200 for the win, the *Lady Stanley* $100 for second, and the *Coral* $50 for third. Belleville's entry, the *Rivet,* finished twenty-two minutes behind the *Coral* and out of the big money.

Mostly local boats made up the race for second-class yachts, and two entries, one from Belleville and the other from Brighton, took home the prize money. The local press regarded this first regatta as a great success and the *Daily Ontario* reported that "The eventful day for the holding of the Bay of Quinte Regatta has come and gone, and deserves hereafter to be set down as a red-letter day in the annals of Canadian yachting."

The regatta was repeated for another two years and then,

Built in Cobourg by Alexander Cuthbert in 1875, the Katie Gray *was one of the original ships to sail under Bay of Quinte Yacht Club colours. She sailed Lake Ontario for sixty-two years, won more honours than any other yacht of her time, and is remembered by the annual* Katie Gray *Race. Courtesy of Hastings County Historical Society, Mika Collection.*

on September 13, 1876, the Bay of Quinte Yacht Club was formed. Thomas Kelso was at the helm as its first commodore and the club roster numbered eleven yachts, including one first-class yacht (the noted *Dauntless*) and four second-class yachts, including the legendary *Katie Gray*.

The new club's first regatta took place on October 6, 1876. According to the *Intelligencer* reporter, "the racers fairly flew along," driven by "a rattling good breeze" from the southwest.

The success of local sailors and yacht-builders would become legendary within a few years with the entry of the *Atalanta* in the America's Cup races of November 1881. Designed and built by Alexander Cuthbert, the *Atalanta* was seventy feet long and was constructed of the "finest Hastings County timber."[13] Despite losing to the American entry, the *Mischief,* the international fame the *Atalanta* achieved led to a group of Belleville yacht enthusiasts being invited to take part in the World Cup races in England in 2001.

Completing the Market Building/Town Hall[14]

BELLEVILLE CITY HALL is the most recognizable public building in the city. What is not generally realized is that it was not built as a city hall, since Belleville was only a town when it was constructed. In addition, its original primary function was not even as a town hall, but rather as a market building.

In fact, it was built with several other purposes in mind. In the early 1870s, Belleville's citizens wanted a clock tower that could be seen by people downtown and on the east and west hills, known respectively as Taylor's Hill and Murney's Hill, after two prominent early families. The citizens also wanted a fire bell that could be heard in all parts of town. Serious losses from fires had occurred because existing bells could not be heard, and the churches had stopped ringing their bells in case of fires. What better location for a large fire bell than a tall tower! As the *Ontario* editor pointed out, "Even slow little Picton, as some of our friends call it, can boast of a Town Clock, and an alarm bell, while the 'City of the Bay' with all its boasted enterprise is totally without either...." Furthermore, weather vanes on top of the tower would show the wind direction.

In addition, a large public hall on the second floor could host public meetings and gatherings and town officials could find office space. If council could meet in the building, that would be good, too. After all, the existing council room over the fire hall near the Upper Bridge was crowded, the chimney sometimes backed up, and smoke forced the councillors to flee to the street.

Council employed architect John Dunlop Evans to prepare the plans for the new building. Evans was a relatively recent arrival in Belleville, settling here in 1867 when he was only twenty-four. Born on a farm near Goderich, he had trained as a land surveyor and, after opening a

Belleville office, became a self-educated architect. His first major project was the new Union School, which housed the Belleville High School and Queen Victoria Public School. His second major project was the new market building. Council instructed him not to exceed the $20,000 budget and to provide first-class accommodation for an inside market, keeping in mind that two other market buildings would be attached to it — a 30 x 100-foot butter market and a butchers' market. Evans based his plan, in part, on Kingston's classical city hall and market building. To crown his architectural masterpiece, he envisaged a 118-foot tower that would rival the best that Kingston or any other centre had.

John Forin (or "Foran" as he originally spelled his name to reflect his early Roman Catholic background) was the builder. A native of Ireland, he had come as a three-year-old with his family in 1835 and settled in Tyendinaga Township. After studying architecture in New York City from 1851 to 1853, he returned to Tyendinaga, where he designed and built the township hall at Melrose. His first construction project in Belleville was the impressive Commercial Bank (1855), which later served the citizens as the public library until 2006.

Forin was one of nine builders to tender on the Belleville market building. Unfortunately, although his was the lowest bid ($22,557), the 1871 council rejected it because it exceeded the $20,000 budget. The 1872 council reconsidered the project and sought ways to save money. Some councillors suggested eliminating the separate butter market and moving the vegetable market from the first floor to the basement, or making other major changes. However, Councillor J. Vandusen called for council to put up a building that would be "a credit to our growing town, and not to mutilate the appearance of the building." After two motions calling for the contract to be split between two parties were lost on 6–6 tie votes, council awarded the contract to Forin.

The project did not go smoothly. Even before the contract was signed, two unhappy council members stated that some parts of the building

Belleville City Hall as it appeared circa 1900, a quarter of a century after its completion by builder John Forin. Courtesy of Hastings County Historical Society, Neg. B-27.

would be too weak. They wanted "a practical architect" to examine the plans. Councillor Samuel B. Burdett, a lawyer, objected that "they were about to commence making changes before a brick was laid." Councillor John Northcott, an experienced contractor who was then building the town hall in neighbouring Thurlow Township, said that some people, including John Forin, thought the walls "would answer," but the roof would certainly have to be altered. No matter their profession, each member of council had become a construction expert and each had his say.

The result was that Northcott took Evans' plans to Kingston to "a practical and experienced architect" who shared Forin's view that the walls, especially the north one, would not be strong enough. Council then altered the specifications, adding buttresses. Forin signed the contract, although he warned council that the changes were not entirely satisfactory and that he would "not be responsible for the *substiality* of the buildings as set forth in the plans." He did not define "substiality," but councillors apparently knew what he meant.

Evans the architect and Forin the builder certainly had differences of opinion. It is possible — indeed, probable — that Forin, with his architectural training in New York City and a growing number of impressive buildings designed and constructed in Belleville, resented being supervised by Evans, a surveyor and self-taught architect. The two disagreed on many things. The result was that both men appeared before council on more than one occasion to air their grievances. Forin's main complaint was that the structure would not be strong enough. Evans responded by making some modifications, including moving the joists closer together. Evans' litany of complaints against

The original bell in the Belleville City Hall tower was cast in London (England) by the firm of John Warner and Sons. The original supporting framework was of wood, rather than metal. John Forin charged $800 to install the bell and had to change its position several times until it could be "heard distinctly in all parts of the town." Photo by author, 1989.

Forin included inferior brickwork, the use of too much small stone in the foundation (thereby weakening it), and copious variations from the plans and specifications. Building Committee Chairman John Lewis, a prominent hardware merchant, said that he had spoken to Forin about the poor brickwork near the main entrance. John Northcott said that the brickwork was the worst he had ever seen and that it was a "shamefully bad job."

Meanwhile, other factors slowed progress. Early in 1872, the journeymen carpenters met to consider the propriety of demanding an advance on their wages. They wanted 25 cents more per day. The employers offered only 12½ cents, and the carpenters threatened to strike. Fortunately, a settlement was soon reached.

In addition, council did its part to slow construction. As they saw the plans translate into the actual market building, councillors concluded that they would like to see changes made. For example, after Mayor Thomas Holden recommended the ceiling of the first storey be raised at least three feet to make the market more comfortable in hot weather, council agreed. The additional cost was $400. Further, council had been persuaded (possibly by John Forin) to raise the tower to 144 feet, 26 feet higher than Evans' original proposal. Considered individually, such extras were insignificant. Taken together, they posed a major financial problem. The result was that the separate butter and butcher markets were cancelled and some other economies were affected.

Nevertheless, by the spring of 1873, only $700 of the original $22,557 contract with Forin remained, with $6,000 worth of essential work still to be done. Forin told council that he was not prepared to continue work until $1,000 more had been advanced him or until council recognized the extras he claimed. These extras included items that had not been listed in the contract, but that Forin felt to be essential or desirable. Council replied that he must resume. If he did not, council would instruct the town solicitor to contact Forin's sureties (people who had guaranteed that he would faithfully fulfill the contract) and take steps to collect the guarantees. Other contractors would then be hired to complete the work. Councillors said they were prepared to deal fairly with Forin, whereupon he replied that justice was not enough: he must have more than justice "or he was a ruined man." Reluctantly, Forin agreed to resume work, leaving his claims for extras for arbitration, if necessary, until after the building was completed.

Finally, although late by almost a year, the building was ready for use. On December 24, the police magistrate held court for the first time in the upstairs courtroom. After reprimanding the first two clients, both charged with drunkenness, he freed them so that they would not have to spend Christmas Day in the cells, or "dongon [sic] keep," as the *Intelligencer* called them. Five days later, town council held its first meeting in the new council chambers and heard Councillor George Henderson report that prospects were good for the settlement of the dispute between the town and the contractor.

Henderson was overly optimistic. The settling of accounts took more than a year. Forin already had received more than $20,000, but he submitted accounts for an additional $4,500. The town offered $486, and Forin launched legal action. The parties agreed on a Kingston architect as arbitrator, and his decision, in May 1885, was that Forin was to receive $785 and must pay his own legal costs. Forin was most unhappy. He had built a market building and town hall of which the citizens could be proud and council had refused him what he thought was his rightful compensation. Perhaps partly because of this treatment, he ran for one of the two Ketcheson Ward council seats in the December election, but finished a distant third.

Nevertheless, Forin remained a prominent Belleville citizen and builder for many years. His many contributions to the Belleville streetscape, and the fact that architect John Evans shortly moved away, meant that his name has been most closely associated with the building.

Usually referred to as the "Market Building" throughout the planning and building stages, the terminology for the building soon changed. There were increasing references to a "town hall over the Market Building" and by the end of 1873, council minutes referred to the site of the next council meeting as "the New Council Chambers in the New Town Hall."

However, it was more than just a town hall or a city hall. Many groups and activities made use of the town hall (or "Auditorium" as it came to be known) on the second floor of the market building/town hall. From its completion in 1874, there had been a steady demand by potential users, especially during the years when there was no opera house. One of council's first actions was to set conditions for its use. Rental fees were $10 per night (almost immediately reduced to $8), and the renter was to pay for gas for the lamps. Early users included the West Hastings Agricultural Society and the Dairyman's Association of Ontario (holding annual meetings and conventions). The Belleville Cemetery Company held an early meeting to plan the establishment of a cemetery west of Belleville.

On January 14, 1874, Doctor Peter Dorland addressed the Native Canadian Society "with pleasing effect," outlining that new group's aims in promoting "patriotism, progress and union."

Banquet in the Market Room on first floor of Town Hall (now City Hall) in honour of Educators of the Deaf from North America in the summer of 1874. Courtesy of Library and Archives Canada, C-61352.

The next evening James Clark spoke. The press heralded his coming. "God is Light! God is Love! Come and hear the Glad Tidings to be preached in the Town Hall, Belleville, by Mr. James Clark...." Albert College held its convocation there. Because of limited space in the Belleville High School, the examinations for third-class teaching certificates were held in the hall on at least one occasion. The Law Student Society conducted debates. To conclude the activities of 1874, the "Bachelors of Belleville" held their Christmas Assembly (party and dance) in the hall. The following year, the federal government conducted a moving ceremony highlighting presentations to surviving veterans of the War of 1812. These included 102–year-old Frederick Killer [sic], Peter Dempsey (90), Luke Ostrom (89), and James McWilliams (89). The youngest veterans to be honoured were 78 years of age.

Although many of these events attracted considerable attention in the community, few created such intense interest as one that occurred on May 23, 1882 — the visit of renowned Irish wit and author Oscar Wilde.

Where Do We Bury the Dead?[15]

THE EARLIEST KNOWN cemetery, used by the United Empire Loyalists, was a family plot on land that John Taylor purchased from Captain George Singleton. Now known as the Taylor Burial Ground, this site was on a slight elevation, within sight of the Bay of Quinte.[16] The first burial is believed to have been that of Lieutenant Israel Ferguson, who died during the winter of 1789–90.[17]

When a town site was laid out in 1816, land was reserved on the proposed Church Street for a church, rectory, and burial ground. Although no denomination was identified, it was understood that this meant the Church of England. The first Anglican rector recorded the first official burial on August, 30, 1821. It was that of Mary Rosborough, "lately from Ireland," who had given birth to a son only a week previous.[18] Some controversy surrounds the second burial — that of Captain John W. Meyers. Although the parish register does not indicate a burial site other than the churchyard, the family believes that he was buried in White's Cemetery, west of Belleville. In fact, at a family reunion held in 1990 to celebrate the bicentennial of Meyers erecting Belleville's first industry, the Meyers family dedicated a new stone at White's Cemetery in memory of Meyers, his slaves, and the Mohawk Loyalists.[19]

Not long after the opening of the Anglican cemetery, the Roman Catholics and the Scottish Presbyterians also opened burial grounds on Church Street, adjacent to their new churches. Given the limited space, the small plot at St. Michael's was soon filled, and, in 1857, a larger site was purchased east of the town. It was named Mount St. Patrick, but is generally referred to as St. Michael's or the R.C. Cemetery.[20] Unfortunately, little is known about burials in the St. Andrew's Presbyterian Church Cemetery. A fire in the 1890s probably destroyed the records. However, photographs indicate a substantial number of gravestones.

Unlike the Anglicans, Roman Catholics, and Presbyterians, who received government land grants for their churches and burying grounds, the Methodists could not own land. Their early burials were probably in the Taylor or St. Thomas' cemeteries. Then, in 1828, "the year of great Revival and the first year in which Methodists in the province could legally hold title to land," they purchased an acre for a burying ground.[21] Like the Taylor Burying Ground, a few feet to the west on Dundas Street, the site overlooked the Bay of Quinte. There is almost no record of burials.[22]

Where records of burials survive — in the case of the Anglican and Roman Catholic congregations — they often indicate the state of health of the local population. For example, the peak year for burials was 1854, when the clergy at St. Thomas' recorded 80 burials and those at St. Michael's 118. Many were victims of Asiatic cholera.

The five cemeteries were active burial grounds until May 1, 1874, at which time a town bylaw was passed, as a result of health concerns, that banned further burials within the town limits. As early as 1847, an editorial in the *Intelligencer* spoke of potential health problems associated with burials within the town and asked if it was now "essential to arrest all further interments … within the limits of the Town …."[23] Then, in 1853, author Susanna Moodie warned that "[the] time will come, as the population increases and the dead accumulate, when these burying-grounds, by poisoning the springs that flow through them, will materially injure the health of the living."[24]

The issue of public versus private cemetery ownership loomed large. In the mid-1850s, several leading citizens considered forming a cemetery company to work co-operatively with town council. A newspaper editor wrote that "nothing is more needed for the health and comfort of the Town than a Cemetery."[25] Nevertheless, when the mayor called a public meeting, few citizens attended.[26] In 1870, the issue revived because some church burial grounds were almost full and the issue of public health had become more important. On September 8, council convened a meeting at the Town Hall of representatives appointed by the churches. Despite "limited attendance," Mayor Thomas Holden chaired an informal meeting and the majority favoured a cemetery of about forty acres to be administered by council rather than a joint-stock company.[27] After a council committee worked on the idea for ten months, a proposed bylaw was introduced.[28] There was much disagreement over the proposed site. One councillor suggested that it was the "very worst." However, his alternate site was said to not have "soil enough to bury a cat without taking the earth there." Council decided to submit the issue to the voters.

There were letters to the editor. One letter writer, "Vox Populi," felt that public ownership was not the way to go. He argued that:

1. caretakers and trustees of a public cemetery would have to be paid and would become "permanent pensioners on the public purse;"
2. council members would always be open to charges of favouritism with respect to employment openings and purchases;
3. friends of councillors would get the best plots;
4. the money was needed for more important things such as a new high school, a new market, and water works; and
5. council would appoint members to "a travelling committee" to visit cemeteries in the United States, in effect "a pleasure holiday."[29]

About three-hundred citizens attended a public meeting in the Town Hall on August 23, 1871, to consider the "Cemetery By-Law." Again, the issue of public versus private ownership came up. Finally, Grand Trunk Railway Solicitor John Bell said that he was ready to subscribe to a private company and Mackenzie Bowell, editor of the *Intelligencer* and the member of Parliament for North Hastings, added that if the bylaw was defeated, it was desirable that a private company be formed.[30] Two days later the citizens turned down the bylaw by an 88-vote margin — 152–64.[31] The way was open for a private company.

On August 27, 1872, a group of influential citizens formed the Belleville Cemetery Company.[32] They chose a site in Sidney Township, a few kilometres west of town on the shores of the Bay of Quinte. Capital stock was set at $10,000, with 500 shares of $20 each. The list of subscribers was a "who's who" of the town's business and political elite, and included John Bell, Mackenzie Bowell, and senator and lumber king Billa Flint.[33] There was such a ready response to the offering of shares in this joint-stock company that the directors regretted not having offered more shares.[34]

The company was fortunate to have the services of landscape designer Heinrich A. Engelhardt readily available. That year, Engelhardt had authored the first Canadian book on landscape gardening.[35] Engelhardt, who had earlier helped lay out Central Park in New York City, and would later design Mount Pleasant Cemetery in Toronto, described himself as "Professor of Agriculture and Landscape Gardener," and may have been associated with Albert College. He had just completed an ornamental grounds layout for the Ontario Institution for the Deaf and Dumb at Belleville. Now the cemetery directors contracted him to lay out their grounds.

By early July 1873, Engelhardt had prepared his plans for the initial block and shareholders were able to make their selections. Newspapers advertised "A Free Trip to the Cemetery" on July 18. Chartered for the day, the steamer *Prince Edward* carried many shareholders to the cemetery, while others drove. The mayor presided at the lottery for lots, drawing first from the names of shareholders who had five shares, then four shares, and so on. One reporter wrote, somewhat humorously: "The rain, which at intervals throughout the afternoon, came down in torrents, interfered somewhat with the grave business in which the shareholders were engaged." He went on to describe the reaction to the architect's planning: "Mr. Englehardt, the architect, has succeeded in a very short time in transforming a large portion of the Cemetery grounds into a most delightful park-like spot, with winding roadways, and paths diverging in almost every direction.…When the grounds become ornamented with trees and shrubbery, and choice plants and flowers, it will be one of the prettiest homes for the dead to be found in the Dominion."[36]

One month later, the *Intelligencer* reported that the cemetery was already a favourite destination for pedestrians on Sunday afternoons.[37] Presumably, these were shareholders or lot proprietors and their friends, because this was a private cemetery with very specific rules and regulations. Each lot proprietor was entitled to a ticket of admission to the cemetery that would admit the holder and a vehicle. This privilege would be forfeited if the ticket was loaned or if any rule was violated. These rules limited vehicle speed to six miles per hour, banned smoking, prohibited dogs, and forbade anyone from picking any flowers, *wild or cultivated*, or breaking any tree, shrub, or plant.[38]

The company celebrated its achievements when the shareholders held their annual meeting the following January. President Francis McAnnany reflected that, "we have set apart the loveliest spot upon the banks of the Bay of Quinte, as the final resting place of our beloved and honoured dead … Soon the mortal remains of hundreds among us, who are now walking our streets in the beauty of health shall slumber there."[39]

Decoration days at the cemetery were important occasions. For example, on July 16, 1890, representatives of ten lodges and societies co-operated in decorating the graves of deceased brethren.[40] The mayor proclaimed a civic half-holiday, and most businesses shut down. Crowds of people "were seen wending their way to the cemetery … The people went on foot, in carriages, in row boats, whilst the larger number took advantage of the steamer *Hero*, which was crowded every trip she made."

Unfortunately, not all visitors behaved themselves, as evidenced

Furniture, upholstering, and undertaking business of George S. Tickell on Front Street, just south of Victoria Avenue, circa 1878, as pictured in Belden's Historical Atlas of Hastings and Prince Edward Counties. *The building and carriageway to the rear parking lot still survive.* Courtesy of Hastings County Historical Society, Mika Collection.

by a Grounds Committee report in 1903 requesting the superintendent "to patrol the grounds occasionally at and after dusk in order to see that no approaches by the water be made by others than those having rightful entrance to the cemetery, and also that every endeavor be made to stop the plucking or removal of flowers from private lots."[41]

Today, the Belleville Cemetery Company continues to operate the cemetery. Its mission statement begins: "The Belleville Cemetery Company, a not-for profit corporation, is dedicated to the provision and maintenance of burial locations for the citizens of Belleville and the surrounding area in a serene park-like setting. The Company is committed to treating death with dignity and grieving families with respect."[42]

The opening of the Belleville Cemetery, to the west of the town, and the fact that the Roman Catholic Cemetery was east of the town meant that council could now act to safeguard citizens' health. Effective May 1, 1874, there could be no further burials within the town limits.[43] The penalties for infractions were from $20 to $50 plus costs or, if in default, ten to thirty days in the county common jail. The penalties were increased dramatically three years later, after a clergyman was found to have buried a deceased eighty-six-year-old widow in a church cemetery two years after the deadline.[44] Even though he had been aware of the regulations, he had performed the burial so that her body might be near to that of her husband. The clergyman appealed his penalty to council, but was refused an exemption.

Today, there is some evidence of each of the five early burial grounds, particularly in the case of St. Thomas' Church. However, the passage of time, the relocation of many markers, and the installation of paved parking lots have made it difficult to see the burial places of our ancestors.

From Picnic to Parliament

IN THE MID 1870s, at a time when Alexander Mackenzie had replaced John A. Macdonald as Canada's prime minister, Mackenzie Bowell gained a prominent position in the Conservative Party (sometimes known as the Liberal-Conservative Association). Bowell helped organize the Conservative political picnics of 1876, which were credited by Macdonald biographer Donald Creighton and others as key steps in Macdonald regaining the position of prime minister of Canada.[45]

The final picnic in a series of seven occurred at Belleville on September 12. There were supposed to have been nearly 15,000 people there, a larger crowd than any Belleville had seen since the abortive visit by the Prince of Wales in 1860.[46] Macdonald and the many other guests were driven through the streets, through ceremonial arches and past decorated homes, to the

View of the 1876 picnic decorations welcoming Sir John A. Macdonald to Belleville, as depicted in the
Canadian Illustrated News. *Courtesy of Library and Archives Canada, C-64596.*

fairgrounds, where Macdonald spoke on the need to bring back prosperity. Though sixty-one years of age and considering stepping down in favour of fresh, young blood in the leadership of the party, he felt rejuvenated by the successful picnics and determined to unseat Mackenzie.

Macdonald was successful in the 1878 election, and Bowell was appointed as minister of customs, in which post he helped implement Macdonald's "National Policy" of increased tariffs to help Canadian industry. Macdonald continued as prime minister until his death in 1891, owing in no small part to the political picnic at Belleville in 1876.

Trouble on the Railway Tracks

BELLEVILLE HAS BEEN an important railway centre ever since the first train arrived in October 1856. For the most part, the relationship between the community and the railway has been excellent. Whereas citizens of Edmonton and Saskatoon can complain that passenger service is limited to a total of six trains each week — and in Saskatoon's case they all arrive in the early morning hours — Belleville residents have that number of trains going each way on a typical day.

The major exception to this first-class relationship took place at New Year's in 1876, when labour unrest among locomotive engineers employed by the Grand Trunk Railway resulted in the Belleville Riot. This riot would require the presence of the Queen's Own Rifles of Toronto to restore law and order.

Shortly before this unhappy event, the townspeople were very pleased with the community's railway prospects. The Grand Junction Railway was nearing completion from Belleville to Madoc Junction, and the Grand Trunk Railway had announced plans for new engine sheds, a passenger station, and repair sheds at Belleville. Town council estimated that these projects would cost $150,000, and would provide considerable employment.[47] Unfortunately, a worldwide recession had deepened, leading the Grand Trunk to announce slight wage reductions for engineers. Then, at the end of November, the company announced that it would not proceed with its building program at Belleville until times improved.[48] This was followed by a reduction of about 20 percent in train service, and then a similar reduction in staff.[49] Almost 70 of the company's 357 engineers were laid off. Those engineers who survived the cut remained the highest paid railway employees, receiving $3.01 per day.[50]

The timing of the layoffs was terrible. It was only two days before Christmas. The weather was very cold. There was little chance of finding other satisfactory employment in the dead of winter, and unemployment insurance was not even a dream. Some employees felt that several senior engineers had lost their jobs while the company kept junior and lower-waged employees. Furthermore, it was suggested that some employees lost their jobs because they had joined the Brotherhood of Locomotive Engineers, then gathering strength throughout North America.

The engineers and firemen did not take immediate strike action, leading a Montreal paper to report happily that rumours of a strike have "turned out to be entirely without foundation."[51] This was only true for a time. The engineers and firemen did take their grievances to management, but they made it clear that if their demands were not met, they would strike at 9:00 p.m. on December 29. Their demands included the immediate reinstatement of all dismissed engineers and firemen, the importance of seniority, and the need for a system of arbitration to settle problems.[52]

General Manager J. Hickson was unwilling to meet these demands, although he did agree to give preference to former employees in the hiring process. Knowing that a strike was looming, Hickson advertised for engineers to report for work at Belleville and Stratford. He said that he would train new men as fast as he could, and use non-union men who were willing to work. In short, he would use renegades and scabs to break the strike.[53] On Friday, with the deadline fast approaching, the company held most trains in terminals. Unfortunately, the last train to leave Montreal for Toronto was stranded three miles from Cobourg. The passengers were reported to have "spent the night in the middle of a snow storm, and virtually cut off from all outside communications."[54] The Toronto Board of Trade and Montreal City Council bitterly condemned what they called the "monstrous and illegal strike." The recently appointed railway president said the engineers who left trains stranded had sunk "almost to the level of burglars."

At Belleville, the strikers were determined to stop the trains. They put two snowplows off the rails, one at each end of the yard. The strikers and their supporters, some allegedly armed with pistols, successfully intimidated the company's replacement workers, who soon found themselves joining the Brotherhood of Locomotive Engineers.[55]

Alarmed by this threat to law and order, Belleville's magistrates felt that action was needed. But who would restore calm? Early in December, the chief of police had been fired for physical inability, and the senior sergeant had been dismissed for drunkenness on duty. A former chief had been reappointed, but the number of constables had been cut by one, to six.[56] Unfortunately, neither chief went to the station. In fact, the police situation had deteriorated so much that, three weeks after the strike, the new chief was dismissed. This followed the theft of police records from the chief's desk, and the opening of the town clerk's safe by duplicate keys.[57]

Town authorities, headed by Mayor W.A. Foster, now called on the senior local militia officer and member of Parliament, James Brown, to provide a detachment to help restore order. As

Grand Trunk Railway · 1867

commanding officer of the 49th Rifle Regiment, Brown instructed Captain Edward Harrison of the First Company to take a detachment to the station. With no ammunition in the armouries, Harrison was forced to borrow some from a private citizen. He and twenty-five men then proceeded to the station late in the evening. With bayonets fixed (and two rounds of ball ammunition each), the detachment assisted the railway superintendent in the safe removal of a locomotive from the sheds. For the rest of the night, the men kept moving from point to point to protect the railway employees while they replaced the derailed cars on the tracks. However, no sooner had they replaced one car

Grand Trunk Railway locomotive, 1867, silk-screened by Nick Mika for a series of pictures on Canada's railway history. Courtesy of Hastings County Historical Society, Mika Collection.

at the eastern end of the yard than it was derailed again while the soldiers were busy at the other end of the yard. At 5:00 a.m. on December 31, the Rifles escorted an engine from the shed. The engine proceeded to Shannonville and returned with the Toronto Express.

Fearing that some serious act of violence might occur, Harrison called the remainder of his company to the station. The order to "fix bayonets" was given, and the soldiers surrounded the engine and began to escort it from the siding to the main line. However, the strikers and their supporters did not stand idly by. They became desperate. Some of the mob brandished revolvers and hurled car bolts at the engine. Just before the engine reached the train on the main line, one of the strikers stepped behind the last soldier and passed an iron bolt into the engine's machinery. A loud noise followed and the engine was disabled. When the mob resorted to several acts of personal violence, the company gave up the idea of moving the Toronto Express. Harrison marched his detachment back to the armouries, relieved that no one had been seriously injured to that point.

The 49th Rifle Regiment's role in the event later led to two criticisms: First, there was the unfortunate shortage of ammunition. The Adjutant General answered that criticism when he suggested that it was "not prudent" to keep a supply of ammunition in company armouries since it was "liable to become useless or stolen."[58] The second criticism, levied by a Kingston military officer, was that civil authorities allowed the 49th to withdraw from the station "at a time when the aid of the military appeared to be most required."[59] Belleville authorities replied that the presence of the 49th seemed to aggravate the situation, and that there was nothing that could be done with this limited force in view of the large number of strikers and sympathizers.

Within two hours of the 49th's withdrawal from the station, Mayor Foster returned with two companies of forty men of the 15th Battalion Argyll Light Infantry under Major S.S. Lazier. Unfortunately, this regiment had not drilled for a year, many men were absent because of holidays or lumbering, and some refused to turn out because of "a strong feeling of sympathy … for the men on strike."[60] Moreover, the soldiers had to borrow overcoats despite the fact that more than a hundred had recently been issued to them. A subsequent military investigation reported that the 15th Battalion was in a "disorganized state" and "utterly wanting in all the requisites which make a military force useful on such occasions." However, the investigator felt that the regiment would "improve vastly under Major Lazier, who is capable of commanding and has a good reputation in Belleville."[61]

At the station, the men of the 15th Battalion found things fairly quiet, the strikers being content as long as no attempt was made to move any train. One company of the 15th guarded each of the two large engine sheds. When the remaining company employees felt that they could protect the engine shed without military assistance, the soldiers were allowed to go home at 8:00 a.m. on New Year's Day.[62]

Civil authorities met in the town hall two hours later. It was obvious that the local police force and militia units were inadequate to the task of reopening the Grand Trunk line. No train had moved for three full days. Accordingly, Mayor Foster sent a telegram to Militia Headquarters in Toronto stating that, because of the "riot and disturbance of the peace," a military force was needed to restore law and order.

The telegram reached Lieutenant Colonel W.S. Durie at 3:00 p.m. on New Year's Day. By 7:30 the next morning, Lieutenant Colonel Otter had a force of 167 officers and men of the Queen's Own Rifles ready to come to Belleville. Their special train consisted of two engines and eighteen or nineteen passenger cars, with pilot engines in front. Owing to threats of violence, guards were placed in the cabs of each engine, and at every station guards immediately surrounded the engines and tenders. At Sidney Station, ten kilometres west of Belleville, the train was met by Mayor Foster and the railway's solicitor, John Bell, a resident of Belleville. Foster spoke of the "wildest rumours" concerning violence and said that he had issued a proclamation warning all parties not having business at the station "to refrain from going thereto, and to disperse therefrom."[63] Unfortunately, the local strikers, numbering about a hundred, had refused to leave the station.

Prepared to deal with any threats, the commanding officer ordered the engine crew to proceed slowly into Belleville. It took more than an hour to cover the final ten kilometres. Arriving at 10:30 p.m., the 167 officers and men of the Queen's Own Rifles found a mob of some seven hundred "riotously disposed" persons awaiting them.[64] Three hours later, with a guard of one company on board for protection, the train left Belleville for Montreal. According to one report, the strikers attempted to disconnect the coaches as the train was leaving, but were driven off by the passengers using camp stools.

Unfortunately, while the Belleville railway employees were attempting to put the other engines into the carefully guarded engine house, one engine ran off the tracks "by some unlucky means."[65] To protect the employees who were working on the very cold but moonlit night, the troops had to "advance with fixed bayonets in order to press the mob back."[66] Some injuries resulted. One man was seriously wounded in the thigh by a bayonet, but the military doctor saved him from bleeding to death. Two soldiers suffered head injuries from thrown stones or ice.

A four-hour meeting that evening in Montreal between management and the workers brought an end to the strike. To a large extent, the settlement was a victory for the engineers and firemen. The company allowed all the strikers to return to work, except those who were guilty of personal violence. The work was to be evenly distributed, and a later meeting would deal with the question of wages and promotions.[67]

Railway officials were less than pleased with the settlement. General Manager J. Hickson blamed Prime Minister Alexander Mackenzie's Liberal government for this setback to the company. Mackenzie had repeatedly refused Hickson's requests that regular troops from Quebec or Montreal be used to reopen the line, stating that the permanent forces could only be used in "case of war, invasion or insurrection."[68] Later that year, however, the Mackenzie government passed the Breaches of Contract Act, designed to protect the public against unreasonable suffering in the event of another strike.

The settlement of the strike relieved tension at Belleville. On the evening of January 3, the Queen's Own Rifles left town via special train. Several of the men were the worse for the wear. Two had been wounded. Three men on engine guard had their feet frozen, and many more suffered frozen fingers. This illustrated the hardships caused by sending men on service in winter without fur caps, boots, and gloves.[69]

Each Queen's Own Rifles volunteer received mementoes of their service in Belleville — a woollen muffler, a souvenir medal made from part of one of the torn-up rails, and $3 in pay. The pay was several months late, because Belleville council initially refused to pay the costs, believing that the railway company or the Canadian government should bear part of the expense. Because the council had called out the troops, the regiment's commanding officer sued the town. On October 2, 1877, the court ruled in favour of the regiment.[70]

The strike was an important event in Belleville's history. The dismissed Grand Trunk Railway employees were again employed. The inefficiency of the police force was clearly demonstrated, and steps were taken to remedy that situation. The need to rebuild the 15th Battalion Argyll Light Infantry was shown, and Major Lazier moved ahead with that process. Further, the role of the town officials was questioned. Mayor Foster and the other magistrates had involved the city in a violent situation that led to a court case, costs of several hundreds of dollars, and charges that the city fathers had favoured the railway company over the workers. Only in Belleville were the troops called out, and only in Belleville were there injuries. Yet, caught up in a crisis for which they were not responsible, and for which they were not prepared, the council members and magistrates had reacted in a conscientious manner.

In the words of historian A. W. Currie: "In a sense the fuss over the strike was ridiculous but at a time when industrial violence was rare and employers expected workers to be subservient, it attracted great attention." For a brief time, Belleville was in the national headlines.

A Glorious Day, July 1, 1878

THIS WAS A red-letter day for Bellevillians — not just because it was the anniversary of Confederation, but also because it was a time to celebrate Belleville's new status as a city. An Ontario statute of March 2, 1877 had granted city status, effective the end of 1877. However, the celebration was delayed to the following Dominion Day, when the weather would be nicer. It was a large celebration, certainly one of the largest in the community's history.[71]

The citizens celebrated Belleville's growth to a community of over 10,000 people with a booming economy based on the products of the area's forests, farms, and mines. Each spring, thousands of logs came down the Moira River. Local foundries produced ploughs and other implements. The Grand Trunk Railway had announced plans to spend $150,000 to improve its shop facilities. Later that year, the Belleville and North Hastings Railway carried iron ore from Madoc to the Belleville harbour, where it was placed on ships destined for the iron-smelting furnaces in Pennsylvania. As a result of two plebiscites, Belleville ratepayers approved bonuses in the amount of $125,000 to the Grand Junction Railway. Belleville was acting, more and more, like a prosperous, growing community. To assist businesses and visitors, the Belleville Novelty Company was authorized to number all the buildings that fronted on any street, and council began to consider the use of standard street name signs. Although the 1871 Canadian census had found the town's population to be only 7,305 — too small a number for city status, a council-sponsored census found it to be 11,120.

Planning for the July 1st celebration did not start until late May. Council was more concerned about other matters, including an economic recession, the closure of the Rathbun Company's lumber mill on Mill (or Rathbun) Island at the mouth of the Moira (after a dispute with council), and a provincial investigation into municipal finances relating to a recently deceased town employee. Only after the Victoria Day celebration on May 24 did council call a public meeting to commence planning. When no private group was prepared to take the lead, council decided that it would serve as the organizing committee. Nine sub-committees were set up, and a maximum of $500 of public money was allocated. Expenditures included $200 to Professor Hand of Hamilton to put on the fireworks display and $35 to purchase a set of colours for the new steamer *City of Belleville,* scheduled to enter service on or about July 1. Council duly noted the honour done to the city in having the vessel named after it. So that as many people as possible could participate in the day, council instructed that admission fees be kept low. Entrance to the agricultural grounds for the fireworks display in the evening was set at 15¢ for adults and 10¢ for children.

Planning went remarkably smoothly. The only major problem came on June 24, when council passed a resolution calling for the July 1 civic dinner to be conducted along Temperance

lines. The treasurer was instructed not to pay for any wines or intoxicating liquors. Despite objections from a few councillors, who wanted the decision left to the civic dinner committee, council refused to budge. Anyone wishing to drink wines or liquors would have to pay the tab themselves. This emphasis on Temperance was part of a strong movement then sweeping across much of the province. A Temperance leader by the name of Rine addressed five local meetings in the fall of 1877. Two were in the thousand-seat opera house, whose manager had just been prosecuted for allowing the sale of lager beer. Over 1,600 persons signed the pledge.

On July 1, Belleville's powerful Temperance associations erected three arches over the lower bridge. The motto "Rescue the Fallen and support the Weak" was displayed prominently. However, one block south on Front Street, the Corby Distillery arch featured — even more prominently — empty liquor barrels, emphasizing the importance of the liquor market.

The day was a long one. According to newspaper coverage the following day, the cannon on the courthouse lawn, accompanied by the discharge of smaller arms, roused the "denizens of Belleville" at 3:00 a.m. The night had been warm, and many had slept uneasily, if at all. Within a few hours, excursion boats began to arrive. About 6:00 a.m., the *Kincardine* docked with 125 firefighters from Watertown, New York. Their band played "God Save the Queen," after which the Belleville Odd Fellows Band, hastily assembled because the Watertown boat had arrived an hour early, saluted the visitors with a beautifully played rendition of "Yankee Doodle." Within a short time, boats arrived from Cobourg, Napanee, Trenton, and Picton. Thousands of other celebrants came by land from neighbouring communities.

The highlight of the morning was a procession composed of the city's various trades and businesses. Some 25,000 citizens and visitors watched as the half-hour parade passed. Viewers of the *Intelligencer* float were treated to copies of the special "July First Extra," which

Front Street decorated for the celebration on July 1, 1878. Barrels advertised brands of liquor produced by Corby's, whose business office was at the extreme right. Corby's Distillery was one of Belleville's leading industries. Courtesy of Hastings County Historical Society, Neg B-88.

was being printed on the float as it passed. On the *Ontario* wagon, nine newspaper employees worked on various jobs, while three Watertown reporters, described as "jolly good fellows," kept an eye on the proceedings. Once at the fairgrounds, located on the southwest corner of West Bridge and Yeomans streets, Mayor Robertson thanked the hundreds who had helped to make the day a success and Senator Billa Flint delivered the inaugural speech. A resident of Belleville for forty-nine years, Flint had held the highest offices in the town and county, making him the logical choice. Unfortunately, he spoke longer than many had expected; the dinner bell rang while he was still speaking and there was a rush for the interior of the Agricultural Hall, where an excellent meal was served for only 25¢. Nevertheless, Flint finished with an "excellent eulogy" of Canada, predicting a brilliant future for Belleville, whereupon, the crowd gave three cheers for each of the queen, the president of the United States, Billa Flint, and Mayor Robertson.

The Caledonian Games, under the direction of Belleville Police Chief Hugh McKinnon, occupied the afternoon. McKinnon, the American champion in these Scottish games, having won the title at the Great Athletic Championship at Philadelphia in 1876, could not compete, but did demonstrate certain activities. Decorated with medals attesting to his athletic accomplishments, Chief McKinnon was a handsome sight. Of the local competitors, Belleville High School teacher E.F. Milburn was the best. Although he was not trained in the pole vault (or leap), he was beaten by only one inch by one of the best competitors. Milburn jumped 10 feet, 10 inches.

While the Caledonian Games were staged at the agricultural grounds, two lacrosse games took place on the old cricket grounds by the bay shore. Teams from Napanee and Picton played two Belleville teams — the Alerts and the Oka club. The Alerts split their four-game series, but the Okas handily defeated Napanee. The first of four games lasted only three minutes.

The civic banquet, scheduled for 6:00 p.m. at the Dafoe House, started two hours late. As some of the guests were leaving the banquet, and as others wished to witness the torchlight procession and fireworks, many toasts were cut short. Nevertheless, the mayors of Watertown, Brantford, Peterborough, and Lindsay all spoke briefly. Meanwhile, the firemen had assembled on the market square. Following some excellent band music that once again included "Yankee Doodle" and "God Save the Queen," the crowd visited the illuminations that decorated Front Street and many private residences. Chinese lanterns and other lighting devices sparkled and shone. The culmination of the day was the magnificent fireworks display at the agricultural grounds arranged by Professor Hand of Hamilton. It lasted from 9:00 p.m. until 11:00 p.m. The program was designed around ten musical numbers, including marches, polkas, and waltzes, among them "The Blue Danube." Unfortunately, however, the bands did not arrive and the display proceeded without accompaniment. The grand concluding scene was the same as Professor Hand had put on before the governor general at St. Catharines. Being 20 feet in diameter, it was the largest ever shown in Canada. In the centre appeared the royal coat of arms and "God Save the Queen."

So ended the very successful celebration of Belleville's birth as a city. Despite a few mild cases of sunstroke, the slight injury of a child (who was knocked down by a fractious horse), a few arrests for drunkenness, and the arrest of a light-fingered gentleman (who was found to be in the possession of five pocket-books, two silver watches and chains, thirteen handkerchiefs, and other items), the day had gone off with few problems. Moreover, the citizens and visitors agreed that this had been a tremendous event, one that showed their fellow citizens in Canada and elsewhere that Belleville could put on a celebration that was second to none.

Sex in the Seventies

WHEN MANY PEOPLE think of late Victorian times, they picture the dowager Queen Victoria dressed in black, prim and proper ladies and gentlemen, and high moral standards. Certainly there would be no reference to sexual matters, and words such as "prostitution" would never appear in the newspapers.

This may have been the case in a few Canadian communities, but it was certainly not true for Belleville. In the mid-1970s, a group of students at Moira Secondary School researched the *Intelligencer* of the mid-1870s to find out what Belleville was like on the eve of achieving city status in 1878. The students were very surprised by what they found. For example, several advertisements related to sexual disorders. One weekly advertisement proclaimed that William Gray's Specific Medicine was "especially recommended as an unfailing cure for Seminal Weakness, Spermatorrhea, Impotency, and all diseases that follow as a sequence of Self Abuse as Loss of Memory, Universal Lassitude … and many other diseases that lead to Insanity or Consumption and a Premature Grave…" To counter these possible problems, druggists A.L. Geen & Company and L.W. Yeomans & Co. offered Gray's Specific Medicine for a dollar a bottle.[72]

The news columns were filled with crimes of passion. Love, sex, and violence were closely linked in many stories. For example, the *Intelligencer*'s Tweed correspondent wrote, "Last Monday Jas. Johnston ran away with Miss Tot Cool, daughter of Isaac Cool, and Mr. Cool and his son Peter are on the track of the fugitives fully determined to shoot both parties unless Mr. Johnston is prepared to make the amende honourable. [*sic*]"[73] In another well-publicized case, correspondents for the *Intelligencer* and the *Ontario* reported on an interview with the prisoner Mr. Shannon, a schoolteacher accused of shooting Bertha Wynn in Seymour

Township. Wynn was a fifteen-year-old girl who, according to the *Ontario,* had learned to be a flirt from her mother. Shannon denied having had any intention to shoot the girl, and spoke of her in the highest terms. "He stated that the woman calling herself his wife, is not his wife, as will be shown by him at the first opportunity." The paper noted that Wynn was recovering nicely "although her wounds were at first pronounced fatal."[74] From this brief description of events, it would appear that the case was an involved one and that Shannon might have required mental evaluation.

In a third case, one of indecent assault that took place on Zwick's Island, the crown attorney noted that "the facts of the case were so disgusting in their details that Justice Moss, at the last trial, had said that it was a case that should never be brought before a jury in an Open Court. In the interests of morality, and in view of the fact that the complainant appeared to have been a consenting party, he would offer no evidence in the case." The prisoner was then discharged.[75]

Commencing on April 2, 1878, the County Court House was the scene of a sensational trial before Justice Morrison of the Ontario Court. Morrison's opening remarks dealt with the nature of the crime, abortion, which he regretted was "becoming prevalent of late years." Doctor Thomas A. of Sidney Township was charged with having "feloniously killed a female child of which Amarilla K. was the mother, through the administration of some deadly drug or by the use of some instrument." The charge followed the discovery of a newly born infant's body beneath the ice of the Moira River near the corner of Front and Dundas streets in downtown Belleville. The baby had been born one or two months prematurely to a twenty-one–year-old unmarried woman in poor health. Doctor A. had attended during the last part of the delivery and had taken the baby away to save the family from the great scandal. So quietly was this done that the woman's father did not know about the birth until two weeks later, when police informed him.

Doctor A's defence was that he had taken the child, which had been stillborn, for a post mortem and then buried it. The crown prosecutor insisted that "Society needs all the aid the law can give it to secure the chastity of women, and prevent the frequency of birth out of wedlock." The jury's decision was that Doctor A. was "guilty of concealing the birth of a child." When he was asked if he had anything to say, the doctor stated that the child found in the river was not the one he had taken away. Moreover, he did not see how a charge of concealment of birth could be made, since this was a miscarriage and not a natural birth, much less an abortion.

Judge Morrison then chastised the doctor and said that he was lucky not to have been convicted of procuring an abortion, for which crime the judge had sentenced persons to death, though the sentences had been commuted to life imprisonment. He then sentenced the doctor to twelve months in the county jail at hard labour. There was much public interest in the sexual aspects of this and similar cases, and the newspaper published detailed accounts of the trials.[76]

In Ontario, circuit judges handled such cases as murder, abortion, and indecent assault while local courts, often incorrectly referred to as "police courts," dealt with lesser crimes. The two Belleville newspapers competed with each other with respect to crime coverage, and April 1878 was a particularly good month for stories about prostitution. Under the headline A DRUNKEN CAROUSAL, the *Daily Ontario* of April 8 reported that "The people of North Front Street were very much pained and shocked last evening by a gang of prostitutes with their drunken companions making the night hideous with their lewd utterances. It was kept up for some time and so startled were many in the neighbourhood that they had to bar their doors for fear of an attack. How long will this state of things continue?"

Perhaps surprisingly, the same newspaper revealed the reason the police may not have been on the scene on North Front Street:

> A RAID — We are glad to observe that during Saturday night our police made a raid on some of the houses in West Belleville to which we drew their attention a few days since. The net was well laid, and they succeeded in making a good haul, so good that the cells could not contain any more, else they would have made a stronger 'pull'. But two houses were visited, one kept by a man named P... and the other by Mrs. D. L.... Seven of the frail sisterhood were captured and brought to the cells, and along with them as many more of the sterner but equally disreputable sex. To Sergeant Snider and officers Rankin, Cook, and Downs is due the credit of making this raid.

Prostitution was not confined to North Front Street and the West Hill. On April 30, *The Daily Ontario* described "yet another pull" in which "two more dens of iniquity" were visited and "a good haul made." Both houses were "on Pinnacle Street and in respectable neighbourhoods." The owners were identified by their full names, although the four women were not.

The police kept very busy during the entire month of April; Police statistics indicate that more arrests were made for prostitution and related acts that month than in the rest of the year. Of the sixty-seven persons arrested in April, twenty-eight were charged for sex-related crimes — keeping houses of ill-fame (seven), being inmates of houses of ill-fame (fourteen), frequenting houses of ill-fame (six), and exposure of the person (one). This represented a veritable crime wave, since in

April of the previous year there had only been nineteen arrests for all offences. It is interesting to note that a century later (April 1978), Police Chief Douglas Crosbie indicated that there were no arrests for prostitution but six arrests for indecent exposure. More recently, on July 31, 2008, in a headline on page 1, the *Intelligencer* proclaimed CITY'S GOT A HOOKER PROBLEM and police actions to deal with the problem were described in subsequent issues.

Almost a century after the police arrests of 1878, the Belleville Police Department was still housed in the former market building on Market Square, as seen in this 1963 photo. Courtesy of Hastings County Historical Society, Mika Collection, MG1.1, Box 6.

Where were Belleville's prostitutes coming from in 1878? A search of the 1871 Census and the *1878–1879 Hastings County Directory* revealed only one identical surname in both sources. A possible explanation is that the young ladies came from outside the city and stayed briefly. Evidence for that theory is found in a newspaper article describing the arrest of an operator of "a disreputable house" and three of his boarders. Two of the women, probably sisters, were described as "nymphs" of "Bunker Hill" (Napanee) notoriety, and one was referred to as "the notorious Ellen G." The newspaper noted, "We are glad to see this work prosecuted, and hope it will be continued until such characters are either driven from the city, or else placed where they will not be in a position to pester society with their presence."[77]

Justice came quickly to those charged with these crimes. Following the police raids of Saturday, April 6, Police Magistrate Abram Diamond dealt with the prisoners on Monday morning in the small courtroom over the police station. Charges of keeping a house of ill fame against Henry P. were dismissed, as it was proven he was not the lessee of the house. Francis W., "who took the place of the prisoner above named" was fined $20 and costs, or three months in jail. Mrs. Jane L. met with the same fate. Six women charged with being inmates of the houses were each fined $10 and costs or two months in jail. Charges against five men of being "frequenters of houses of ill fame" were dismissed, it being their first offence. In mid-afternoon, the prisoners were brought back to court and two who were able to pay were allowed to leave. Those unable to pay were remanded for one week to allow them to raise the money.[78]

On the Monday afternoon of the trial, a most unusual event took place at the police court. Police Magistrate Abram Diamond dropped charges (of being an inmate and a frequenter of a house of ill fame) against Nellie T. of Camden, near Napanee, and Hugh C. of Trenton, since they professed a desire to marry. Accordingly, at 3:00 p.m., the Reverend Mr. Rose and Anson G. Northrup, the issuer of marriage licences, attended the court. The bride and groom were escorted from their cells, and, after the necessary preliminaries, the couple were united in marriage. Police Magistrate Diamond "heartily congratulated the newly wedded couple," who had professed a desire "to mend their ways and unite their destinies." The ceremony, described as being performed "in a highly impressive manner," was conducted in private in the clerk's office, and the couple was allowed to leave by the back door. This was "a great disappointment to the crowd in the Court Room, who had expected to be spectators of the interesting event." Newspaper coverage headlined the event as TWO HEARTS WITH BUT A SINGLE THOUGHT and AN UNFASHIONABLE WEDDING.[79] The *Intelligencer* coverage concluded, "It is to be hoped that both parties will reform and lead respectable lives in the future. May they do so and be happy." If the couple had children, any descendants who are genealogically inclined will find this story to be an interesting, unusual, and challenging part of the family tree.

7
END OF THE VICTORIAN ERA

A New Hospital and Home for the Friendless

ONE OF THE most important developments in local medical history took place, in large part, as the result of a serious accident on the Grand Trunk Railway near Shannonville on June 21, 1872. Five passengers died instantly, and fifty, thirty-two of whom died soon afterwards, were injured. When the injured were brought to Belleville, they were treated at first in a large freight shed and, later, in the Roman Catholic convent, thanks to the Right Reverend James Farrelly, second pastor of St. Michael's Church.

The *Intelligencer* soon pursued the need for a hospital, noting that the provincial government had set aside a lot for such a purpose in 1816 and that major accidents and diseases, such as smallpox, made a hospital essential. However, for health reasons, the *Intelligencer* argued that the hospital should be located further from the centre of town than the original site. The paper rejoiced that "a number of ladies, particularly those who had been acting as nurses at the temporary hospital, purpose (*sic*) taking action to induce the Council to proceed in this matter at once."[1] On January 30, 1873, town council responded with the announcement that a special committee had been formed to select a site and construct a hospital.

Unfortunately, planning proceeded very slowly, partly because some citizens were becoming increasingly concerned about elderly and poverty-stricken residents and children who were begging in the streets, and wanted their needs considered, as well. Although the majority of citizens in the 1870s appear to have felt that such matters were not a concern for the general populace, and that members of a family should look after each other's welfare, some felt differently. Among these was Anselm Schuster, a Jew who had converted to Christianity and minister of the Bible

Christian Church. "Concerned with the plight of dockworkers, coal heavers and immigrants to the town's Foster Ward, he resigned from his ministerial post to devote more time" to the temporal needs of these people. He wrote articles describing the "horrible conditions of the jail where the poor and insane were placed in cells together with hardened criminals."[2]

Fortunately, Anselm Schuster was not alone. Accompanied by his wife, he collected food and clothing for needy families. Others concerned about the plight of the poor included Mrs. J.J.B. Flint, Reverend Farrelly of St. Michael's, and Reverend M.W. MacLean of St. Andrew's. They were soon joined by Mrs. Harriette Lyon Jaques, the wife of Doctor J.R. Jaques, recently appointed principal of Albert College. Mrs. Jaques began to attend council meetings and soon came to the conclusion that councillors wasted too much time arguing about where to build the hospital and how to finance its construction. Accordingly, during the summer of 1879, she approached some of the leading women from various churches and suggested organizing a society to spearhead the establishment of a hospital and house of refuge. On November 18, 1879, a meeting, to which only women were invited, was held for that purpose, and the Women's Christian Association (WCA) came into existence. Mrs. Jaques became president, and directors included women from each of the city's thirteen churches.

Just three weeks after the formation of the WCA, the group approached three prominent businessmen and asked them to form a delegation to go to city council and propose the establishment of a home for the poor. Council agreed to give some financial support, and Mrs. Jaques and her associates set out in January's cold and snow to canvass for furniture, clothes, and other items necessary for the opening of the house for the poor. However, the exertion proved too much for Mrs. Jaques, and, despite her intense wish to continue canvassing, her doctor ordered her to bed in March. She died on April 24. Her funeral, held in the chapel of Albert College, saw a tremendous outpouring of grief.

While Mrs. Jaques was confined to bed, the WCA opened a "Home for the Friendless" in an unpretentious frame house on Coleman Street, near the junction of Water Street. The work that Mrs. Jaques had so successfully begun was carried on by other women, including Mrs. Jane C. Jones, wife of well-known and respected merchant Nathan Jones. During Mrs. Jones' term as president (1880–85), the members of the WCA improved the house of refuge and sought an official charter from the provincial government. Registered on June 2, 1880, the charter empowered the WCA to establish and maintain "a House for destitute orphans, aged, and friendless persons, and also a Hospital for the care of those injured by accident, or who are sick."[3]

Despite the reluctance of some members of Belleville council to financially support the project, such aid came from the province, the county, and many community members canvassed by the WCA. Fundraising ranged from children making and selling candy door-to-door, to people pledging one cent a day. After five years of fundraising, Mrs. Nathan Jones officiated at the laying of the cornerstone for the new structure to serve as "a hospital for the suffering and a home for the friendless" on September 25, 1884. Almost two years later, the formal opening took place. Initially, the hospital contained only ten beds, compared to 432 in 1986; 206 in 2008, following a provincially ordered reduction in beds; and approximately 283 after a major expansion is completed.

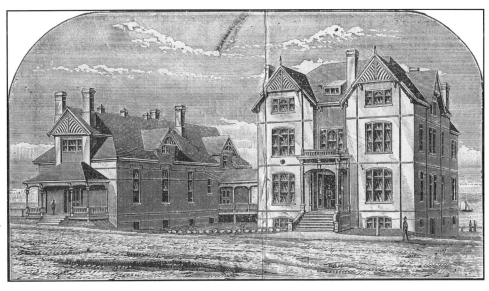

The new hospital (right) and the Home for the Friendless as shown in the Daily Intelligencer *of July 2, 1891.* Courtesy of Hastings County Historical Society, Newspaper Collection.

The hospital would not have been possible without the initiative and support of the Women's Christian Association. In fact, it was said to be the only hospital built, owned, and operated by laywomen in Canada. Accordingly, for many years after the city assumed ownership of the hospital in 1948, two members of the Association were called upon to sit on the hospital's board of governors.[4] Also, in keeping with its concern for the aged, the WCA operated a home for elderly women on Highland Avenue from 1956 to 1996. Today, the WCA continues to follow its original mandate by providing funds for local agencies, as well as the hospital.[5] Certainly, the community is greatly indebted to the Women's Christian Association for its leadership in the health field for more than a century.

Mary Merrill: Dead or Alive?

MATHEMATICIAN MARY MERRILL was, and still is, at the centre of a medical mystery. Her death, on April 7, 1880, puzzled local medical doctors, who, for two days, debated whether she was actually dead or in some inexplicable state of suspended animation. The Belleville *Intelligencer* reported "a very wide divergence of opinion amongst the medical men."[6] Some doctors kept ministering to her until, finally, decomposition set in, and she was declared dead. Even then, several doctors (including specialists) could not agree on the time or date of her final passing.

Mary Merrill's case became the subject of "a thinly disguised biography" by her younger sister, Flora MacDonald Denison, the mother of noted Canadian writer Merrill Denison.[7] In this biography, Mary Merrill became Mary Melville, Belleville became Bellview, and Alexandra College (the ladies' college within Albert College) became Prince of Wales University. In the 1970s, Merrill Denison assisted Doctor Cyril Greenland of the Clarke Institute of Psychiatry in Toronto in further researching the case. What Greenland discovered was somewhat inconclusive. He determined that Mary Edwards Merrill was an excellent mathematician, but not necessarily the "Mathematical Prodigy" who was described in the biography as representing Canada at a meeting of the Mathematical Societies of Europe and America at Philadelphia in September 1876. At that meeting, she was said to have been selected vice-president, an honour never before conferred upon a lady, especially one so young — only eighteen years of age."[8]

The psychic story of Mary Melville was encouraged by her contemporary at Albert College, the Reverend Benjamin Fish Austin of Brighton, whose publishing house printed the alleged biography in 1900, and who contributed a preface with this comment: "Mary Melville's life was prophetic of the New Era of Psychic Unfoldment [*sic*] upon which the human race is now entering."[9] Interestingly enough, the preceding year, Austin had been expelled by the General Conference of the Methodist Church for heresy, for subscribing to the beliefs and practices of spiritualism.[10] Like Susanna Moodie and Kate Fox earlier, some local people continued to believe in the use of spiritualism and psychic powers to create an earthly paradise.

A Wilde Event

FEW VISITORS TO Belleville have attracted as much public attention and created as much excitement as the Irish author and lecturer Oscar Wilde (1854–1900), who made a public appearance on May 23, 1882. Wilde was famous for his wit. For example, when he landed in New York City at the beginning of a year-long North American tour, he allegedly told the customs official, "I have nothing to declare except my genius." Wilde was also noted for his eccentricity in dress, taste, and manners, and was the centre of a group glorifying beauty for the sake of beauty itself. In 1881, Gilbert and Sullivan satirized him in their opera *Patience* as Reginald Bunthorne, a maudlin and fluttery poet who walked "down Piccadilly with a poppy or a lily in his medieval hand." Richard D'Oyly Carte, the producer of *Patience*, arranged to bring the opera to North America in September 1881, then offered Wilde a lecture tour to promote the opera and speak about subjects of his own choosing.

A week after speaking in Ottawa, where he apparently met Prime Minister John A.

Macdonald, Wilde arrived in Belleville for a brief visit. Actually, it was shorter than intended because the architecture of Kingston (including Fort Henry and St. George's Cathedral) had captivated him and he lingered there. Instead of catching the morning express on May 23, he delayed his departure until the afternoon train.

Wilde did not travel alone. He was always accompanied by Mr. Davenport, a black valet who handled all the baggage (a trunk, two suitcases, and several hatboxes), and usually by a manager as well. Like a Hollywood star, Wilde travelled first-class and his entourage, cloak, and general appearance must have attracted his fellow passengers' attention. No doubt, as was his custom, he spoke freely to them as he smoked cigars and cigarettes during the trip.

He arrived at Belleville at 7:00 p.m., only an hour before the lecture. However, before proceeding to the lecture hall, he "would not move a peg until he had regaled and strengthened himself with viands much more substantial than dewdrops and the petals of roses and lilies." Accordingly, he arrived an hour late to the auditorium on the second floor of City Hall where he found the room half-filled by an audience of about 230, mostly women. They had been remarkably patient, but were becoming somewhat anxious.

Wilde's topic was the "Practical Application of the Aesthetic Theory to exterior and interior House Decoration and to Dress and Personal Ornaments" — or "The Decorative Arts," for short. In fact, Wilde might be described as a nineteenth-century Martha Stewart or Debbie Travis.

The audience seemed appreciative and sympathetic. His message, however, was less significant than his appearance, which caused the hearts of many women to flutter. On stage he wore tight-fitting patent-leather shoes ornamented by large silver buckles, black silk hose, black silk knee ties, and a "court dress of wine-coloured velvet." The *Intelligencer* reported that "a perfect cascade of rich lace enveloped his neck and rested on his breast, and his hands were partially hidden by lace ruffles." Arriving on stage, he would throw off his cloak and reveal his stage costume to the audience.

As was his custom, Wilde ended his lecture abruptly and left the stage. Many women approached him, hoping to speak with him or, as one reporter put it, "touch the hem of his garment" and gaze into his poetic eyes. However, Wilde did not stay. He hastened the two blocks to the Dafoe House (the site of the later Quinte Hotel and Clarion Inn and Suites), where he sat down for dinner, his second major meal in less than three hours. Meanwhile, the treasurer of the Belleville Mechanics' Institute, sponsor of both the lecture and the city's small library, was no doubt working on the accounts; the net profit would be $16.

Wilde might enchant and impress some people, but he did not capture the fancy of the *Ontario* reporter who wrote, "Oscar is aestheticizing the people of Canada at 50 cents a head … Oscar Wilde is said to live on glistening dew drops and sunflowers … seed merchants say here that there never before was such a demand for sunflower seeds. It must be the result of Oscar Wilde's visit to this country." Moreover, although agreeing that his appearance certainly created a stir, the *Ontario* went on to say that much of what he said was "stale and stupid." Other critics might agree. Many found his delivery boring, especially from such a youthful and fun-loving young man only twenty-eight years of age.

The famous lecturer had little time to see Belleville. He left early the next morning for Toronto and spent most of his time in the breakfast car eating and speaking with John Hague, a financial journalist who described Wilde as "a gentleman to the core" and a great social reformer.[11]

It would be interesting to know if Wilde stressed the threat of pollution in his Belleville talk, as he had done elsewhere. For example, a week earlier in Ottawa, he had attacked the sawdust pollution of the Ottawa River, which was killing fish and befouling the water and the river's banks. He said, "This is an outrage; no one has a right to pollute the air and water, which are the common inheritance of all; we should leave them to our children as we have received them."[12] Certainly, the lumber mills at the mouth of the Moira River were still very active in 1882, but Wilde would not have had time to see them because of the short duration of his stay in Belleville.

The Teacher, the Novelist, and Iceboating

ICEBOATING WAS A popular recreation in the late nineteenth century. The Bay of Quinte provided ideal conditions — sheltered waters and no strong currents. Unfortunately, iceboating could also be a tragic activity, as evidenced by the tombstone of deaf educator Samuel Greene, who lies buried in the Belleville Cemetery. The stone indicates that he died (age 46) on February 17, 1890 from injuries suffered in an iceboat accident on the bay. His unusual marble grave marker, with his name "fingerspelled" on the base, was "erected by his mute and hearing friends." When the base recently became worn, private funds paid for its replacement. Just who was Samuel Greene and why is he remembered?

Samuel Thomas Greene was "the first hearing-impaired teacher of hearing-impaired pupils to be employed at a recognized educational institution in Ontario — the Provincial Institution for Education and Instruction of the Deaf and Dumb in Belleville (now the Sir James Whitney School for the Deaf)."[13] Born, apparently without hearing, in Portland, Maine, in 1845, he attended the American Asylum for the Education and Instruction of the Deaf and Dumb in Hartford, Connecticut, where he learned sign language and determined to dedicate his life to the teaching of hearing-impaired children.

In 1870, Greene received a Bachelor of Arts degree from the National Deaf-Mute College (now Gallaudet University) in Washington, D.C. Greene's degree was personally presented to him by Ulysses S. Grant (Civil War hero, American president, and patron of the college). After graduation, Greene moved to Belleville to become the only hearing-impaired instructor of the three original teachers. Greene was present when John Sandfield Macdonald, Ontario's first premier, and William Pearce Howland, the lieutenant-governor, officiated at the school's opening on October 20, 1870. Belleville Mayor Alexander Robertson had declared the day a public holiday. Throngs of Belleville residents and out-of-town visitors, accompanied by a militia band, formed a procession from the railway station to the school. Others arrived by steamer. The *Prince Edward* sailed between the town "and the dock at the Asylum" every hour that day for a round-trip fare of 25¢.[14] Although only a handful of students were present on opening day, the number increased to seventy by the end of the first year, and by 1875, attendance would increase to beyond the original capacity of approximately 225.

For the next twenty years, Greene usually taught a class of beginning students, recognizing the need for students to have a good foundation. This led him to write *The Proper Method of Teaching New Pupils,* "an amazingly precise and graphic account of his teaching methods."[15] His inspired teaching earned high marks from provincial inspectors.

Outside the classroom, he proved to be an excellent informal counsellor and confidant to hundreds of hearing-impaired students. On the provincial level, he presided over the initial convention of the Ontario Deaf-Mute Association in 1886. He chaired the association's second convention at Belleville in 1888, where he entertained the delegates with a spirited sign-language rendition of Tennyson's "Charge of the Light Brigade." Shortly after being re-elected unanimously to a further two-year term as president, Greene had a tragic accident. Greene had always been interested in sports. Starting with baseball, he had turned his attention to sailing and iceboating. At Belleville, he built and sailed boats and was a founding officer of the Bay of Quinte Yacht Club in 1876. With his students, he also built and operated iceboats. Unfortunately, while returning from Trenton with two friends on February 3, 1890, he was thrown from a boat while attempting to adjust the rigging. He was able to walk home, but that evening lapsed into unconsciousness. He died two weeks later, without regaining consciousness. Ironically, the iceboat was one of several that he

Samuel Greene, celebrated teacher of the deaf, after whom Greene Street on the West Hill was named. Courtesy of Hastings County Historical Society, HC-4562.

and his students had constructed. Greene's funeral was held at the school, whose students, graduates, and staff mourned the loss of a man who had done so much to "promote the well-being of the children of silence."[16]

In the Belleville Cemetery, he is interred near the burial site of Susanna Moodie and the tomb of Sir Gilbert Parker (1862–1932), a novelist closely associated with Belleville and the Quinte area. Not only did Parker enjoy "international fame as a novelist who romanticized Quebec and the Canadian Northwest and as a public figure who spoke for Canada and the British Empire," but he romanticized iceboating on the Bay of Quinte.[17] Parker recalled travelling twelve miles in eleven minutes on the bay about 1880:

> The journey was made on a day of days. The land white with snow, the trees along the shore glittering with frost, the air stirring strongly, the sun as hot as summer and as bright as a diamond, the whole world open to the eye, washed, starched and laundered to a perfect cleanness, and the long stretch of bay a noble race-course, where the sails of the iceboat spread like the wings of arctic birds. No complicated machinery to work…. It is a simple and primitive contest, where dangers clutch at you every second, and you drive down the wind with strained, enthralled eye and flaming cheek, striving for the first place home. That is sport and it is speed; it is flying on the wings of the wind.[18]

Iceboating set world records for speed in the late-nineteenth century, and was very popular locally. Even as late as the 1920s, as many as twenty-four iceboats were said to have been present at a hockey game played on the bay near the Belleville Cemetery. The sport declined in popularity, however, and when Belleville resident teacher Dick Bird became interested in the sport in the 1950s there were no iceboats in the area. Bird helped to revive the iceboating, but, like Samuel Greene and many other iceboaters, he fell victim to a pressure ridge. He spent a week of the 1966 Christmas vacation in hospital recovering from cracked ribs and numerous other injuries. Unfortunately, changing climate conditions have reduced the number of opportunities for iceboating. Where the bay ice would be thirty inches thick in the 1950s, it is only twelve inches thick today. Moreover, heavy snow in the winter of 2007–08 made iceboating impossible for the half-dozen surviving Belleville iceboaters.[19] Perhaps memories and stories of great years of iceboating will be all that remain of the sport in the future.

The "Least Objectionable" Mr. Bowell

ONE OF BELLEVILLE'S main claims to fame is that Mackenzie Bowell, Canada's fifth prime minister (1894–96), was closely associated with the community for all of his adult life. Not only was he editor and owner of the *Intelligencer* for many years, but he chaired the local school board, helped found the board of trade, was president or director of several companies, and saw active military service during the 1860s. Moreover, he was a leading member of the Orange Order, serving as grand master of the lodge in British North America from 1870–78. Politically, he represented Hastings North in the House of Commons for twenty-five years before being appointed to the Senate in 1892.

Unfortunately, some historians and journalists have downplayed his importance as prime minister, or even ridiculed him. For example, a *Maclean's* magazine survey in the late 1990s rated Bowell near the bottom of the prime ministers, and an ongoing Internet survey by *rateitall.com* in June 2008 placed him nineteenth out of twenty-two, slightly ahead of Arthur Meighen, Stephen Harper, and Paul Martin. Such ratings tend to ignore the fact that Bowell held office longer than four prime ministers (Charles Tupper, Joe Clark, John Turner, and Kim Campbell), and conscientiously tried to resolve the controversial Manitoba Schools Question, even if it meant angering some of his friends and supporters in the Orange Order. Furthermore, Bowell was never an extremist, and was independent enough to vote against the Conservative Party when he felt justified.

The late Belleville historian Betsy Dewar Boyce attempted to remedy this Bowell slighting a few years ago when she meticulously examined resource materials in Belleville and elsewhere and wrote the first and only complete account of his life and career. Unable to find a publisher — a Bowell book was not seen as a potential best-seller — she arranged for its publication on CD-ROM by the Seventh Town Historical Society in 2001.[20]

Her book, *The Accidental Prime Minister,* took its name from the fact that Bowell became prime minister almost by accident — the result of an unusual chain of events. The death of legendary Sir John A. Macdonald in 1891 was followed by the resignation of Sir John Abbott (1892) and the sudden death from a heart attack at Windsor Castle of Sir John Thompson (1894), Macdonald's early successors. Faced with the prospect of leadership disputes among the remaining cabinet ministers, Governor General

Mackenzie Bowell in uniform as a leading member of the Orange Lodge, circa 1870. Courtesy of Hastings County Historical Society, HC-1482

Ribbon distributed to citizens of Hastings County to honour Sir Mackenzie Bowell, following his appointment as prime minister. Courtesy of Hastings County Historical Society, HC-785-1.

Belleville's
WELCOME
To her distinguished Son.

MARCH 12TH, 1895.

Hon. Sir Mackenzie Bowell, K.C.M.G.

From Belleville Schools
—TO—
PREMIERSHIP OF CANADA.

Aberdeen turned to Mackenzie Bowell as the minister most likely to be trusted and least likely to offend. After all, Bowell had served with distinction in several cabinet posts, largely because of his administrative talents. He had proven to be "conscientious, hard-working, and scrupulous."[21] Moreover, although he had been sitting in the Senate since 1892, he had been appointed "acting premier in Sir John's absence."

In her diary, Lady Aberdeen, wife of the governor general, described Bowell as "rather fussy, and decidedly commonplace," but she also believed him to be "a good and straight man … [with] great ideas about the drawing together of the colonies and the Empire…."[22] In fact, Bowell had visited Australia the previous year to explore the possibilities of increasing Canadian trade, and a full-scale conference had been arranged for Canada. On this trip, Bowell also apparently stopped in Hawaii, where he met with President Dole and addressed the Honolulu Chamber of Commerce. At least one Canadian newspaper felt that he was hoping the Canadian government might annex or establish a protectorate over Hawaii, if the United States did not do so first.[23]

Bowell's term as prime minister was doomed from the start. Lady Aberdeen wrote of his inability to write letters, his failure to make up his mind on certain questions, and his sense of importance: "He is altogether in the seventh heaven at being premier and fancies that he can emulate Sir John A. Macdonald's genius in managing his party."[24] Fellow cabinet members worked behind his back and, in January 1896, about half of his cabinet walked out. In vain, Bowell struggled against this "Nest of Traitors." On April 27, 1896, he resigned, and Sir Charles Tupper, considered a better vote-getter, took over, only to lose the 1896 election to the Liberals under Wilfrid Laurier.

Subsequently, Bowell was chosen leader of the Opposition in the Senate, but played only a minor role in politics. Ten years later, he retired to private life at Belleville, where he died on December 10, 1917, a few days before his ninety-fourth birthday. There was no state funeral for the deceased prime minister. Canada was too busy fighting a war in Europe.

Had Bowell taken office in the prime of his life, rather than in his early seventies, he might have become one of Canada's outstanding political leaders. Honest and conciliatory, he was a man of steadfast character, courage, and integrity. He "recognized his own shortcomings as a national leader and did his utmost to put honour and the country's welfare above his personal, religious and racial sympathies."[25]

A Leisurely Life

THE CLOSING DECADES of the nineteenth century had a grand and leisurely side to them. Some of Belleville's largest and finest homes were being built, such as Glanmore, erected in 1882–83 for wealthy banker John Curran Phillips and his wife Harriet Douglas Phillips.[26] Designed by Belleville architect Thomas Hanley, the house was built by Francis McKay. Its outstanding Second Empire architecture, with mansard roof, elaborate cornices, dormer windows, and multi-coloured slate, led to its designation in 1969 as a National Historic Site of Canada. The home to four generations of the Phillips family, the house was sold in 1971 to the City of Belleville and the County of Hastings by Philippa Faulkner, the last resident family member. Glanmore served for several years as the Hastings County Museum and was operated by the Hastings County Historical Society. Today, it is operated as a restored dwelling by the Recreation and Community Services Department of the City of Belleville. Much restorative work has been done, both inside and outside.

This was also a time for grand public projects. In 1833, for example, an attractive post office was built on the southwest corner of Bridge and Pinnacle streets. Privately constructed by a Watertown (New York) company in 1886–87, the Belleville Waterworks was purchased by the City of Belleville in 1889. Two years later, the city was a major shareholder in building a bridge between Prince Edward County and Belleville.

City lawyer and councillor William N. Ponton played an important role in Belleville's industrial development. As chairman of the city's Industrial Committee, Ponton communicated with many companies in Canada and the United States in 1891, asking if they were interested in relocating to Belleville. Interest was expressed by companies in Boston, Detroit, Oswego, Toronto, and elsewhere. For one such company, the Steel Rolling Mills of Boston, the city was prepared to offer "special inducements" such as "a free site with a water frontage" near a railway. Also, the company would be exempt from city taxes for 10 years, would receive fire protection (if hydrants were not near the chosen site), and would earn a cash bonus of $500 in one year if at least 30 men were employed.[27]

In addition to the "special inducements," the city advertised such advantages as excellent rail transportation east, west, and north; nearby mineral resources; the new Bay Bridge; and the recently completed Murray Canal (linking the Bay of Quinte with Lake Ontario). Fine residential areas, new hotels, and "delightful summer resorts in the area" were also noted. Some advertisements stressed that "Labour is cheap, rents low and living economical."[28] Such advantages and inducements were successful in attracting a steel-rolling mill and other industries in this and subsequent years.

Culture was not ignored. Two opera houses were built during these years. The first, which contained an art gallery, was built on the site of the present Belleville Public Library and John M. Parrott Art Gallery. Its grandiose interior enthralled local audiences for several years before the building was destroyed by fire. It was followed by a second opera house, completed in December 1883 on the southwest corner of Bridge and Church streets.

Likewise, churches were being built or rebuilt. Destroyed by fire on January 6, 1886, Bridge Street Methodist Church was rebuilt and improved. The tower was heightened and given a fancy top. Stained glass windows were added, including round, fifteen-foot diameter gallery windows in the north and south walls — crafted by the world-famous McCausland firm of Toronto. The church reopened in May 1887. The following spring, the church was the scene of a celebrated Crossley & Hunter six-week evangelistic crusade, after which the Reverend John E. Hunter named his new daughter Ethel Belleville Hunter because of the event's success. Bridge Street received 365 new members, "the greatest one-year increase it had ever experienced in its history."[29] Other Methodist and Presbyterian churches also had many new members.

One of the largest conferences ever to take place in Belleville was held in mid-July 1897. The Epworth League of Christian Endeavour (renamed the Young Peoples Union of the United Church after 1925) attracted 20,000 young people from the United States and Canada to its energy-charged event. More than two-hundred speakers stressed the need for good literature.[30]

A new Roman Catholic church building for St. Michael the Archangel was constructed in 1887–88, not long after Bishop James Cleary concluded, after his first visits to Belleville, that the church building, which he described as "too small, insecure, and mean for this little city," had served its purpose.[31] The new church was dedicated on October 7, 1888.

Meanwhile, some Belleville homes attracted attention for unusual reasons. John J.B. Flint, adopted son of lumber baron Billa Flint, mayor of Belleville in 1872, and police magistrate, resided at 215 Charles Street. The large, attractive building had been built circa 1870 and was known as Randolph Place. Writing in a family newspaper in January 1893, Flint related some unusual experiences:

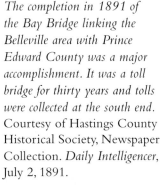

The completion in 1891 of the Bay Bridge linking the Belleville area with Prince Edward County was a major accomplishment. It was a toll bridge for thirty years and tolls were collected at the south end. Courtesy of Hastings County Historical Society, Newspaper Collection. *Daily Intelligencer,* July 2, 1891.

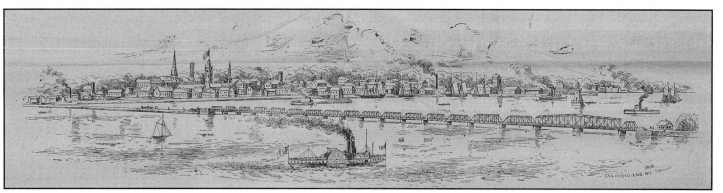

A few weeks ago, I was sitting at the organ, in our drawing room, when some impulse caused me to turn my head quickly to the left, there was a large chair between me and the folding doors, and by the side of this chair, stood the figure of a man, facing the door leading into the hall. It wore a black frock coat, turn down collar, black hair, strongly marked features and black side whiskers — I took in every detail. It remained only sufficiently long, so as to indelibly stamp it on my mind.[32]

Flint went on to describe a similar event a few weeks later, when a black substance "like a lady's dress" disappeared through the hall door. He concluded: "I can give no explanation of what I have seen and although not a believer in ghosts know I am not mistaken."

In the same newspaper, he wrote about 226 Charles, the residence of Mrs. Phillips. Going into her kitchen late one evening, "she saw standing before her, a young girl, in white, with what seemed a halo of light radiating from her entire person, — the dress seemed to be of some light material — the collar of white lace — the face very pale — eyes and hair dark — The figure remained motionless for about a minute and then disappeared…. Mrs. Phillips is a person of strong nerves, cool and not excitable."[33]

On the sporting field, cricket was among the favourite team sports of the 1880s. One of the most unusual games was between the married and single men on July 5, 1882. The game was not finished on that day because of rain, nor was it finished the next day "as very few of the bachelors appeared on the scene of action. No doubt they were otherwise engaged."[34] Unfortunately, the halcyon days of cricket came to an abrupt end in 1899 when the cricket fields on the bay shore were sold as a site for the steel-rolling mills.

Meanwhile, Belleville was "bicycle crazy." The Ramblers Bicycle Park at the corner of Queen and William streets was the site of bicycle races, musical concerts, and other entertainments. Other popular sporting activities included lawn bowling (commencing in 1886), hockey (the first hockey

Front Street looking south, circa 1880, showing a horse-drawn street-railway car of the Bay City Company, with the City Hall in the distance. Courtesy of Estate of Joseph Post of Belleville.

match was played on February 5, 1892, with Belleville losing 8–0 to Trenton), and canoeing (legendary Ned Hanlan of Toronto appeared in 1896).

Public celebrations were important. Dominion Day was celebrated annually with various activities. The 1887 and 1897 celebrations of Queen Victoria's fiftieth and sixtieth years as Queen of Canada and the British Empire were special occasions. Among other actions, city council changed the name of Hotel Street to Victoria Avenue, the school board gave the queen's name to the part of the Belleville High School building that housed elementary students, and the former island at the mouth of the Moira River, which had housed a major lumber mill, became known as Queen Victoria Park.

Preserving Our Heritage

FOR ALMOST 150 years, there have been attempts to form a local historical society in Belleville. Before Confederation was achieved in 1867, Doctor William Canniff interviewed residents to discover what the pioneer days were like. He published some of his findings in his highly respected histories of Upper Canada and its medical profession.[35] On February 19, 1884, Chief Justice Shelden, a distinguished member of the Buffalo Historical Society, visited Belleville, explained what a historical society was, and outlined its benefits, including the establishment of a museum in which relics of the community's past could be preserved and displayed. Citizens who met with the judge in J. Lyons Biggar's hospitable home included lawyers J.J.B Flint and William N. Ponton. Their efforts did not immediately bear fruit.

However, Ponton and others tried again a few years later, this time with more success. On February 11, 1899, with Mrs. William Ponton as president, the Belleville and Bay of Quinte Historical Society approved a motion to affiliate with the newly organized Ontario Historical Society. Thanks to Ponton's influence (he was now a lieutenant colonel in the militia), the society was allowed to hold regular Saturday afternoon meetings from 4:00 p.m. to 4:30 p.m. in the drill hall on Church Street. Among the speakers at these unusually brief weekly meetings was Arthur McGinnis, who told of early local churches. Other members brought interesting historical pictures and documents to share, and Colonel Ponton kept some of these items for public displays. Again, this group soon ceased to meet.

Sometime before 1910, a number of citizens set up the Belleville Historical Society. Under the leadership of Corresponding Secretary Arthur McGinnis, it compiled a handsome souvenir booklet with almost one-hundred pictures of Belleville, both past and present. The publisher was C.B. Scantlebury, stationer and interior designer. In the introduction, McGinnis described the city in glowing terms: "Belleville is an ideal residential town.... It occupies one of the finest sites in the Province. It has handsome residences and beautiful lawns. Its streets are well made and lined with rows of Maple and other shade trees, and in summer, when dressed in all its variegated foliage, it is without doubt the most charming spot in Canada."

He went on to praise the Bay of Quinte as "one of the most beautiful and picturesque sheets of water on the Continent … whose shores are replete with historic incident." Moreover, the angler would find "excellent sport" with black bass and "Maskinonge, the latter of which … have been known to [reach] the weight of fifty-one pounds." In addition, featured pictures included views of such recent achievements as the 1891 Bay of Quinte Bridge linking the counties of Hastings and Prince Edward (the 1,869-foot-long iron superstructure described as "the longest bridge in Ontario"), the Belleville Rolling Mills and the Belleville Portland Cement Company's works at Point Anne. No wonder that the booklet was entitled *The Beautiful City of the Bay*, and that McGinnis was active with the board of trade (Belleville Chamber of Commerce) in promoting the city. Nevertheless, the historical society failed to survive.

Twenty years later, on the eve of the Great Depression, there was yet another effort to start a historical society. Energetic Belleville lawyer and former mayor (1924) W.C. Mikel set up the Meyers' Creek Historical Society. Unfortunately, there is no evidence that the group included more

Top:
Dr. William Canniff's career as described in the government of Canada 1952 plaque at the Hastings Heritage Centre in Cannifton. Photo by author, 2006.

Bottom:
Noted nineteenth-century historian Dr. William Canniff, who helped popularize the United Empire Loyalist movement. Courtesy of Archives of Ontario, S-409.

Glanmore National Historic Site, a treasure of the heritage movement, as seen in 2007. Today it houses several important collections of furniture, lamps, and paintings. Photo by author.

than Mikel and a handful of others. None of these early attempts to form a historical society was successful.

The formation of a long-lasting society would only occur on October 1, 1957, when a meeting was held in the council chambers of City Hall. Chaired by Irene Haig (known to her radio listeners and *Intelligencer* readers as Harriet Stevens), the meeting was a final attempt to organize a society. Antique dealer Tom Wrightmeyer agreed to assume the presidency for the first year and the executive included Ken Bird, Veva Robson, Tom Ransom, and Gerry Boyce. From these difficult beginnings, the society has gone on to establish two county museums (one in the former registry office and one in Glanmore) and the Hastings Heritage Centre in Cannifton.

Farewell, Victoria

THE DEATH OF Queen Victoria on January 22, 1901 — less than a month after the close of the nineteenth century — was a major event in world and local history.[36] Most Belleville residents could not remember the day when Victoria was not on the imperial throne. After all, coming to the throne in 1837, in her nineteenth year, she had ruled during the Rebellion of 1837, the selection of Ottawa as the capital of Canada, Confederation, the granting of city status to Belleville, the Northwest uprisings, and Mackenzie Bowell's term as prime minister. During her lifetime, many local homes displayed pictures of Victoria, sometimes with her husband and several of their nine children.

Evidence of her reign could be seen in the school, the park, and the streets, all named in her honour. Moreover, Hastings County had been known as the Victoria District for almost ten years. No wonder that churches such as St. Andrew's Presbyterian held special services to celebrate her life.

Her royal consort, Prince Albert, who had predeceased her by forty years, was also remembered in the name of the college and several streets. In 1874, the *Bird's Eye View of Belleville* showed Victoria and Albert streets running north off West Moira: Albert is now Boswell and Victoria has disappeared under the fire hall. On the East Hill, Albert was the north part of the present Albert (then known as Centre Street), and Victoria was at the east end of the recent housing development known as Victoria Square; Though deceased for more than a hundred years, Victoria's name lives on in many ways.

Victoria, Queen of Great Britain and the British Empire, including Canada, 1837–1901. Courtesy of Hastings County Historical Society, HC-1988.

8
DAWN OF A NEW CENTURY

The Century Begins

THE EARLY YEARS of the twentieth century saw Belleville resume its growth. Although the 1891 and 1901 federal census returns had recorded a decline in population of almost 800 (from 9,916 to 9,117), Belleville had replaced almost all of the loss by 1911. The city's name and fame was carried abroad by the Kilties Band. Hailed as "the greatest Scottish Band in the World" and "the Pride of Canada," the band visited more than twenty different countries and twice played before Edward VII, who, as Prince of Wales, had visited the Belleville harbour in 1860. When marching, the band was headed by its seven-foot-tall drum major, Donald MacCormack.

Belleville was also interested in attracting visitors, including former residents. The summer of 1905 saw the first of a series of highly successful old boys' reunions. Thousands of former residents joined local citizens for four days in August to celebrate their mother city. Belleville's leading citizen, Sir Mackenzie Bowell, served as honorary president. So successful had the 1905 reunion proved that it was repeated on regular five-year intervals until 1930, with the exception of the war year 1915. Events ranged from athletic contests to concerts.

Life in Belleville was undergoing major changes. Certainly, the introduction of the automobile was one of the most important. According to historian W.C. Mikel, Adolphus Burgoyne of Pinnacle Street was the first man in Belleville to own a car — a 1904 wine-coloured Packard. It also served as the community's first motorized taxi, since Burgoyne had been operating horse-drawn taxis. To quote Mikel's description of the car's arrival:

Grouped around a strange looking contraption that resembled an oversized buggy, all dressed up with big brass headlamps and other shining accessories, in the freight shed yards of the old Grand Trunk Railway on that spring morning in 1904, stood a knot of curious citizens. Small boys pushed through the crowd to better observe the strange thing, and were repeatedly ordered away by the two men who were busy unwrapping the last few yards of cheese cloth and paper that had covered the machine on its journey from New York to Belleville…. Housewives opened doors and stood goggle-eyed at their passing. Small boys lined the walks and

In 1911, William James Topley's camera recorded (left to right) City Hall, the post office, businesses on Bridge Street, and the newly rebuilt southern entranceway to the Quinte Hotel, with its barbershop pole and manicured lawn. Courtesy of William James Topley/Library and Archives Canada, PA-9972.

proceeded with measured pace alongside them, keeping up easily with the speed. Down Pinnacle Street they proceeded without incident, other than scaring the wits out of a number of weaker hearted citizens, and the daylights out of a placid horse that had never before been known to shy even at a thunderstorm.[1]

Strict provincial laws governed early car operators. In 1903, speed limits were set at ten miles per hour in cities and towns and fifteen miles per hour on the open highway. The operator had to sound an alarm bell at every intersection. Two years later, the law was changed so that motorists had to keep to seven miles per hour when near horses.

City council recognized the importance of its road system. In May 1913, council approved concrete paving for Front Street, marking a major step in road improvement. Off-street racing for motorcycles came the same month, with the first race held at the driving park (at the southeast corner of Sidney and Bridge streets) to celebrate the birthday of King George V. Belleville "rider extraordinaire" George Pepper would later become famous for his racing exploits. On Labour Day 1936, the twenty-four-year-old Pepper outdistanced the top thirty-five riders in North America in a two-hundred-mile race through the streets of Belleville.[2]

Meanwhile, there were changes in one of the community's oldest institutions — the post office. First opened in 1816, residents had grown accustomed to visiting the post office to pick up their mail and chat with the postal clerk and their neighbours. For many years, the local newspaper printed lists of people for whom mail was waiting in the post office. Finally, after almost a century of postal service, home delivery began in 1913. It was a "red letter" day for residents. For many years afterward, there were two deliveries each weekday and a single one on Saturdays.

Postal authorities prided themselves on excellent service. It was possible to take mail to the Belleville railway station, where it would be sorted aboard a mail car. Or the sender could take packages to the station and the station's baggage staff would sort them quickly and put them aboard the train. The late Eugene Lang remembered when an individual living a few miles east of Belleville, at Shannonville, could come to market on Saturday morning and order a roast from a Front Street butcher shop. The butcher would deliver the roast to the

Post office officials and city dignitaries gathered on the steps of the post office as the letter carriers began their first deliveries on May 24, 1913. Courtesy of Hastings County Historical Society, Mika Collection.

station, and it would arrive in Shannonville in time to be cooked and on the table for dinner when the individual arrived home from Belleville.

Concern for the welfare of children led to the formation of the Children's Aid Society in 1907. Through the generosity of Thomas Ritchie, a children's shelter was erected on land adjoining the Belleville hospital.

On the recreational front, "a well attended meeting of lovers of aquatic sports" took place in June 1907 and launched the Belleville Yacht Club under Commodore Thomas Ritchie. The same month, the Southern Theatre Company announced that it would be bringing moving pictures to Belleville. For a five-cent admission fee, residents could view "a series of moving pictures and illustrated songs" guaranteed to please old and young. The pictures would be changed twice a week in "a moving picture place" on Bridge Street, not far from Front.[3]

In 1911, the YMCA was constructed on Campbell Street, and city police moved into new quarters in the former market building at the east end of the Market Square. The constables were said to have "commodious rooms" and there was a "spacious cell block available."[4]

The city could be said to have come of age on April 4, 1914, when the Belleville Club was incorporated. Every major city was expected to have its exclusive club, intended for members of its business, professional, and political elite. The club continues to be a prominent city feature, and is still located on the upper floors of the club building at the northwest corner of Bridge and Pinnacle streets.

Blow Belleville's Bugle

BELLEVILLE HAS BEEN called many things. Among others, it has been known as the Gateway to the Golden North (after the gold rush of the 1860s), the Friendly City, the Sports Fishing Capital of Ontario (or even Canada), the Ball Hockey Capital of Ontario, and the Volunteer Capital of Canada. Currently, the chamber of commerce calls it "Belleville on the Bay of Quinte." Almost a century ago, on May 10, 1914, the *Intelligencer* sponsored a contest to find a suitable (and preferably polite and imaginative) slogan to boost Belleville. Readers submitted a number of entries, which the paper found to be first-class. These included "East or West, Belleville's Best" and "Ho! For Belleville and Prosperity!" One of the longest entries, and certainly one that would soon become dated, was "Belleville has Launched Her Boat on the Sea of Prosperity — Come Along With the Coal, Boys." One of the favourites was "Blow Belleville's Bugle." However, on May 14, the judges gave the prize to "A Bigger and Better Belleville."

Right:

Although the Portland Cement Company at Point Anne was just outside Belleville until Thurlow Township joined Belleville on January 1, 1998, local residents regarded the company as a Belleville company, in much the same way that they consider hockey legends Bobby and Dennis Hull, natives of Point Anne, to be Bellevillians. Photo circa 1920. Courtesy of Archives of Ontario, 10004151.

Below:

Rolling Mills of the Steel Company of Canada, 1912, along the shore of the bay in the vicinity of the present Water Pollution Control Plant. Courtesy of William James Topley/Library and Archives Canada, PA-10476.

The question of a suitable slogan or motto surfaced again in the 1920s. Newspapers suggested "A Better and Brighter Belleville" and "Build Up Belleville."[5] Then, in 1923, the chamber of commerce launched an official search. Readers submitted 124 suggestions, and members of the chamber voted on them. The first-place prize of $10 went to Mrs. H.J. Parker of 141 Charles Street. The voters selected the top seven entries, which are listed below. Find out if you agree with their decision by trying to pick the first-place winner. The answer is in the Notes.[6]

1. "Share Belleville's Opportunities"
2. "The City of Opportunity"
3. "The Gateway to Central Ontario"
4. "Why Not Belleville?"
5. "The United Empire Loyalist City"
6. "Belleville Suits Me — It Will You"
7. "Belleville — Beautifully Situated, Beautifully Endowed"

Not long after this contest, there were frequent references to "Belleville the Beautiful."[7]

"Scandal in River City"

WHILE CONDUCTING RESEARCH for his excellent book *Dockside Democracy*, C.W. "Bill" Hunt uncovered an interesting scandal involving several Belleville city councillors and officials. The scandal first surfaced on December 27, 1910, when the *Daily Intelligencer* published a letter from local bank manager and Glanmore owner J.P.C. Phillips. He accused certain city officials (especially the mayor and treasurer) of having family members purchase city lots at low prices and then quickly resell them at prices two or three times higher. The eventual buyer was usually an agent for the Canadian Northern Railway (CNR), which was quietly assembling land in Foster Ward (at the south end of Belleville) for a right-of-way for its proposed rail line, as well as land for a station and homes for its employees.

What Phillips found particularly annoying was that he had hoped to buy these lots himself and then sell them to the railway for a handsome profit. However, City Treasurer David Price had stalled him. Accordingly, Phillips went public. In his letter, he wrote about Club 13, the property committee of city council, which included Mayor Lorne Marsh. He quoted a member of the club as saying that "he had made a barrel of money out of acquiring city lots for a song and by selling

them to the CNR." Phillips continued, "Personally, I have no wish to cast blame at any one, as guilt has not been proven against any city lot purchaser to my knowledge." Nevertheless, he stated that the mayor's mother-in-law and the city treasurer's son-in-law were among the purchasers.

Other letters describing variations on the same theme appeared in the newspaper. The authors were members of the recently formed Property Owners' Association, whose leading members included former MP Henry Corby. This group had hired an attorney to carry out a search at the

View of the Canadian Northern / Canadian Pacific Station on South Church Street, circa 1913. Today there is no CPR passenger service and the station has been demolished. Courtesy of William James Topley/Library and Archives Canada, PA-12539.

registry office. He found that some lots, purchased for as little as $15 each, had then been sold to the railway for $150. The association then called a public meeting to discuss the matter.

Among the participants who spoke against the mayor and treasurer were three prominent Conservatives: Sir Mackenzie Bowell (former prime minister, then eighty-seven years of age), J.W. Johnson (MLA for Hastings West) and Henry Corby (retired MP). Interestingly enough, both Mayor Marsh and Treasurer Price were Liberals. It was clear that Corby not only wanted to force an investigation into the trading of the city lots, but also to guarantee the election of Alderman H.W. Ackerman as mayor in the approaching election.

Mayor Marsh was absent from the public meeting. In answer to Corby's request that the mayor be present to explain his actions, Marsh stated that his presence in Montreal "is of more importance to the building up of Belleville's industries and to Belleville's mechanics than my presence in Belleville to refute any slander you may utter. I have not sinned...."[8]

The following day, the headlines in the *Daily Intelligencer* (a traditional supporter of the Conservative Party) read: MAYOR AND TREASURER ARE PUBLICLY BRANDED AS VIOLATORS OF THE PUBLIC TRUST REPOSED IN THEM — PEOPLE AROUSED AS RESULT OF EXPOSURE — PROBE DEMANDED.[9]

As C.W. "Bill" Hunt suggests, "By modern standards, Mayor Marsh and his Treasurer Price would be guilty of profiting from insider information."[10] The railway company was assembling land quietly, hoping to keep its plans private. Some city officials must have known of its plans and hoped to profit from this knowledge.

The January 1911 election saw Ackerman narrowly defeat Alderman George Thomas (who was supported by Marsh and "the alleged gang behind him") to become mayor. The new council set up a committee to investigate the sale of city lots, and council subsequently decided to appoint County Court Judge Deroche to investigate and make a report. The hearings lasted for several months, and heard numerous witnesses. Judge Deroche's decision was that "the city's bylaw which regulated such matters did not prohibit members of the city's property committee or any other of its officers from trading in city lots."[11] He did recommend that council consider passing a bylaw "prohibiting the Property Committee from selling city property to any relative without first having the sale approved by the Council itself."[12]

The lot scandal was not the only one that concerned the residents of Belleville, especially those in Foster Ward. In December 1913, another scandal surfaced. An investigative reporter for the *Daily Intelligencer* found that council had approved a personal tender from city engineer James G. Lindsay to build and repair three streets in Foster Ward. Not only had Lindsay used public works employees to do much of the work while they were on the city payroll, but he had also used city materials. After this discovery, Lindsay quickly returned to his homeland, England. The city launched a lawsuit to recover the money, but it was not successful.[13] Together, these two scandals may have led to the establishment of one of the city's most famous institutions; the Wharf Street Debating Club was formed about this time "as a protest against civic corruption and to defend the interests of the people in Foster Ward against the machinations of their alleged betters."[14]

Still later, in the 1950s, the troubles surrounding a famous Belleville hockey team, and players on the city payroll, would remind taxpayers of the "city engineer scandal."

"The Funniest Woman in the World"

KNOWN IN THE mid-twentieth century as "The Funniest Woman in the World," and the outstanding comedic actress of her time, Beatrice Gladys Lillie received some of her schooling in Belleville.[15] Born in the downtown Toronto neighbourhood of Parkdale on May 29, 1894, Beatrice (often simply referred to as Bea) studied voice and drama in her youth, and was part of a family trio that travelled Ontario. She was billed as a "character Costume vocalist and impersonator." On the eve of the First World War, when her mother took her older sister to Europe to finish her education, Beatrice stayed in Canada to complete her formal education in Belleville at St. Agnes' School. Incorporating the former home of lumber baron Billa Flint, on Bridge Street East, the school stood on five acres of land with beautiful gardens and various amenities, such as a swimming tank. According to the school prospectus, "Character-building is the end to which all energy is directed."[16]

Judging from her comments on St. Agnes' School, Beatrice did not take kindly to the school or its proceedings. She described the building as a "fifty-year-old brick monstrosity, originally built for a lumber baron by a contractor who must have copied it from a patternbook. There was a Tuscan watchtower over the front doorway, whose design was lifted intact from a sixteenth-century Venetian palace."[17] Apparently school life resembled the popular Madeleine stories, since the young ladies "took a walk every morning, sedately, two by two, alike as peas in a pod in our dark green blazers, straw hats and sensible brown oxfords."[18] The good girls walked at the head of the line, and the bad ones brought up the rear. Once, just once, Beatrice was put at the front as the leader. She led the procession into a Front Street bank, where a handsome young teller had caught her eye on previous excursions. Without a word, she then led the group out of the bank and back to the school for chapel service. The bank must have notified the school, since, immediately after service, the headmistress quizzed the students, individually, as to which one was responsible for the bank visit. Nobody snitched on Bea; however, she confessed, fearing that she'd be expelled if she was found to be lying.

Probably the other highlight of her brief stay at St. Agnes' school was the one occasion during the year when boys were admitted. Much to her delight, the "beautiful bank teller" attended, talked to her, and offered to fetch ice cream. When the party ended, "Beatrice Gladys was nowhere to be found." When located, she and the bank teller were up in the Tuscan watchtower where they had eaten ice cream and "talked a bit to each other, and it was just as innocent as that."[19] Subsequently, she summarized her school days as a flop. "It was all a waste of time.... None of it left any permanent trace."

Bea soon joined her mother and sister in England, and her entertainment career took off as the war began. Although she hated rehearsing and was slow to learn lines, she soon upstaged other performers on the world scene. Noted composer Cole Porter wrote songs for her. She acted or appeared in films with Bing Crosby, Bert Lahr, and Tony Randall. She won a Tony award in 1953 for her revue "An Evening with Beatrice Lillie," which was a smash hit. Her final stage appearance was in *High Spirits*, the musical version of Noel Coward's *Blithe Spirit*. Certainly, Beatrice Lillie had an amazing career, from school in Belleville to success on the world stage in revues and light comedy.

The Airplane in City Hall

A LOCAL NEWSPAPER recently printed a 1914 picture of an airplane in the former inside market of Belleville City Hall. At least one reader asked if he could see the plane if he went to City Hall today.

Unfortunately for the reader and others interested in the history of flight, the plane was only on display for a brief time in 1914. It had been built by the Polly brothers of Belleville, who commenced construction on October 6, 1913, and completed it on February 11, 1914. It was then disassembled, moved into City Hall, and reassembled for display. Belleville historian W.C. Mikel, who helped the Pollys build the plane, included its picture in his 1943 history of Belleville, and described it as "the First airship built in Ontario."[20] Unfortunately, this claim cannot be verified.

The Wright brothers and other early aviators had inspired the Polly brothers. Perhaps they witnessed the first airplane flight in Belleville, which took place on June 3, 1913. The site was the driving park at the fairgrounds, then located south of Bridge Street, across from the present fairgrounds. The pilot was Earl Sandt of Erie, Pennsylvania, one of the earliest "barnstormers" and the first person to fly across Lake Erie. The Citizen's Celebration Committee had invited Sandt to attend the celebration of King George V's birthday. So great was the interest of many local residents in examining the plane up close that, prior to the scheduled flights, hundreds paid 10¢ each to view the plane, which was encircled by canvas. Sandt's plane was a pusher-type biplane, in which the pilot sat out front while a rear-mounted engine and propeller furnished the power. It was an improved version of the type used by the Wright brothers in their first successful heavier-than-air flight in 1903.

Aircraft similar to Earl Sandt's plane. Hundreds of onlookers turned up to see the early "legends of flight" on their visits. Courtesy of C.W. "Bill" Hunt.

As flight time neared, the *Intelligencer* reporter noted that the "Expectation was at a fever heat and many were the apprehensions of disaster by the thousands who for the first time were to witness such an event," yet the apparent confidence of the daring aviator, an expert in his line, tended to calm the fears of many. Finally, the plane was wheeled from its enclosure and the engine was started. Sandt then mounted the seat and sent the plane whirling along the ground for perhaps one-hundred fee. Then, like a bird, it spread its wings and sailed the south. As the plane circled the grounds, dippi ess operator waved to the spellbound crowd. Then, wanting to be the f Quinte, he covered a portion of Prince Edward County and return admiring audience with greater aerial performances. After a flight lasting nutes, he sailed over the grandstand and dropped like a feather in the field to the we 15,000 people within the fairgrounds, along with many in other parts of the city and across the bay, witnessed this history-making flight. Later in the day, Sandt took off again and accompanied the motorcyclists in their last race around the track at the fairgrounds. It was evident that the motorcycles, swift as they were, were no match for the bird man.[21]

The *Intelligencer* reporter and many citizens hoped that Earl Sandt would make a return visit to Belleville for the fall fair. Unfortunately, this would not be possible. Nine days after his performances here, Sandt crashed at Grove City, Pennsylvania, and died on June 22.

Exactly one year after Sandt's visit, Lincoln Beachey, arguably the most accomplished and popular of all the exhibition aviators, came to Belleville to celebrate the king's birthday. Described as "all the stars of stage and screen combined, with a touch of Superman thrown in," Beachey was known as "The Man Who Owns the Sky." From November 1913 to November 1914, he entertained more than seventeen million people in 126 cities, including Belleville. Like Sandt and many other "barnstormers," Beachey died while exhibiting in March 1915, at the young age of twenty-eight.[22]

Communications from the front were censored during The Great War. However, pictures that showed normal activities, often taken on leave, were encouraged. Private Ernie Pigden of the 155th Overseas Battalion sent this card from France in 1917, showing him as a lacrosse goalie. After the war, he became a locomotive engineer with the Grand Trunk and CN railways. Photo in author's collection.

9
THE FIRST WORLD WAR AND ITS AFTERMATH

A World at War, 1914–18

BELLEVILLE DOES NOT take a back seat to any Canadian community when it comes to patriotism. From the Loyalist participants in the American Revolution to the present, Belleville's fighting men and women have demonstrated their loyalty. Nowhere was this more evident than in the First World War. The lists of names on the cenotaphs clearly show that they were prepared to give their lives for their country. In 1899, thirty local soldiers even went to the Boer War (1899–1902), which was strictly a colonial war between Britain and the Dutch settlers (Boers) of South Africa who wanted to live away from British control. This was the first official dispatch of Canadian troops to an overseas war. Local church bells were rung to signal British victories.

Fortunately, the experiences of the soldiers of the First World War (1914–18) have been recorded in several articles and books.[1] Arguably the most significant and detailed account from a local point of view is a collection of forty unpublished letters written by Sergeant Garnet Edmund Dobbs covering his service in the Canadian Expeditionary Force from his departure from Belleville in June 1917 to his return to England in April 1919. A native of Belleville, Garn (the usual name by which he was known) served in the military band under bandmaster Reg Hinchey, and was second in command.

Garn Dobbs' letters reveal that the military band was an important morale booster. The music made the soldiers' marching easier, and every time the band stopped playing it would get a chorus of "good old band, good old band." In addition to his work in the band, Dobbs dug trenches, strung wire, and moved supplies to the men during the night. "Sometimes we got lost and believe me it is some sensation to be out in strange country wandering aimlessly around (in the dark) and not knowing what minute you were going to walk into the Boche trenches…."

Belleville factories, such as Marsh Engineering Works Ltd., produced war materials, including shell casings. A few industries continue on the site near the bay. Courtesy of Canada. Dept. of National Defence / Library and Archives Canada, PA-25211.

Front Street on Armistice Day, November 11, 1918, showing vehicles and dogs decorated for the occasion. Courtesy of Hastings County Historical Society, HC-9386.

The men were frequently cold and wet, and complained about marching all day in the rain with a "dose of the grippe," a form of influenza.

In one of his last letters, written from Belgium three months after the end of hostilities, Dobbs laments the slow passage of time. "No doubt it's all due to our impatience," he writes to his sister, Millie Dobbs, "but who wouldn't be impatient to get back to the only country on God's green earth and home. Don't ever get the notion that you'd like to try and find a better country than Canada. There ain't no sech [*sic*] animal." After the war, he returned to Belleville where he owned and operated a heating, plumbing, and sheet-metal business on Victoria Avenue.

Meanwhile, the home front was very supportive of the war effort. The Belleville Branch of the Canadian Red Cross was organized on August 28, 1914, and added the work of a patriotic league to its activities. Thousands of field comforts were sent to officers and men in the trenches, to hospitals in England, and to prisoners of war in Germany. Supplies also went to hospitals overseas and to Belgian refugees. Belleville industries and food-processing plants provided large amounts of war material and dried food for the war effort.

Women played an important role in many war activities on the home front, such as working in factories and knitting for the troops. Their contribution helped to increase their political influence and, in 1916, partly as a result of that influence, the government of Ontario passed the Ontario Temperance Act. Almost at the same time, the legislature granted women the right to vote. The extension of the franchise was due, in no small way, to the efforts of a Belleville educator and politician. Principal of the renowned Ontario Business College, John Wesley Johnson had begun his political career in Belleville, where he served as mayor for four years, from 1897 to 1900. In June 1908, he was elected as a Conservative to represent Hastings West in the Ontario legislature. Johnson, an accomplished speaker and independent thinker who was extremely popular, was acclaimed in 1911 and returned by a wide margin in 1914. During several sessions, he introduced a bill to confer the franchise upon women. Finally, his efforts and those of others were rewarded with success. To quote historian C.W. "Bill" Hunt, Johnson's efforts should grant him status as "the father of women's suffrage in Ontario."[2]

After the Conservative government of Sir William Hearst brought about women's suffrage, an editorial in the Conservative-inclined *Daily Intelligencer* supported the move, though reluctantly: "It is too late in the day to relegate them (women) to the sphere of the home and the church ... (but) when it comes, woman suffrage will make little difference to the ordinary course of affairs ... women usually imbibe the political views of the husbands or brothers, and vote as they do."[3]

Also on the local front, the volunteer fire service that had protected Belleville since the community's early existence became a permanent fire department on January 1, 1916 under Chief W.J. Brown.

The Better Understanding Meeting

ON THE AFTERNOON of May 26, 1917, Sergeant Garn Dobbs left Belleville on the Grand Trunk Railway to join the Canadian Expeditionary Force fighting in Europe. On June 14, he wrote from Sussex, England, to his brother Walter, describing his journey to that point.[4] Dobbs commented on "a great send off from a large crowd at the Belleville station." He had tried to persuade his wife, Nell, "to stay away from the station but 'nothing doing' so she and the Folks were all there which of course didn't make the going away any easier." He didn't take much interest in the surrounding country until the train reached Quebec, but then:

> We could tell almost as soon as we struck Quebec too, by the reception of the people at the different towns. We were the last of seven troop trains and several of those ahead of us had windows broken by stones thrown by civilians at different stations. We were held up in Montreal at St. Henri station for a couple of hours and learned that there had been rioting there and demonstrations against conscription. We got through however: without any 'rough stuff' reaching Halifax Monday night about 8 p.m.

Dobbs' comments indicated a serious problem in Canada, and some of Belleville's leading citizens set out to improve the situation not long after the war ended.

On July 25 and 26, 1918, Belleville was the site of a "Better Understanding Meeting." Instigated by W.C. Mikel, the president of the Canadian Fraternal Association, the meeting brought together almost thirty representatives of fraternal societies from Ontario and Quebec "for the purpose of discussing ways and means to arrive at a better understanding between French- and English-speaking Canadians."[5] Speakers included Lieutenant Colonel Mulloy of the Royal Military College,

Aerial view of Belleville, circa 1919, showing the Lower Bridge (Bridge Street) and the intersection of Bridge and Front streets in the lower right corner. Note the late nineteenth-century architecture, the occasional four-storey buildings (some later lowered to lessen taxes), the YMCA (centre), St. Michael's Roman Catholic Church (top left), and the array of billboards. A small boat is anchored upstream from the bridge, something that is often impossible in 2008. Courtesy of Archives of Ontario, C 285-1-0-0-43.

Kingston, an executive member of the Bonne Entente, an organization with similar aims. Napoleon Champagne of Ottawa, "an Ontario Frenchman and politician," and others argued that "the whole of the French people and the whole of the English people cannot be judged by a few hotheads who are fomenting trouble for a purpose and who represent perhaps only two or three percent of their nationalities. They cause all the trouble and all the strife, and they are dangerous people."[6] Others argued that the media was to blame, for placing inflammatory remarks in very large type.

The participants spoke frankly on such matters as bilingualism in education, separate schools, and other issues important to French-English relations. Colonel W.N. Ponton of Belleville summed up the meeting with these words: "I think the characteristic of this meeting is that we have not accentuated our differences nor have we minimized them, but we have just had the will to be one, to be tolerant and fraternal."[7]

Service to All

BELLEVILLE'S FIRST SERVICE club was organized in 1920. The instigator was Norman Tovell of Toronto, who had been in charge of the federal victory loan campaign in Belleville and had come in contact with Belleville's leading business and civic leaders. Tovell believed that Belleville was at the beginning of a large industrial expansion period and that a "Rotary Club will help keep things moving."[8] The Rotary Club of Toronto, of which Tovell was a member, enthusiastically agreed to sponsor a club in Belleville. On February 11, the organizational luncheon meeting was held at the Hotel Quinte, which served as the club's meeting place for many years. Prominent charter members included President E. Gus Porter, William B. Deacon, S.R. (Sandy) Burrows, and William J. (Billy) Hume. Over the years, the club became famous for its camps, variety shows, youth exchanges, junior achievement programs, student clubs, music festivals, Rotary Park, and a host of fundraising efforts to support worthwhile activities.

Other service clubs soon followed Rotary. The Kiwanis Club, organized in 1923, introduced the Victorian Order of Nurses to Belleville the following year, sponsored annual "Kiwanis Carnivals" and sporting teams, and helped police with children's safety programs. The Lions Club, organized in 1953, sponsors the summer "Music in the Park" program and is involved with the Lions Park development on Station Street. The Kinsmen Club promotes recreation and safety through its pool on East Dundas Street. Other clubs include the Probus Club, with programs for seniors.

Animals were not overlooked in the citizens' efforts to provide improved services. The Belleville branch of the Ontario Society for the Prevention of Cruelty to Animals was established on a permanent basis in April 1920. To encourage participation, membership fees were set at only 50¢ per year.

Although not defined as "a service club," the Belleville and District Chamber of Commerce is an organization that provides many services to its members and the community. Organized in 1860 as the Belleville Board of Trade, the organization has a proud history. One of its most active periods followed the First World War, when it was renamed the chamber of commerce and set up a very active program of community development and improvement. It published a regular bulletin, actively recruited new members, and worked to bring in new industries. On June 15, 1920, the *Intelligencer* proudly announced that seven new industries had been attracted the previous year. They included the Elliott Machinery Company (housed in the former Burrell Building on the Moira River) and the Judge Jones Milling Company, producers of quality flour. The same month, the chamber held its first tour, visiting the mining areas at Deloro and Marmora.

So successful was the chamber in attracting industries that it held a "Made in Belleville" Exhibition on October 24–28, 1922. Three quarters of the hundred businesses invited to participate did so. The event was a rousing success.[9]

The chamber gave city council much of the credit for its success. The chamber experienced a difficult first year or two, until city council appointed an industrial commissioner who also served as manager and secretary of the chamber of commerce. It "proved to be a happy arrangement." The chamber was purely an advisory body, and the council had the "legislative and administrative functions to secure the carrying out of suggestions, recommendations and promotional policies."[10]

One of the chamber's main concerns was the acute power shortage that Belleville was experiencing in the early 1920s. On July 24, 1922, the *Intelligencer* reported that "there are many factories closed down." Power shortages in Belleville and elsewhere in eastern Ontario were blamed on "difficulties with the water levels in the Trent System" and a clash between the Dominion Department of Railways and Canals and the Ontario Hydro-Electric Commission over the control of rivers.[11] Fortunately, the dispute was resolved in short order.

According to pioneer Belleville businessman W.C. Springer, this was only the second power interruption in twenty-one years — not a bad record.[12] Nevertheless, the *Intelligencer* felt that any interruption was unnecessary. On July 8, the editor noted: "This is the day of big projects. We are so bent upon harnessing Niagara, or making a highway to the sea via the St. Lawrence River, that we are apt to neglect opportunities that are right under our noses." Great visions were commendable, but the editor felt that the Moira River must be harnessed, a suggestion that would be acted upon in 2007–08.

The Bun Feeds

THE TERM "BUN feed" may not mean anything to many readers. But to long-time Belleville citizens (especially of the male gender), it means a municipal election is at hand. The origins of the bun feeds and of their sponsor, the Wharf Street Debating Club, are lost in the mists of time. Even C. W. "Bill" Hunt, the author of the club's unofficial history, has been unable to determine when they began — whether 1903, 1909, 1912, 1913, 1919, or some other year.[13] What seems certain is that the club and the bun feeds are about a hundred years old, and that the first reference to the annual bun feed was in the *Daily Intelligencer* on November 30, 1923.

After meeting in rented quarters elsewhere in Foster Ward, the members of the Wharf Street Debating Club organized a building fund in 1921, raised $105, and created their own clubhouse. Originally a boathouse on the corner of Wharf and South Front streets, it was a small building, perhaps 25 x 25 feet in size, although it has been lengthened several times since. Interestingly, the club did not buy the land under the clubhouse. That belonged (and still belongs) to the city. For many years, the bathroom was "nothing more than a thinly disguised outhouse. It was located on the north end of the back wall and featured a single wooden bench into which a round hole had been cut. The toilet discharged directly into the Moira."[14] In recent years, a number of improvements, many dictated by the Building Code, have been made. Also, Fire Chief Gord Gazley issued an ultimatum in 1986 that, unless the building was brought up to current fire standards, it would have to be demolished.

The unique bun feed events were held, and are still held, just before municipal elections in order to give candidates the chance to explain their platforms to the voters of Foster Ward and the rest of Belleville. Actually, the voters didn't, and don't, give them much of a chance. In the early years, candidates were expected to sing, dance, and otherwise entertain while the voters taunted them and made all sorts of nasty (often clever) and risqué comments to and about them. When a national television network taped parts of the event in the 1980s, it could use the pictures, but not the soundtrack. Members of the club paid annual dues — originally a dollar a year — for the "privilege" of hearing and jeering the candidates. For their money, each member also got a hot dog (usually passed from hand to hand), a piece of cheese, and a "cold" soft drink. The air was blue with comments and smoke.

Although there was no formal attempt to keep women out in the early years, they did not attend. It would have been unladylike to be there. After the Second World War, there was a deliberate effort to limit the events to men. Female candidates were allowed to speak at the start, and were then piped out to the tune of "Good Night Ladies."

The legendary, and now much modernized, Wharf Street Debating Club on South Front Street. Photo by author, 2006.

It took the ladies several attempts to gain entry to the small clubhouse. In 1972, a woman protesting her exclusion threw a metal construction rod through the window, narrowly missing a man. The club promptly gilded the bar and mounted it with a suitable plaque for all to see. In 1982, a woman sought the assistance of city police to gain entry, but was told that she would need a court order. Finally, in 1988, Julia Drake, a reporter with the *Intelligencer*, assumed an alias (Bill Blake, roving reporter for the *Loyalist Pioneer*), disguised herself as a man, and persuaded the officer at arms to allow her to enter. She and a female friend remained for the entire meeting.

Nevertheless, the issue of women in the Wharf Street Debating Club's bun feeds did not go away. Prior to the 1991 event, Donna Chambers phoned the candidates for council and school board and suggested that they not attend, because of the unseemly conduct of some parties likely to be present. Chambers was unsuccessful in her efforts. However, in retaliation, the club executive decided to name the club's new ladies washroom "The Donna Chamber Pot." On the same weekend, someone tossed a large rock through the club's front window. The club executive "assumed — or pretended for propaganda purposes — that the missile had been thrown by an unknown person of the feminine gender" and had the rock mounted on a board with the inscription "Thrown through the Window of the Warf [*sic*] St. Debating Club on Nov. 10th 1991 by 2 unknown women jealous of the policy of the Club."[15]

Since Julia Drake broke the sex barrier at the club in 1988, a few women (mostly candidates) have remained for entire meetings and have acquitted themselves extremely well. Particularly notable were performances by former mayor Shirley Langer (at the end of her term) and Councillor (later mayor) Mary-Anne Sills.

In the twenty-first century, Belleville's waterfront and the people of Foster Ward have changed. Some question the continuing need for the Wharf Street Debating Club, now used only for a few club meetings, social events, and skate changing and hot chocolate when winter weather permits skating on the harbour. Let C.W. "Bill" Hunt have the final word: "Without its raucous, brutally honest, and often hilarious bun feeds, the city's political life would be much the poorer. Belleville needs the Wharf Street Debating Club. It's in the soil."[16]

Dedicating a Cement "Log" Cabin

THE MAJOR CELEBRATION of this period took place from June 15–19, 1924, to mark the 140th anniversary of the arrival of the United Empire Loyalists in the Quinte area. The event was arranged in large part through the efforts of W.C. Mikel, Belleville lawyer, United Empire Loyalist, historian, and, of greater importance, mayor of the city in 1924–25. Mikel and other like-minded citizens wanted the world to know that Belleville was a key part of Loyalist country.[17]

Gwen Lazier meeting President Calvin Coolidge at the White House in 1924. Courtesy of Queen's University Archives, Florence Gwendolyn (Lazier) Braidwood Fonds – photograph 3147.

To publicize the event, the city dispatched two representatives to invite Americans and Canadians to attend. Gwendolyn Lazier was the representative chosen to visit the United States. She left Belleville on April 14, 1924, travelling by horseback, after the manner of the early pioneers, who had neither railway nor mechanized vehicle. Riding "Tip," kindly loaned by Alexander Moore, justice of the peace of Belleville, Gwen rode east from Belleville, across the American border, and south to Washington. Along the way, she was well-received by the mayors and officials of the cities and towns through which she passed. Newspapers gave front-page coverage to her mission, especially as she rode up the steps of New York City Hall to present the invitation to the mayor. She later met American President Coolidge on the White House lawn in Washington. (Apparently, life at the White House

was more informal in 1924 than it has been in recent years.) Following her meeting with the president, Gwen returned to Belleville by rail and the horse was shipped back by express, although somewhat delayed by border crossing procedures.

To cadet Allan Dempsey, a seventeen-year-old student of Belleville High School, went the somewhat less exciting role of walking along Highway 2 to Toronto to invite the mayor of that city, and officials and citizens along the way, to attend the June celebration.

Although President Coolidge did not attend, many thousands of visitors from both sides of the border did. Military participants came from neighbouring communities and from Toronto, which was represented by more than seven-hundred members of the famous 48th Battalion, with its three bands. Under the heading "Highlanders catch fancy of the city," a reporter for the *Daily Intelligencer* of June 16 wrote:

> The 48th Highlanders have captured the city. From the time the stalwart, upright soldiers swung into the city streets from the lower [CPR] station on Saturday night until the present, they have been the centre of keen admiration, which has repeatedly found expression in cheers from Belleville people and visitors.
>
> Large numbers were out to watch them pass through the city towards the Fair grounds on Saturday night and the streets were jammed yesterday afternoon when they joined with the Argyle Light Infantry and the 34th Field Battery in a drumhead service. In the evening when the famous band of the regiment came back to the Armouries lawn to give a concert hundreds gathered around to listen. Windows of nearby buildings swarmed with people and three or four score even climbed to the roof of the General Post Office in order to see and hear well.

On Monday, June 16, throngs of people, many carrying and waving flags, gathered on the courthouse lawn for the official opening. A descendant of the Loyalists, Colonel S.S. Lazier, UE, as chairman of the ceremonies, called the event "the greatest epoch in the history of Canada." Lazier introduced Mayor W.C. Mikel, who read an address of welcome. On Tuesday, nearly a thousand people from the county and leading Masonic officials from all over the province attended the ceremony for the laying of the cornerstone of the United Empire Loyalist Memorial at the entrance to Victoria Park. Lieutenant Colonel W.N. Ponton, immediate past grand master of the Grand Lodge of Canada in Ontario, acted as grand master for the ceremony and poured the symbolic corn, wine, and oil over the stone. On Thursday evening, a "stupendous and beautiful" historical pageant and panorama of Upper Canada's early years took place at the fairgrounds.

Three months later, on September 8, the Honourable Colonel Henry Cockshutt, lieutenant-governor of Ontario, unveiled the finished monument. Thousands of citizens and students of all the city schools witnessed the removal of the large Union Jack that covered the structure.

Unfortunately, the passage of time seriously affected the monument's appearance. Members of the Masonic Order and the Bay of Quinte branch of the United Empire Loyalist Association supported plans that called for the monument's demolition and replacement by several small markers. The Hastings County Historical Society strenuously opposed the demolition of the original 1924 monument, which had been designed by Belleville architect J. Arnold Thomson. Fortunately, the John M. Parrott Foundation came to the monument's rescue, donating a substantial amount of money to have it moved and restored on a more suitable site across Dundas Street. Other private and government bodies (including the Hastings County Historical Society) assisted. The unveiling ceremony took place on September 10, 2005.

Below: The United Empire Loyalist Monument, circa 1980, before the move north across Dundas Street, and (right) after the move in the summer of 2004. A rededication service took place on September 10, 2005. Photos by author.

The Fate of the Cradle Roll

MANY PEOPLE TAKE religion very seriously. Nowhere was that more evident in Belleville's history than in the discussions that led to the formation of the United Church of Canada in 1925. Prior to that time, there were three main Methodist churches in the city — Bridge Street, Tabernacle, and Holloway. There were also two Presbyterian churches — John Street and St. Andrew's.

There was almost overwhelming support for church union among the Methodists. In 1912, the Bridge Street congregation voted 99 percent in favour, and Tabernacle and Holloway Street churches also gave clear approval to the union.[18]

The two Presbyterian congregations did not deal with the issue as easily. From time to time, there had been discussions about a union between John Street and St. Andrew's, especially after the Free Church and the Kirk (the two main branches of Presbyterianism in Canada) came together in a union in 1875. However, the congregations could not agree on the terms. A proposal, approved by St. Andrew's in 1917, called for the two congregations to unite under the name of St. Andrew's. Worship services would be held in St. Andrew's church, while lectures and entertainments would be in the John Street building. The John Street congregation was not in favour of the proposal. Each congregation valued its own heritage — John Street as a Free Church congregation with American influences and St. Andrew's with ties to the Church of Scotland.

Both congregations also debated the possibility of a larger union of Methodist, Presbyterian, and Congregational churches in Canada. On two occasions, in 1912 and 1915, the members and adherents of St. Andrew's voted overwhelmingly in favour of such a union. On the third and most important vote, in January 1925, the majority rejected church union by a 185–141 vote. Colonel William Nisbet Ponton, a grandson of William Hutton and a prominent lawyer, effectively led the opposition and convinced the majority that they would be deserting the church of their ancestors.[19] There was much ill will. The Reverend Andrew S. Kerr immediately left St. Andrew's because he was a strong supporter of union.[20] Almost 120 congregational members also left and joined Bridge Street. No doubt others joined the John Street congregation, whose members had voted 139–123 to enter union. Some fifty-two members of the John Street congregation, wishing to retain the Presbyterian tie, went to St. Andrew's. By the end of the year, St. Andrew's had received 138 new members, either by transfer or profession of faith. Five years later, St. Andrew's had a larger congregation than ever — 521 communicant members.

A final act of defiance came from one or more former Presbyterians who left St. Andrew's after the vote. An envelope in the church archives holds the 1925 cradle roll listing the infant members of the church's families. The roll is in pieces, and a notation on the envelope reveals that it was "destroyed by Unionists when they left in 1925."

The Klan Rides Here

FEW PEOPLE KNOW that the Ku Klux Klan was active in the Belleville area in the 1920s and 1930s. Although the Klan is normally associated with white supremacists, especially in the southern United States, there were chapters throughout Canada. I first became aware of the local Klan when I received a one-page letter in June 1959 from Flora Bell of Coleman Street, a member of the newly founded Hastings County Historical Society.[21] She enclosed pictures of Klan members on horseback at Belleville. The members were wearing white robes and hoods, and their horses were sheeted and masked, with crosses on their face hoods. Mrs. Bell wrote, "The Klan (KKK) if I remember rightly was active from 1925–1936, perhaps a little longer, and did a good work, when and where it was needed, strictly protestant and of good character … do not connect them with the actions of the U.S. The organizer was from Nova Scotia." She also suggested that if the historical society "did not like to have these pictures, a match will do the deed."

Two years later, when I and other members of the historical society were sorting through old records (some dated back to 1839) in the basement of the original county courthouse prior to its demolition, we uncovered a further reference to the Klan. It was a cryptic message, perhaps a warning, bearing the letters "KKK." We were unable to determine the origin of the message. However, the fact that it had been saved in the official court papers (or perhaps in the unofficial papers of a clerk or county official) attached some importance to the discovery.

Over the years, more information has become public. For example, the first Klan organizers arrived in Ontario from New York early in 1925. They began in Toronto, and, according to one writer, "built on a ready-made base of bigotry provided by the powerful Loyal Orange Lodge,"[22] Certainly the Klan was in Belleville by July 29, 1925, for late that night passengers on the steamer *Brockville* "sighted a burning 30-foot cross standing on the promontory between the Bay Bridge and Zwick's Island."[23] The untoward incident was reported in the *Daily Intelligencer* the next day. An investigation by the Belleville Police Department proved fruitless.

Eight days later, three more crosses simultaneously illuminated the summer sky. One was on a small island north of the Bay Bridge. A second was at the fairgrounds on the West Hill, and the third was at the Dundas Street Burying Ground at the southwest corner of East Dundas and Newberry streets. At 2:00 a.m. on September 14, a huge cross burned brightly on the front lawn of a South John Street home. It was the sixth cross to be burned in Belleville. The Klan had arrived, apparently in force.

Meanwhile, handbills had been circulated announcing an outdoor Klan meet at Victoria Park. It was advertised as a free Sunday afternoon public lecture under the auspices of the KKK of the British Empire, about its "Principles and Purposes." On the afternoon in question, Mayor W.C. Mikel, accompanied by a detective, went to the park planning to tell the Klan that there would be no meeting. However, rain had forced the rally to an indoor location.

The largest local rally was held on Sunday, June 27, 1926, in a vacant field on the southeast corner of Sidney and College streets. All members were robed and hooded; only the speakers' faces were visible. Their robes were made of white duck material, with a green maple leaf set in a red circle on the right breast, and a white cross on a red background on the left breast. A red tassel ornamented the top of the hood. The chief officials wore purple robes. During the afternoon, the imperial commander of the Ladies' Ku Klux Klan of Kanada spoke, and a ladies' group from Kingston performed a splendid drill. Speakers stressed that the Klan was a great and essentially patriotic, fraternal, benevolent, and educational social order. They claimed that the Klan did not discriminate against men because of religious or political creed when the same did not antagonize the rights and privileges guaranteed by civil government, Christian ideals, and institutions.

At the same time, the speakers stated the Klan was dedicated "to the preservation and pre-eminence of the White Gentile Protestant race," so that the ideals of the British Empire would be passed on to future generations. They pointed out some problems. For example, it was suggested that white Protestant men feared failure if they opened a restaurant in Belleville because all downtown restaurants were owned and operated by "foreigners." In Vancouver, it was stated, that "white girls were living with Chinamen and Mongolians and other foreigners," and that "mixed marriages between white and yellow and white and brown couples would lead to national ruin."

The rally lasted well into the night. A huge eighty-foot cross and three smaller crosses were burned as sixty new candidates, both men and women, were initiated into the Klan. The ceremony was conducted by Klansmen from London (Ontario), and the inductees, marching to the tune "Onward Christian Soldiers," were led by a fiery cross from station to station within a circle. At each of the ten stations, the inductees had to commit to a pledge of commitment. Three of these included:

#2. Are you a White, Gentile, and Protestant patriot devoted to Klan principles?

#5. Do you esteem the British Crown and its institutions above any other government, civil, political, or ecclesiastical in the whole world?

#7. Do you believe in and will you faithfully strive for the eternal maintenance of White Supremacy?[24]

According to the newspaper account, there were 1,150 Klansmen in attendance, as well as 10,000 spectators.[25] The sightseers were kept at a distance by the constant surveillance of hooded horsemen acting as outriders. The spectators sat on top of cars, climbed trees, and seized every vantage point about the area.

The *Intelligencer* editorial that accompanied two lengthy articles called the rally "the outstanding event of the day," and called the speeches patriotic. It agreed with the Klan declaration that "mixed marriages between white girls and Orientals are harmful and terribly wrong."

Since that time, several writers have shed light on the Klan's activities in Belleville. In addition to freelance writer Rick Mofina's excellent article in the *Intelligencer*, Stirling historian Lewis Zandbergen, the Tweed Heritage Centre's Evan Morton, and author Ian S. Robertson have all touched upon this topic. At a meeting of the Hastings County Historical Society on May 29, 1974, *Intelligencer* reporter Lenny Williamson spoke on the history of the local Klan. Wearing an authentic white Klan hood from the collections of the Hastings County Museum, Lenny described how the Klan had burned crosses in different locations, how the Klansmen liked to travel by horse, and how their horses wore booties so they would not be heard as they moved through the night. She based much of her talk on Flora Bell's reminiscences.[26] At the end of the talk, a Klanswoman who had served as an executive member showed some official records of the local group.

Elsewhere in Hastings County, the Tweed Heritage Centre has an invitation to the Klan's Third Annual At Home (a social gathering) on January 29, 1929. Further, Glanmore National Historic Site has an official seal of a local Klan chapter, and, in 1990, Bill Seabrook of Belmont Township took an interesting document in to the Stirling office of *The Community Press*. It was the program for the Ku Klux Klan of Canada Field Day, held at Belleville on Sunday afternoon, September 15, 1929.[27] The program highlighted the religious nature of the event and included hymn lyrics. The first hymn was "Let the Fiery Cross be Burning," sung to the tune of the hymn "Let the Lower Lights be Burning."

Newspaper coverage of the September 15 event stressed the Klan's claims to be a law-abiding religious organization. The Reverend George Marshall, rector of Belleville's Reformed Episcopal Church (and later to become the imperial wizard of the KKK), stated that the Klan was a new means to meet new conditions. Its aims included a British Canada without domination by any religious group. The Klan was anti-Communist, because in Communist schools there was propaganda to destroy religion; Communists were teaching children that there was no God and no Christ. Other speakers claimed that Canada's press was afraid of the church, that there was an effort to give Canada a new flag, that Canada's press was not fair to the Klan, and that there should be one language. Although "many of the Klansmen and Klanswomen wore their cloaks and hoods, Rev. Mr. Marshall did not appear in uniform, but in clerical garb."[28]

No individual in recent years had a better knowledge of the Klan than the late Ed Buckley, a Belleville educator and historian who wrote the history of St. Michael's Roman Catholic parish. Buckley grew up on Station Street and experienced the burning of a cross first-hand on Pinnacle Street, just east of the Front Street bridge. He remembered the Reverend George Marshall as a tall, thin man who lived on Victoria Avenue. He knew that the Klan frequently burned crosses on the lawns of homes inhabited by philandering husbands. And he knew the history of the local Klan because he had read every surviving issue of the *Intelligencer*. In fact, the most complete history of the local Klan — almost five large pages — is to be found in his church history.

In the *Daily Intelligencer* of October 22, 1926, Buckley found evidence of a serious conflict between the local Klan and the president and manager of the paper, S.B. Dawson.[29] Dawson had taken over the paper three years earlier, and had just reorganized his staff. A more elderly supervisory employee had been moved into a less demanding position because of "his advancing age and state of health," with no loss in pay. However, the young man promoted into his position was a Roman Catholic. As a result, two representatives of the local Klan, Mr. Canniff and A. Ruttan, along with the Reverend George Marshall, visited the editor. Although they admitted that the young man was honest, capable, and a good husband and father, they objected to a Roman Catholic being given a position of authority over Protestants. They asked that he be demoted, and suggested that the paper would be well advised not to hire Catholics at all.

To quote Buckley, "Dawson rose like a fish to bait and printed the story of the interview...."[30] Dawson began, "When the Ku Klux Klan of Kanada first came to Belleville, it was greeted with tolerant amusement. It was good fun to watch the 'hooded warriors' manoeuvre on unaccustomed horse-back when they held their field days and their fiery speeches and fiery crosses were entertaining and innocuous." However, he continued, an attempt to dynamite a Roman Catholic church in Barrie by three men, including two Klan officials, had awakened the public "to a realization of the folly of stirring up sectarian strife and bitterness in Canada. To allow an imported organization from the United States to come to this country and set class against class and church against church is to invite destruction. The ugly head of bigotry and intolerance has now been raised in Belleville."

Dawson maintained that, carried to its logical conclusion, the Klan's attitude would mean the expulsion from Belleville of some five-hundred families totalling between 2,500 and 3,000 members. "Through the Rotary Club, the Kiwanis Club, the Chamber of Commerce, and similar organizations,

"Gathering of the Klan at Belleville . . . a little of past history," circa 1930, according to the donor, a Klan member. Courtesy of Hastings County Historical Society, HC-2029.

good citizens are striving to build a bigger and better city here. They work together, regardless of private differences of religion. Why is the Ku Klux Klan allowed to nullify the efforts of these broad-visioned public-spirited men?" After Dawson told Ruttan and Marshall that they were "interfering in a private manner in an unwarranted manner," a veiled threat was made that the paper would suffer for its attitude, and a number of people cancelled their subscriptions.

The delegation then claimed that Dawson's interpretation of the interview was incorrect and invited him to attend a public meeting at City Hall on October 25 to debate the truth of the matter. Dawson agreed to the debate, and the second-floor public hall at the east end of the building was packed with Klansmen, Klanswomen, and their supporters. The Reverend George Marshall spoke first, stressing that he did not want all Roman Catholics at the newspaper office to lose their jobs. He did agree that the men for whom he spoke were Protestants, but claimed that he had not said anything against Roman Catholics. Moreover, he claimed that neither he nor Ruttan were Klan officers. Ruttan supported Marshall's comments, and thought the whole newspaper story was false.

With "all the cards stacked against him," according to Buckley, Dawson rose to speak.[31] He said that the account in the newspaper was correct, and that the two gentlemen had attempted to interfere in the paper's operations on purely sectarian grounds. Moreover, he stated that Canada had no place for an organization such as the Klan, which was based on bigotry and intolerance. Members of the audience then became angry and some shouted "Throw him out the window" and "Pitch him out." Some Klansmen soon formed a guard and escorted Dawson safely out the front door of City Hall.

The next morning, Dawson restated his views on the front page of the *Intelligencer*. Moreover, he denied Marshall's statement that the earlier delegation was not from the Klan. Dawson stated that Ruttan was "the Klan Keagle (or whatever they call it)," and that Marshall had preached at every Klan function attended by representatives of the press.[32] As to Marshall's claim that the Protestants have a right to an organization of their own to protect their religious rights, Dawson said they already had it — the Orange Lodge "an Order of high standing made up of a fine class of Canada's citizenship…." For many local residents, Dawson's letters on the front page of the newspaper seemed to close the Klan issue. However, the Klan continued to function in Belleville until at least 1936, and its influence survived much longer. For some, it was simply a benevolent organization that was "Protestant and of good character." For others, it was an organization based on "bigotry and intolerance."

Veterinarian, Bootlegger, and Rum-Runner

THE STORY OF "Doc" Hedley Welbanks, owner of three rum-running boats by 1925 and a noted bootlegger, is a story that waited many years to be told. It was only in 1988 that Belleville historian C.W. "Bill" Hunt shone a light on it in his excellent book *Booze, Boats and Billions*.[33] Subtitled "Smuggling Liquid Gold," the book offers an "anecdotal and often very amusing account" of "a miniature war zone in which the forces of the law never quite caught up with the ingenuity of an endless crop of liquor smugglers."[34]

Rum-running flourished from 1920 until the end of 1933, when the United States government ended Prohibition. Many ordinary Canadians were attracted to liquor smuggling because Canada's federal government chose not to prohibit the production of beverage alcohol, and refused to stop the export of Canadian liquor to the United States until June 30, 1930. There was big money to be made, and the activity was not considered against the law in Canada for the first ten years. These factors, and the nearby presence of the huge H. Corby Distillery, encouraged Belleville citizens, as well as those in Prince Edward County, to participate in rum-running. Vessels of all sizes were used, and many boats cleared from Belleville and other lake ports were listed as sailing to Mexico City, Havana, and other distant ports. Most of the boats returned, allegedly from these destinations, within a day or two.

The United States government tried to put an end to these operations, and, by 1924, the coast guard had twenty-eight speedboats actively searching out rum-runners on Lake Ontario and elsewhere. The boats were armed with machine guns, and more than one smuggler died from "lead poisoning."

According to C.W. "Bill" Hunt, one of the leading rum-runners was "Doc" Hedley Welbanks, the likeable "cigar-champing horse doctor" who could legally dispense alcohol to sick horses as he made his rounds of local farms during the Prohibition years in Ontario.[35] Initially, he employed members of "the Foster Ward smuggling fraternity," and, later, farmers and fishermen from Prince Edward County, to work on the three boats he used to smuggle liquor to American importers.[36]

Perhaps the most unusual Welbanks story involved the hijacking of the rum boat *Rosella*. This liquor-laden Welbanks boat had been seized by the American coast guard on July 26, 1927, near Main Duck Island. The *Rosella* was towed to Oswego, where Fred Sprung (the alias used by skipper Bruce Lowery after his capture by the coast guard) was brought before Commissioner Charles Bulger. The evidence favoured the defendants, who were supported by two lighthouse keepers and a minister who all affirmed that the *Rosella* was in Canadian waters at the time of seizure. Bulger set the crew free and ordered the coast guard to return the boat and her cargo to Welbanks.

Unfortunately, the coast guard had already turned the boat over to the collector of customs, and it was put up for auction. Welbanks travelled to Rochester and bid US$350 for his own boat, but was outbid by an American fish buyer. The new owner repaired and improved the boat, renamed her *Verna*, and sent her out to haul fish to Rochester. Hearing that the boat was in port at Brighton, Welbanks, accompanied by a Canadian customs officer, went to Brighton and seized the boat at gunpoint. This touched off a minor diplomatic row, and Welbanks was summoned to court. A somewhat involved and confusing hearing followed, and Belleville Magistrate W.C. Mikel ruled that, inasmuch as the coast guard had seized the *Rosella* in Canadian waters, it rightfully belonged to Welbanks. Mikel then went on to censure the coast guard, calling its action "a high-handed act of piracy."[37] As a result of the court case, "Doc" Welbanks had ensured himself a prominent place in the list of interesting, noteworthy, and controversial local citizens.[38]

Slaughter of the Canada Geese

As a schoolchild in the early 1940s, I remember making a donation — I think it was only a dime — to help Jack Miner in his efforts to save an endangered species, the Canada goose.

Miner (1865–1944) had established a sanctuary at Kingsville for the conservation of migrating Canada geese and wild ducks. I was not aware, until recently, that he also helped establish a small sanctuary north of Belleville. Miner gave twenty-three wild Canadian geese to the sanctuary, operated by the Hastings branch of the Jack Miner League. In mid-October 1928, three unknown men entered the sanctuary when no one was there and killed fourteen of the birds. According to the *Toronto Globe,* "Had the ruthless vandals not been interrupted at their dastardly business they would doubtless have completed their work of destruction and wiped out the little colony of geese….There is nothing 'sporting' about the deed. It could have been prompted only by the basest of motives and carried out by minds of criminal intent."[39]

This slaughter upset one of the sanctuary's leading supporters, Wallace Havelock Robb. Described by the *Toronto Globe* as a "well-known naturalist," Robb was a native of Belleville who was responsible for the establishment of Abbey Dawn, near Kingston, and gained renown as a poet and lecturer. Earlier, he had approached city council for a hundred-dollar grant to assist the sanctuary, to no avail.

Now, Robb took action. He delivered a package to City Hall and placed it on the city clerk's desk. An attached card read: "Four of the Murdered Geese — To His Worship the Mayor of Belleville and City Council from a poet of Canadian Birdland who pleaded before them in vain." When council received the geese ("covered with blood and dirt") and the note, it took no action. The next morning, the four geese were burned in the furnace at City Hall.

Robb also composed a poem to mark the sad occasion, and the careless attitude councillors and citizens displayed with regard to the sanctuary. One stanza read:

> What ho, my fellows! Laugh and have good cheer;
> The geese are dead, but drink! Fill up on beer.
> Let pointing poets take their quills and go,
> The fools make us uneasy when they're near.

Robb was certainly not impressed by council.

Despite this unfortunate incident, Jack Miner's efforts to preserve Canada geese have been very successful. A few years ago, Doctor J. Russell Scott arranged for a few Canada geese to be sent to Belleville, and there is a growing flock in the city, especially in East and West Riverside parks.

An "All-Belleville Night" on Radio

BELLEVILLE'S FIRST RADIO station came on the air in 1946. Almost twenty years earlier, however, Belleville Mayor Morley Duff and local musicians made local radio history when they appeared for an hour on CKGW, described as a "high-class station," at Toronto's King Edward Hotel. The station took its call letters from distillers Gooderham and Worts, was based at Bowmanville, and is now CBC Radio One at 99.1 FM. Belleville followed Peterborough and Galt as the featured municipality of the week. The local press proclaimed that Belleville was "known all over Ontario as the home of musical talent that is not surpassed in Eastern Canada."[40]

The Radio Four, a quartet composed of Messrs. Al Stillman, J. Arnold Thomson, Harry Moorman, and Doctor A.B. Haffner, headlined this talent. The Radio Four had previously appeared on radio station CNRM in Montreal, and had made several recordings for Apex Records. Their numbers included such popular favourites as "John Peel," "Swing Along," and "Steal Away." Helen Sobie, who had appeared on several Toronto broadcasts, sang "Who'll Buy My Lavender?" Also featured were James D. Bankier (a lyric tenor who had appeared before as a "Cheerio" artist) and Leo Riggs ("Belleville's peerless pianist"). Mayor Duff gave a few words about the city.

The program was scheduled from ten to eleven o'clock in the evening, and the participants went to Toronto that day by train. Unfortunately, the broadcast started forty-five minutes late because of a transmitter problem at Bowmanville. Nevertheless, it was a great event. According to the press, the singers performed extremely well, as did Mayor Duff. His message was described as being "remarkably clear," and "delivered with the clarity, enunciation, and the confidence that one might expect of a radio announcer." Not only did he praise Belleville's industrial development (in the preceding five years, American companies had set up seven branch plants), but he spoke of the great fishing and other sporting activities, including the National ball team, which had won the provincial championship two years in a row, spectacular scenery, the excellent Bay of Quinte Golf and Country Club, and other features.

The radio audience was estimated at about a third of a million people in Ontario and well over a million throughout southern Ontario, Quebec, and adjacent parts of the United States. In fact, CKGW was said to be able to reach the whole continent.[41] As the program progressed — and for hours afterwards — listeners from all parts of Ontario as well as Nova Scotia and Chicago flooded the station with congratulatory telephone calls and telegrams. At one time, there were 150 callers waiting to get through.[42] So successful was the program that Alderman Wotten suggested that the city should arrange a program for every other month.[43]

Less than a year after the Toronto broadcast, Belleville gained further prominence in the radio world. On August 21, 1929, Alemite Products of Canada Limited, a subsidiary of the Stewart-Warner Corporation of Chicago, announced that the first made-in-Belleville radio for commercial use was ready. It was the Model 950, a metal-cased, eight-tube "model of beauty." Although most of the parts were imported, the company noted that the new Belleville plant would soon be manufacturing many parts. It would produce one-hundred radios each day by the end of the month, and would employ seventy-five "men and girls." Apparently, no women need apply!

By the end of the year, radio production was climbing and was expected to reach between "200 and 250 a day."[44] In addition, the plant began to produce other models. Cabinets were modelled on seventeenth-century English styles, and each radio had a plug-in for a phonograph link. Perhaps surprisingly, the company announced that it was also looking forward to the development of television. This development offered "enormous possibilities" to consumers, and company representatives informed the local press that all current models "are equipped with television attachments." Amazing!

As of 2008, Belleville still does not have its own television station, although Cogeco has a local-programming channel.

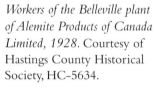

Workers of the Belleville plant of Alemite Products of Canada Limited, 1928. Courtesy of Hastings County Historical Society, HC-5634.

10
DEPRESSION, ROYALTY, AND WAR

The Depression Years

ON THE EVE of the Great Depression, there was optimism. The 1920s had witnessed many improvements, and Belleville residents were upbeat.

In 1921, the Bay Bridge, after being taken over by the Ontario government and made part of the province's highway system, was made toll-free. The collection booth at the south end of the bridge was removed. The same year, the Belleville Amateur Athletic Association was organized in an attempt to consolidate the many areas of sporting activity under one umbrella. It was successful for a decade. The Foster Ward Goyer family, which had enough boys to form a hockey team, did just that. In May, they beat the LaMoore Brothers of Trenton 9–7. Several members of the family went on to achieve distinction in the sporting world. Also in 1921, Bridge Street Church chartered a Boy Scout troop. In December, Agnes McFee was acclaimed to the school board, making her the first woman to hold elected office in the city. Two years later, the Belleville Parks Board was formed, marking the beginning of a city department that would create a parks system that is the envy of many municipalities.

On November 23, 1924, Canada's political elite came to Belleville when Prime Minister Mackenzie King and former and future Prime Minister Arthur Meighen attended a YMCA banquet. In 1924, council gave Fred Rawson a charter to operate buses, and, the same year, the Henry Corby family donated a public bathhouse in Queen Victoria Park. The bathhouse joined the Belleville Public Library and the Corby Rose Garden as examples of the family's generosity.

Later in the decade, on December 6, 1929, a major celebration marked the opening of the city's new arena. Thanks in large part to William J. Hume, described as "a Belleville boy who made good, but never forgot where he came from," funding was obtained for the arena, which was described as "one of the finest ice palaces in Ontario."[1] The opening ceremonies took place before an exhibition tilt between the Queen's University and the University of Toronto's Varsity hockey teams. Hume came to the financial rescue of the community and its arena again in August 1933, when the arena directors decided to close it, return the ice plant, and sell the property.[2]

Even as the Depression began, Canada's leading financial paper could boast that the residential centre of Belleville had become an "important industrial community." In the preceding ten years, Belleville had attracted twenty new industries.[3] New American companies included the American Optical Company (the world's largest manufacturers of spectacles), the Stewart-Warner Corporation (automobile accessories and radio sets), the Stephens Adamson Company (conveying equipment), J&J Cash (woven labels), and Mead Johnson (infants' foods). Furthermore, the Belleville Chamber of Commerce was doing well, and downtown businessmen were promoting an esplanade and parking area along the east bank of the Moira River.[4]

Unfortunately, even before the puck dropped in 1929 to open the Hume Arena (which came to be known as the Memorial Arena and the "Home of the world-famous Belleville McFarlands" in the 1950s), the Depression struck. Belleville still remained "one of the brightest spots in Eastern Ontario," but it was affected.[5] Local effects reflected those in other parts of Canada — unemployment, reduced hours, lower wages, and financial insecurity. Ending a long-time rivalry, the *Intelligencer* and the *Ontario* merged to become the *Ontario Intelligencer*. Churches and community agencies took on more relief work. Beset by additional responsibilities, the Children's Aid Society, first incorporated in 1907, revised its constitution and sought reincorporation in 1933.

Federal and provincial make-work programs operated in the area. The federal government created the Trenton air base, just east of Trenton. In 1934, the province announced the construction of an improved road between Belleville and Bancroft. The Dominion government also helped the local economy in 1936, when it opened the Dominion Parasite Laboratory (usually referred to locally as "the Bug House"). The lab's main purpose was to breed and liberate insects to destroy other insects that injure plants, trees, and animals. It gained world prominence. A new lab, located just north of Dundas Street at the eastern entrance to the city, was constructed in the 1950s. After the lab closed, the building was used by other government departments and has since been converted into the Lakeview Manor Retirement Home. Nevertheless, despite such government-financed programs, it was the Second World War that revived Belleville's economy.

The Axe Murder and Happier Events

> Calmly, exhibiting the same indifference towards death that he has displayed since the final sentence was passed, Harold Worden Vermilyea went to his death at 12:20 this morning. With the same unconscious manner that has characterized his incarceration in the local jail, Vermilyea mounted the twelve steps to the scaffold, accepted the black hood and the hempen slip knot over his head, and without questions, slid almost silently to his death. Only the dull rumble of the trap door, as it slid on well oiled hinges marked his departure.

WITH THOSE WORDS, the reporter for the *Ontario Intelligencer* recorded the execution, on May 2, 1935, of Harold Worden Vermilyea, convicted of one of the most brutal murders in Belleville's history. Shortly after 10:00 p.m. on October 4, 1934, Mrs. Nathaniel Vermilyea, the widow of a prominent former Thurlow Township reeve, was found lying in a pool of blood on the lawn in front of her daughter's home at 101 Bridge Street East. According to the newspaper reporter, her head had been "bashed in" from several hatchet blows and her right wrist had almost been severed. Trying to protect herself from her attacker, she had apparently raised her right arm to her head. Mrs. Vermilyea's daughter, the wife of Doctor A.J. Faulkner, MLA and minister of health in Mitchell Hepburn's Ontario Liberal cabinet, found her body. Mrs. Faulkner recognized her mother by the brooch she was wearing.

A search for the killer was launched immediately. The murder weapon, a new, bloodied lathe hatchet, was found in the nearby bushes. Evidence pointed to her son, Harold Worden Vermilyea, who had lived in California, where he owned an orange grove, for twenty-three-years. Vermilyea was extradited to Canada, and the trial began on February 11, when the grand jury brought in a true bill. Two weeks later, after some compelling evidence had been presented, the case went to the jury. A salesman from Simpsons in Toronto testified that he had sold Vermilyea the hatchet, which had been reduced in price from $3.75 to $1.50. Taxi drivers testified that they had transported him from Toronto to Belleville and back on two occasions, for $15 per trip. Vermilyea's sister stated that Harold had asked his mother to divide her estate and give him money for the orange grove. Despite an attempted insanity plea, the jury found Vermilyea guilty after four and a half hours of deliberation and sentenced him to hang. During his final days, local newspapers commented on his special diet, his meals, and his final letter telling his son to join a church and not to gamble.

The Vermilyea murder was not the only event attracting attention in the mid-1930s. In mid-March 1936, because of prolonged rain, there was a disastrous flood, one of the worst recorded in Belleville. The following year, there were proposals for flood-control measures, including reservoirs on the Moira River.

An earthquake, one of the few ever recorded in this area, struck on November 1, 1935. WHOLE COUNTRY AWAKENED FROM SLEEP AS BEDS SWAYED AND SWAYED read a headline in the *Ontario Intelligencer* of that day. Shortly after 1:00 a.m., the half-minute quake awakened people in eastern Canada from the head of Lake Superior to the Bay of Fundy. In Belleville, the damage mainly consisted of loosened bricks in chimneys and broken china. Down on East Dundas Street, "residents of a double house had a coal bin divided only by a light partition. After the earth tremor had passed, one of the residents had all the coal."

On January 22, 1937, the *Ontario Intelligencer* proclaimed farm water "better than gold." The reference was to the Belleville Aqua Vita Company Ltd., chartered by the provincial government on September 23, 1936, to acquire and develop "springs of natural and mineral waters and medicinal waters."[6] Doctor Ernest Melville Carefoot of Belleville was the president

A view to rekindle or create childhood memories. Today, Reid's Dairy is famous for its "Loonie Milkshakes," ice cream, castle, and farm animals. Courtesy of Hastings County Historical Society, Mika Collection, Business File.

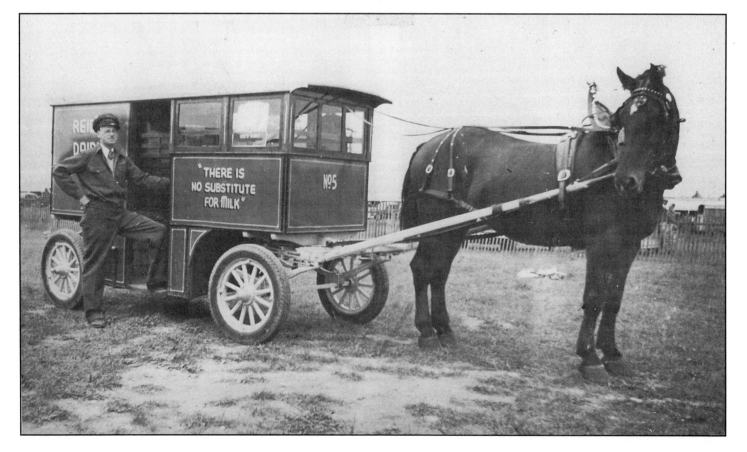

of this controversial company, which promoted the healing powers of an artesian well near Foxboro. According to the *Globe and Mail* of January 19, 1937, the waters were "believed to be able to cure ulcerated stomach, goitre, bladder conditions, arthritis and chronic headache." Moreover, they "may prove an aid in the treatment of cancer." The discovery had been made at the 500-foot level of a shaft dug by miners in search of gold. The medicinal powers remained highly debatable.

A far less contentious medical discovery and award was made the same year, when it was announced that the University of Edinburgh's thousand-dollar Cameron Prize had been awarded to Doctor James Bertram Collip, for many years a resident of Charles Street. He had greatly assisted Doctors Banting and Best in their research into diabetes and the development of insulin.[7]

A major development affecting public services took place in 1937, when the Belleville Public Utilities (BUC) was formed to take over hydro, water, and gas works. The gas works were subsequently disposed of, but electricity and water remained under the BUC until 2000. When city council disbanded the BUC (in the midst of the reorganization of electrical services mandated by the provincial government), it helped bring about the defeat of the incumbent mayor and several councillors in the November 2000 election.

Despite the Depression, Belleville maintained a strong interest in sports. In 1931, local resident Tommy Pedder became a household name because of his participation in the prestigious Canadian National Exhibition swim in Toronto. He continued to participate and set records until the 1950s. Not a tall man, standing barely five feet tall and weighing only sixty-five pounds at the age of sixteen, Pedder's strength "did not come from nature, but from hard work and training. If you were to use one word to describe him it would be 'Heart.'"[8] He also earned fame for weightlifting.

George Pepper was another world-class athlete. On September 8, 1936, he won the title of Canadian Motorcycle Champion by defeating thirty-five competitors from Canada and the United States in a two-hundred-mile race through the streets of west Belleville.[9]

In other sporting news, the South End Athletic Club was founded in 1933 to encourage anyone interested in any branch of sports in Belleville. An offshoot of the Wharf Street Debating Club, it kept its membership rates down to 25¢. The club gained prominence for sailing, especially punt racing.[10] From 1936 to 1941, the Kinsmen sponsored a Kid Kar Derby. Thanksgiving Day, Monday, October 12, 1936, saw the first soap-box derby in Belleville. The course ran down North Front Street, from the CNR bridge to Moira Street. Almost a hundred cars competed. From time to time since the end of the Second World War, attempts have been made to revive local soap-box racing — with limited success.[11]

Belleville was home to some noted writers during the Depression years — notably W.C. Mikel and Farley Mowat. Lawyer and former mayor W.C. Mikel dreamed of publishing the first history of Belleville. He had begun work in the 1920s and had hoped to publish his book in the early 1930s. Unfortunately, the Depression intervened, making finances a problem. Mikel approached people to make donations in return for pictures or descriptions in the book. In fact, one gentleman recently recalled his father throwing Mikel out of his Front Street business when he insisted on a donation in return for coverage.

Nonetheless, Mikel did continue his work, and sections appeared in the local press from time to time. It was finally published in 1943 under the title *City of Belleville History*. Deluxe, leather-bound copies sold for $10 and regular cloth-bound copies for $3.75. Before that time, one of the sections that appeared in the *Quinte Sun* on December 8, 1937, highlighted Mikel's idea that local municipalities should form "Quinte City," made up of land on both the north and south shores of the Bay of Quinte.

Another budding writer, although still only a boy, was the legendary Farley Mowat. He spent some time in Belleville after his father, Angus Mowat, was appointed librarian of the Corby Public Library in the summer of 1928. The family lived in an apartment on the third floor of the library, and Farley reflected on his life in Belleville in *Born Naked,* his autobiography. He recalled fishing used condoms out of the Moira River, near where a sanitary sewer spilled its contents into the stream. Upstairs in the apartment, he and a friend filled a condom with water — perhaps a gallon — then released it onto an unsuspecting citizen. That person was Charles Eardley Wilmot, described as a friend of Angus Mowat and "a dashing young fellow who owned the local Ford dealership."[12] Angus and Wilmot gave Farley and his friend a serious talking-to, and warned them not to tell anyone, especially their mothers.

Among Farley's other memories of Belleville was the state of the harbour, which he described as "a filthy place, full of sewage and industrial refuse."[13] As to his earliest connection with the area, Mowat recalled that his father had told him that he "was conceived in the lee of Indian Island [near the west end of the Bay of Quinte] in the sweetest little green canoe that ever was."[14] Farley would have much more to say about the Belleville area in *The Regiment*, his history of the Hastings and Prince Edward Regiment during the Second World War. Known familiarly as the "Hasty Ps" (or "Hasty P's"), the regiment traced its proud tradition to the arrival of military units that served in the American Revolution."

George, Elizabeth, and the Royal Oak, May 21, 1939

BELLEVILLE HAS HAD its share of memorable royal visits. Although the Prince of Wales' intended visit in 1860 was a fiasco, all subsequent events were highly successful and emotional, though usually very brief.

On Monday, October 14, 1901, the Duke and Duchess of Cornwall (later King George V and Queen Mary) stopped at the Belleville railway station during their tour of Canada. The governor general's train preceded the one carrying the Duke and Duchess, and his train was welcomed with a hearty cheer from the gathered citizens as it came in. "The band played 'God Save the King,' the children waved their flags and the scene was an animated one."[15] His train stayed only a few minutes before pulling out. Again the band played the national anthem.

After a long wait, during which the police and soldiers had their work cut out trying to keep the crowd back, the train carrying the royal couple appeared. Then the cry went up: "Here she comes." The crowds cheered. The soldiers presented arms. The band played and every eye was focused on the Duke and Duchess, "who plainly dressed, stood bowing and smiling on the platform." Members of council were introduced to the couple, as were several other people, including two children from the Ontario School for the Deaf.

Just as the chorus began to sing "Rule Britannia," the train began to move and they quickly changed to "God Save the King." The band played, the soldiers presented arms once more, and the crowd disbanded as the train disappeared from sight.

The *Intelligencer* asked its readers what all the fuss was about. Its answer was "We were cheering for the great nation to which we belong, on whose flag the sun never sets, whose martial drum beat rolls around the world, and under whose government men and women enjoy a greater measure of freedom than anywhere else on earth. And in the person of the Duke we were cheering the grandson of the good Queen whose reign was a benediction to the world, and who was rightly named Victoria the Good."

Thirty-eight years later, on May 21, 1939, Belleville welcomed King George VI and Queen Elizabeth. When the royal couple came out on the lighted rear platform of the royal coach at the station, the *Intelligencer* stated "that no drama was more intense." The crowd of thousands, many of whom had been there for hours, sang, and then sang again "God Save the King."[16] Fearful that the train might leave shortly for Toronto, the crowd began to chant, "We want the King. We want the King." Then, light was seen coming from within the coach. There was a sudden burst of light as the door opened. "Into that light moved with fairy light silence a figure in white."

It was the queen, followed almost immediately by the king. The crowd burst into cheers. The band started to play the national anthem and thousands took up the words. The king and queen "began to wave those significant gestures of theirs. With her left hand she waved with that gracious style of movement which the world has admired so much," a style similar to that of Elizabeth II.

All too soon, the train began to move west. Those at the Cannifton Road crossing had the last, best view of the couple as they stood on the platform, still waving graciously. Within a few months, the royal family would become a symbol of freedom and resistance as the Second World War broke out. Although not seen by the crowd as the monarchs stood on the train platform in 1939, their daughter Elizabeth would return to a royal welcome in October 1951.

The royal tour would be long remembered because of a royal gift. Queen Elizabeth, the wife of George VI and mother of Elizabeth II, gave acorns from Windsor forest in England to rural schools during the tour. Local schools included King George, Cannifton, and Bayview. The royal oak was preserved for several years after King George School closed and the property was redeveloped as King George Square. Finally, the oak succumbed to the same fate as the school, which had been demolished in 1994.[17]

War Again, 1939–45

THE PASSAGE OF time has meant the loss of many men and women who can recall and describe the events of the Second World War. Most countries were actively involved, and all others were affected in many ways. Fortunately, there have been several books and documentaries that vividly record the war years.[18]

Farley Mowat's book *The Regiment* shows the extent of the overseas effort. In the opening pages, he expressed his "gratitude to the soldiers of the Regiment for their understanding of the fact that I could personally identify so few of them in this story, which touches upon the lives of more than four thousand men."[19] Not all of these men came from Belleville and from the counties of Hastings and Prince Edward, but a substantial number did. To quote Mowat: "The Regiment received its mobilization orders on September 1, 1939. Six years later, on October 4, 1945, it laid down its arms. The story of those six years is the story of four thousand volunteers. It is the story of men who came from the relief rolls of the Depression, from the aimless wandering of the unemployed; from law courts; from business offices; from wealthy homes; and from tar-paper shacks."[20]

Mowat was in a particularly good position to describe the campaign, since he was a regimental intelligence officer with the Hasty Ps and wrote with the authority of a man who was there. After the war, Mowat went back and retraced the regiment's footsteps. In flowing prose, he described the soldiers' training in Canada, the sea voyage to England, more training, the Sicilian campaign (July–August 1943), the crossing to the Italian mainland, and the struggle to liberate the Italian peninsula. Towards the end of the Italian campaign, the troops boarded ships to Marseilles and moved overland to Belgium. On April 12, 1945, the regiment tasted action in northern Europe for the first time. Early in May, word came that the enemy in northwest Europe had surrendered. On September 1, the Hasty Ps left Holland, and, after a brief pause in England, sailed for home. The troop train arrived at the Belleville CNR station at 9:00 a.m. on October 4 to a tumultuous welcome. Not all Belleville soldiers returned on that train, because many had served in other units, as well as in the air force, navy, and merchant marine.

Almost twenty years after the publication of Mowat's book, the role of an outstanding local war veteran was remembered in another book, this one by journalist and trade association executive Ken Smith. In *Duffy's Regiment*, Smith recorded the career of Angus Duffy, who served as regimental sergeant major during the war, and later commanded the regiment. According to the Right Honourable Lord Tweedsmuir, a former commander of the regiment who was "mightily proud" of being a Canadian soldier, even though he was not a Canadian citizen, Duffy "was regarded as representing the very spirit of the Regiment."[21] His "devotion to the Regiment was absolute. He drove his men and himself to the ultimate."[22] Although Smith was with the regiment in Italy for only 144 days — he was seriously wounded and forced to leave — he came to know and admire Duffy. In fact, everyone who knew Duffy was delighted when he was made a Member of the Order of Canada for his efforts in both military and civilian fields. The Quinte Region Emergency Measures Organization, scouting, and Belleville City Council were only three groups to which Duffy made outstanding contributions.

In May 1957, Second World War battle honours were awarded and "no unit got more than the Hastings and Prince Edward Regiment's 31."[23] These honours commemorated the battles in which the regiment had distinguished itself. Its honours already included battles in which men of its predecessor units had participated before 1920. They were for Northwest Canada (1885), and nine campaigns in the First World War, including the Somme, Ypres, and Amiens.

It is fortunate that, in 1995, Ruth Howard and the Quinte Writers Guild helped to preserve many veterans' stories. One of the heroes was Lieutenant General Chester Hull, a bomber pilot. Before joining the Royal Canadian Air Force (RCAF), Hull had served in a militia unit in Ottawa and in the Navy. In 1940, he was posted to Camp Borden, where he received his wings

The soldiers of Hastings and Prince Edward counties were welcomed home after the Second World War. Citizens watched from the street and the steps and windows of Belleville Post Office (southwest corner of Bridge and Pinnacle streets). Courtesy of Archives of Ontario, C 5-1-0-131-3.

from First World War flying ace Billy Bishop. In England, he flew Halifax and then Lancaster bombers. On one occasion, flak blew nine holes in his aircraft. Following the war, he stayed with the RCAF and served in various capacities, achieving the rank of lieutenant general (air marshall) in 1972, when he was appointed Vice Chief of the Defence Staff.[24]

Although some veterans were willing to talk about their war experiences, many, especially in the army, where they had witnessed first-hand and up close the violence of war, were not.

Some would talk about the lighter side of war. For example, one army private recalled to family members his experience "liberating" French currency from a bank in Cannes by using powder taken from land mines to blow open the safe. He and others were then subjected to a German mortar attack when smoke was seen rising from the bank.[25]

In 2002, award-winning journalist Andrew Clark wrote a book that showed "another side of what many consider our proudest military campaign" — namely the death by execution of the "only soldier the Canadians had executed since the First World War." Private Harold Pringle of Flinton was put to death by a five-man firing squad on July 5, 1945. A member of the Hasty Ps who had deserted, Pringle was ostensibly put to death for murder. Clark's controversial book shed light on an intriguing case that had been closed for almost a half-century.[26]

On the home front, Belleville citizens responded as they had during the First World War. Companies such as Reliance and Bristol Aircraft produced planes. Airmen from Commonwealth countries trained at Canadian Forces Base Trenton and used many buildings in Belleville. In fact, the RCAF took over the Ontario School for the Deaf, and its students were dispersed throughout Belleville.

Rationing of such items as meat and gas was introduced, and residents carefully guarded their ration coupon books. New cars were impossible to purchase, and tires and replacement parts were scarce.

Although several hundred men were lost overseas, some died at home. For example, Major Charles Eardley Wilmot lost his head to an airplane propeller when he walked into the path of a taxiing plane on the tarmac at Trenton. The pilot had not seen him. One of the first men in Canada to hold a pilot's licence, Wilmot had gained local fame in the First World War by regularly flying above his parents' home on West Dundas Street (near the Ontario School for the Deaf) and dropping his dirty laundry on the lawn. In 1927, he served as mayor of Belleville. There is a rumour that the Wilmot house on West Dundas is haunted, although it is unclear who (or what) is doing the haunting.

Belleville residents took time to relax during the war. Swimming in the Bay of Quinte and the Moira River was an important pastime. Residents with gas to spare went to Oak Lake. Fishing was also popular. On September 27, 1940, W.I. Cole caught a 32½-pound muskellunge in the Moira River near Corbyville. The fish measured four feet, two inches. In 1942, citizens were discussing the possibility of a Moira River walkway; the dream would be realized in 2002. The following year, lawyer/historian W.C. Mikel predicted that Zwick's Island would become the site of a beautiful park. Formerly an island, it had been connected by a roadway to the Bay Bridge Road. The future park was expected to be named Quinte Park; however, it would continue to be

Students at Belleville's only public secondary school, Belleville Collegiate Institute and Vocational School (BCIVS), were famed for their annual Kampus Kapers program highlighting various athletic activities. Unfortunately, one pyramid-building exercise led to a court case (Murray vs. Belleville Board of Education) in 1943. Fortunately for the school board and the supervising teacher, the judge ruled that there was no negligence and the action was dismissed.[28]

War or no war, neatness was seen as important. In 1944, Front Street merchants co-operated in collecting refuse previously swept to the street curb in the morning, after the city street sweeper had made its rounds during the night. Front Street had "presented a dirty and untidy appearance during the day."[29]

The role of Belleville-area residents in the Second World War has been well-documented by historians. These accounts become increasingly important to our memory as our veterans decline in numbers.

known as Zwick's Park after it was developed in 1967 as the city's official centennial project commemorating the centennial of Confederation.[27]

Above:
Angus Duffy, celebrated member of the regiment. Courtesy of Hastings County Historical Society, Mika Collection (Military File).

Right:
The Hastings and Prince Edward Regimental Cenotaph in front of the Belleville Armouries. Courtesy of Hastings County Historical Society, Mika Collection (Military File).

11
THE POST-WAR ERA

Peace: Problems, and Progress

THE SECOND WORLD War was over, but the adjustment to peacetime living was gradual. Rationed items slowly returned to the shelves. Industries converted to peacetime production. Many women left the factories, often reluctantly, and resumed or started home lives. The returning members of the armed forces resumed their work or found new occupations. Many veterans returned to secondary school in Belleville, or to post-secondary institutions elsewhere. Many married their sweethearts and settled down to create families. Displaced people (sometimes referred to as "delayed pioneers") from Europe soon began to arrive.

With the population increasing and no homes constructed during the war, there was an increasing concern for the homeless. Determined to help resolve this serious issue, the Belleville Shriners approached city council on September 7, 1946, and asked for help for the homeless. Council allowed some families to move into the City Hall auditorium, where they remained for two years. Council also provided temporary housing in the city barn.

In December 1946, Angus Duffy, of Second World War fame, was elected as a Belleville alderman "on a platform of expediting housing for veterans. His message was blunt. Ex-servicemen should have priority … but they were being outbid by civilians who had stayed home and made money."[1] A battle followed, with groups such as the Belleville Property Owners and the directors of the chamber of commerce opposed to land for veterans' housing, but, in the spring of 1949, council voted 8–7 to approve the development of the former County Home property on the eastern edge of the city. Streets, from First to Sixth, were opened up for veterans' housing. Streets in the area of Hastings Drive were opened for general housing.

More people meant the need for more schools. In 1954, Quinte Secondary School became the second public secondary school, joining BCIVS. Moira Secondary School followed five years later. The name "Moira" proved a problem on at least one occasion. In its early years, a band scheduled to play at the school ended up at the hamlet of Moira in Huntingdon Township. It was quickly rerouted and arrived in time to entertain the students.

Separate school education took a significant step forward on Sunday, October 23, 1960, when Nicholson Catholic College was officially opened. With its roots in one room of St. Michael's Academy in 1930, the high school had moved into the former convent on John Street in 1941.[2]

The Women's Suffrage movement, with strong roots in Belleville through Ontario Business College principal and MLA J.W. Johnson, continued to be important locally. In December, 1953, voters elected two female aldermen for the two-year term — Effie McCabe and Jane Forrester. They beat out several former aldermen, school board trustees, and veterans. In her first attempt at office, Mrs. Forrester, wife of a prominent surgeon, led the polls with 3,352 votes, setting a new record in the number of votes attained. She became so popular over the next two years that she handily defeated incumbent mayor Jack Both in the election for the 1956–58 council, becoming Belleville's first female mayor. She chose not to run for the 1959–60 council, but continued to devote time to such matters as the need for parks and playgrounds, and the importance of cleaning up the polluted bay.

Returning veterans helped to open up the communications field. Radio came to Belleville in 1946, when CJBQ took to the airwaves. Originally known as "The Voice of the Bay of Quinte" with a frequency of 1230, the station later changed to 800 on the dial. The official opening took place on the BCIVS stage on August 15. The station was housed in a small frame building at 11 Victoria Avenue. The structure was so weak that the floor of the second-storey record library had to be reinforced to support the weight of the old 78 rpm records. Bill Stovin, now of Saskatoon, was the first station manager. The station has several claims to fame. It has only had two sports editors in its sixty-year history — a pair of Jacks — Jack Devine and Jack Miller. Its morning phone-in show is said to be one of the oldest in Canada. Moreover, despite the trend towards giant broadcasting conglomerates, the Morton family has operated the station for its entire history.

The 1950s witnessed a building boom. In 1951, a new Masonic temple was opened on Foster Avenue. In 1955, a new three-storey Dominion Parasite Lab (Bug House) replaced the historic former brick residence that had housed the lab at the corner of Bleecker and Dundas streets.

Health issues were a concern in the growing community. A major addition to the 1939 West Wing of the Belleville General Hospital was opened on October 17, 1956. Although the

Honourable Mackinnon Phillips, Ontario Minister of Health, attended, he was a spectator. Practically everybody assumed that he would cut the ribbon. However, "in a happy gesture," he relinquished that honour in favour of Mrs. W.C. Mikel, the senior member of the board and president of the WCA from 1918–32. Mrs. Mikel "was taken completely by surprise."[3]

The building boom continued. In 1959, hospital "services reached new heights" with the opening of a seven-storey wing, the crowning glory to that point in time. Some 6,000 visitors toured the building on opening day.[4]

What might be regarded as a religious revival took place in the late 1950s and early 1960s, as several religious buildings were constructed. They included: First Pentecostal (1953), Sons of Jacob Synagogue (1955), St. Margaret's-on-the-Hill Anglican (1957), Calvary Temple (1960), St. Joseph's Roman Catholic (1961), St. Columba Presbyterian (1963), Church of Jesus Christ of Latter Day Saints (1964), Emmanuel Baptist (1962), Holy Trinity Lutheran (1963), and College Hill United (1964). These were followed within a few years by the relocation of the Salvation Army on Victoria Avenue (1969), and the building of Eastminster United (1969), and Holy Trinity Greek Orthodox (1973).

As they had done so many times in the past, Belleville's citizens had responded to the challenges of the post-war period.

World Champions: The McFarlands, 1959

Prague, Czechoslovakia, 1959. CJBQ sports director Jack Devine, tired, his voice hoarse, calls the play-by-play action. Thousands of fans in the Belleville area listen, hardly daring to believe that the local team can be making sports history. The game ends, and Devine proudly announces that Belleville has won the World Hockey Championship. Certainly city teams had won many championships — and would win more in the future. But this was a world title, and in hockey, Canadians' favourite sport.

The Belleville McFarlands, a Senior A hockey team usually known as the Belleville Macs, had won the world championship by defeating several of the world's best amateur teams. In the preliminary round they defeated Poland, Switzerland, and Czechoslovakia. The final game was against a very strong Russian team, and the Macs won 3–1. *Intelligencer* sports editor George Carver attributed the victory to the work of the "Four Bees" — Geordie Bell, Red Berenson, Denis Boucher, and Moe Benoit. "The latter trio played superb hockey coming and going. Goalie Geordie Bell was out of this world."[5]

The Belleville McFarlands, Canadian Allan Cup Champions in 1958 and World Hockey Champions in 1959. Courtesy of Hastings County Historical Society, Mika Collection.

Organized in the mid-1950s, the team took its name from Harry J. McFarland, the dynamic founder of a successful construction company in Picton. Originally part of the Eastern Ontario Senior B League, the Belleville team became an original member of the Senior A League in 1956, after hockey legend Wren Blair came from Whitby to persuade Belleville team manager Drury Denyes to move the team up to Senior A. Denyes was reluctant, because he didn't feel that Belleville could get players who were good enough. "Wait a minute," Blair said. "We don't need any more players. I'll tell you what, Drury. If you'll agree to go Senior A, I'll help you build

your team, too, behind the scenes." Denyes agreed. Blair then called "Bep Guidolin," who was the player-coach in Timmins, and asked him how much money he was making. When Guidolin told Blair that he was making $100 a week, Blair responded that he could make $250 in Belleville, but he would have to bring five good Senior A players with him. That evening, Guidolin lined up Geordie Bell, Moe Benoit, Floyd Crawford, Minnie Menard, and Moe Savard. The next day, Blair told an excited Denyes the names of the five and the money it was going to cost.[6] Blair almost regretted helping Belleville get the players, because at the end of the season, Belleville finished second in the league, just three points behind Blair's own Whitby Dunlops. He wondered if he had created a monster that would beat his own team. The league finals between the two clubs went to seven games before the Dunlops won. They went on to win the Allan Cup in 1957 and the World International Championship the following year.

Meanwhile, Denyes had been strengthening the Belleville Macs, and the team followed the Dunlops' lead. In 1957–58, the Macs won the Eastern Division and went west, where they played the Kelowna Packers. Down three games to one, the amazing Macs came back, on May 1, 1958, to defeat the Packers and win the Allan Cup for the first and only time. Belleville goalie Geordie Bell was described as the "hero of the series." The following year, the Macs went to Europe. All of Canada was said to be behind them, and the team emerged victorious. On their return to Belleville on April 1, the players enjoyed a heroic reception. Thousands cheered as team members were driven down Front Street. They were the toast of the town, and several chose to settle here permanently.

Unfortunately, not long after their return, it was discovered that the Memorial Arena Commission and the city were faced with a deficit of over $110,000. Financial problems forced the dissolution of the team, "a team which had done so much to lift the morale of all Canadians and had been such successful ambassadors."[7]

Several businessmen threatened court action unless there was a full investigation into the city's finances, particularly in connection with the arena commission. The Ontario Minister of Municipal Affairs agreed, and cabinet appointed a Royal Commission under Judge A.R. Willmott of Cobourg. Judge Willmott convened the hearing in Belleville and heard witnesses for fifteen days. The *Intelligencer* and CJBQ gave extensive coverage to the hearings, and the citizens were not pleased by much of what they read or heard. On October 31 — Halloween was perhaps an appropriate day given its emphasis on "tricks" — Willmott completed his report. He had worked quickly, hoping to release the report "in the expectation that the 1959 municipal elections should clear the air…."[8]

Judge Willmott began his report on a positive note, commenting that the citizens of Belleville had been "well and faithfully served" by their various boards and commissions, with the exception of the arena commission, which looked after the Memorial Arena and the hockey club.[9]

Willmott then commented favourably on efforts by the city's auditor, J.D. Lewars, to alert councils to certain accounting problems. However, the city auditor had failed to notify council promptly in 1958 that "certain hockey players were on the Public Works' payroll" and were being paid by cheques issued by the treasurer.[10] These payments, listed as "Advances to Memorial Arena" and covering hockey expenditures for parts of three seasons, totalled $95,006.92. Added to other city expenditures called into question in the auditor's 1958 report, the total for such expenditures came to $232,099.18.[11] Had the auditor "read the Minutes of Council with any degree of care … he would have noted that it owned and operated a Hockey Club." Willmott concluded that the auditor should not have accepted the treasurer's word that the hockey club accounts were not any part of the city audit.[12]

Lewars responded to Willmott's criticism by pointing out that he had gone to Drury Denyes to inquire why payments to hockey players were coming from the city Public Works Department. Denyes had assured him that this was merely "a temporary arrangement to finance hockey and that when the season was over and the Hockey Club accounts were settled it would all be repaid." Playoff revenues were expected to cover the deficit. Lewars continued: "Now we have no reason to doubt Mr. Denyes' word. He was the Hockey Manager, the City Manager and the City Treasurer and he had been here for ten years and nothing had occurred to make us suspicious of anything he might tell us."[13]

The city auditor had revealed a main problem. Councils had placed too much responsibility on one person. Drury Denyes had been treasurer since June 1948, city manager-treasurer since October 1957, and hockey manager (directed to follow the instructions of the arena commission) since July 1956. Moreover, fans and council members were pressuring him to maintain a winning team. When Mayor Gerald Hyde told Denyes that he was worried about the calibre of the team and told him to strengthen it, Denyes took the mayor at his word and did just that.[14]

There was inadequate gate revenue, and each week Denyes would submit a list of players he wanted on the Public Works' payroll, and they were put on. Another reason for this move was that it would exempt the hockey club from paying the Ontario Hospital Act tax, which would cost the arena commission nine percent of gate receipts. That tax would have come into effect unless 60 percent of the players earned $20 a game or less. Denyes admitted to not telling any member of the arena commission, or any member of council, what he was doing. Willmott admired "the frankness" with which Denyes told the story of the McFarlands, and of his efforts to give Belleville a successful team.[15] "There is not a scintilla of evidence to show that Drury Denyes appropriated public funds to his own use," Willmott wrote.[16] Nevertheless, he "failed to carry out the duties of his office." He proceeded "to use the City's monies as a secret reserve and never failing source of hockey players' salaries."[17] Ron Cass, the astute Belleville lawyer who represented Denyes at the hearing, spoke of Denyes' preoccupation with the team as "a magnificent obsession."[18] Willmott felt that Cass acted very wisely on Denyes' behalf, although he did accuse the lawyer of having "drawn a magnificent red herring across the real issues" involved in the hearing.[19]

Willmott was critical of council, the auditor, and the Bank of Montreal for allowing payroll cheques with only one signature. Moreover, the bank came in for additional criticism because it accepted other documents with a single signature and allowed the arena commission to operate by way of overdrafts, which it was not allowed to do.[20] The city was advised to do some hard bargaining with the bank.

Much of the blame was attributed collectively to the councils of the mid-1950s. Stanley E. Fennell, Q.C., the able committee counsel, doubted "if any greater exhibition of municipal mismanagement has occurred in Ontario," and a troubleshooter for the Department of Municipal Affairs addressed council with these words, "I said that I was amazed that there were so many lawyers on the Council and yet the City had persisted for several years in doing things in an illegal manner."[21] Among other things, councils had authorized a single signature on cheques, permitted inadequate bonding of the treasurer (only $22,500 when the city budget was over $2,300,000), and had failed to seek Ontario Municipal Board approval for the purchase of a parking lot. Willmott concluded that there had been "gross negligence on the part of the Mayor and Council of the City of Belleville in those years."[22] In summary, "Council had no real knowledge of the state of the City's finances from month to month. They were apparently willing to remain in the dark until the bombshell of the Treasurer's illegal hockey expenditure brought the whole issue of the City's finances into public view."[23]

Individual council members were singled out. At a council meeting on November 5, 1956, Alderman Gerald Hyde spoke of the splendid work of the team manager and said, "Under no consideration will the taxpayer have to pay anything." At the same meeting, Alderman Claude Tice, a ten-year veteran of council and chairman of the arena commission, told council, "I, as Chairman, do not know, nor does any member of the Commission know, the financial arrangements with the hockey team, and that is as it should be." In his report, Willmott described Mayor Hyde as "certainly interested in promoting the Hockey Club activities," and said that "his actions may have been due more to political expediency than to any other reason."[24] As to the arena committee and its chairman, Alderman Claude E. Tice, Willmott suggested that they "be relegated to the limbo of the municipal archives."[25]

Willmott had a flair for dramatic language. He allowed a fair degree of latitude in the hearings and noted that there was "a good deal of vigorous political infighting engaged in by Council members and officials."[26] His hope was that the hearing would clear the air with respect to "amateur hockey" in Canada, and might be a lesson to other municipalities. To illustrate the point, he included a contract Denyes drew up for Fiori Goegan for the 1958–59 season.[27] Goegan was guaranteed $185 per week for 23 weeks, a bonus of $250 if the team finished first, a bonus of $250 if the club won the world championship, and guaranteed employment at a rate of $75 per week during the off-season. Willmott's conclusion was that this matter "might reflect on the price that Canadians are willing to pay for a winning team."

The Royal Commission was a learning experience for Belleville's taxpayers. They learned from City Solicitor Bob Pringle that he was recommending a special assessment on the city's 1960 tax bills. This special levy of $142,000 would include $110,000 for hockey and $32,000 for accumulated arena losses. In addition, future tax bills would have to deal with an additional $469,500 deficit covering a variety of unbudgeted items from 1955.[28]

Willmott included this statement: "The City of Belleville needs, and I have no doubt the coming year will have, a Mayor who will in fact be the Head of the Council and who can and will provide leadership in bringing about the gradual and orderly solution of the City's financial difficulties and make a clean break from the present disastrous policy of political expediency."[29]

To quote the *Ontario Intelligencer* of March 16, 1959:

> This story could only have happened in Canada, where hockey enthusiasm and the obsession to produce the best hockey players in the world might well prevail over reason. When the Macs had caught on fire and defeated team after team, when the desire to beat the last opponent and win the World Championship had gripped the Macs' boosters and supporters, when Bellevillians shouted "Go, Macs, go!" and the hockey fever bordered on hysteria, anything was possible. Nobody asked, "How are we going to pay for this?"

The Amazing Mikas

NICK AND HELMA Mika have been among Belleville's most industrious and talented citizens. Arriving in Belleville from the Ukraine after the Second World War, they worked at various jobs, and began a part-time industrial silkscreening business in the basement of their home. They produced a variety of items for businesses and even silkscreened lines onto running shoes for Bata Shoes, numbers for circular dials on telephones, and covers to conceal land mines.

Their love for their new homeland led them to write and publish books about Canada, especially relating to local history, railways, and the United Empire Loyalists. One of their first books was *Mosaic of Belleville: An Illustrated History of a City*, published in 1966. It featured many silkscreened pictures of heritage buildings and streetscapes. Each picture contained as many as seven colours, and each colour was screened by hand and had to dry overnight before the next one was applied. When silkscreening became too time-consuming and expensive, the Mikas devoted more time to reprinting earlier histories, especially from the Maritimes and Ontario, as well as county atlases. They also made it possible for authors to write local histories by helping them to obtain funding, thereby earning the thanks of the writers and the plaudits of readers across Canada.

Nick and Helma Mika were renowned for their publishing ventures. Here, long-time Belleville Mayor George Zegouras presents them with a certificate of commendation at a special ceremony hosted by the Hastings County Historical Society on June 4, 1985. Photo by author.

Arguably, their major project was the *Encyclopedia of Ontario,* which included three volumes containing condensed histories of no fewer than 5,000 places, all within the province. It opened with Aaron Provincial Park in the Kenora District and ended with Zurich, a village in Huron County. The first volume, published in 1977, "was the dedicated occupation of Nick and Helma Mika and their staff for four concentrated years." The other volumes appeared in 1981 and 1983. William Morley of Queen's University wrote: "The result of these Herculean labours is a comprehensive work of reference which, though it will eventually require a supplement, is not likely ever to be superseded."[30] Researchers will find copies of this encyclopedia in many archive locations, including the Reading Room of the Archives of Ontario, where I recently made use of the well-thumbed volumes.

The Sixties and Seventies

THE 1960S AND 1970s brought about many changes, both to Belleville's appearance and to the lives of its citizens.

As the sixties began, Belleville lost one of its most important buildings. The historic Hastings County Court House, erected in 1838–39, was demolished and a new County Court House and Administration Building was erected. Many people opposed the demolition, including members of the Hastings County Historical Society, who examined and toured the building, stressed its historical nature, and persuaded county council to reconsider the demolition. However, the building's deteriorating condition and the various aromas coming from the attached jail convinced council that it had to go.

Actually, the demolition of the courthouse benefited the historical society. Not only did the county allow the society to use the 3,000-square-foot former registry office as a museum and archives, but the county also transferred various records and paintings to the society. Among the transferred records were "misplaced" stock certificates from transportation companies, which the society was able to return to their proper owners.

The view from the Court House Hill changed in 1964. For almost a century, railway tracks had run through the centre of Belleville, along Pinnacle Street. Motorists travelling east and west along main streets (such as Dundas, Bridge, and Victoria) frequently had to wait for the trains. As well, motorists travelling north and south on Pinnacle Street had to share the road with the trains. Fortunately, most of the trains were very short. Although passenger trains of the former Grand Junction Railway had originally used the line, by the 1960s the CNR used the line only to move a few freight cars from industries in the southern part of the city and the CPR line near the waterfront to the main CNR line. Belleville residents were pleased when the railway decided to abandon the line and lift the rails. The event was celebrated during Railway Week, in May 1964. To mark the occasion, the CNR brought a special train down Pinnacle Street to the Quinte Hotel so that Rotarians could hold an excursion by rail to Cobourg.

Veterans were in the news. On May 17, 1964, before an estimated 5,000 people at the fairgrounds, the Hasty Ps received new colours and the freedom of the city. The following year, on February 16, many veterans were upset when Canada's new Maple Leaf flag flew for the first time atop City Hall clock tower. For some time, the new flag was unpopular with many veterans because they had served overseas under the Union Jack and the Canadian Red Ensign.

Belleville's population was changing. After Chinese troops stormed into Tibetan monasteries and rounded up Tibetan spiritual leaders some fifty years ago, approximately five-hundred Tibetans sought refugee status in Canada. They settled in three main locales in Ontario: Belleville, Lindsay, and Toronto. Belleville "claimed to be host to Canada's earliest Tibetan community, providing a base on which its unique culture could thrive in this country," and for many years it held the largest number of Tibetans in Canada.[31]

Anniversaries were important. In May 1966, the Hastings County Historical Society held a celebration to mark the 150th birthday of the official beginning of Belleville as a town site in 1816. Then, in 1967, the city celebrated Canada's centennial. A committee selected Zwick's Park as the city's official centennial project. Funding was shared equally by the federal, provincial, and municipal governments, and the amazing improvement of Zwick's Park, home of major celebrations over the years, began. Other local centennial projects included *Historic Hastings*, a history of Hastings County by Gerry Boyce, and *The Rambling River*, a history of Thurlow Township (now part of Belleville), by Mary Plumpton. Many local schools used *Historic Hastings* as a textbook.

Centennial Secondary School is a reminder of the importance of Canada's centennial year. It is not the only such reminder. Originally paired with Sir Sandford Fleming Community College in Peterborough as part of the new system of colleges of applied arts and technology, Loyalist Community College had its start in 1967.[32] Until a permanent home was soon found on a 138-acre site on Wallbridge Road (later known as Wallbridge-Loyalist Road) in Sidney Township, Loyalist occupied the second floor of Centennial Secondary School. Centennial teachers were envious of Loyalist teachers (later to be called professors), with their small classes and telephones in every teacher's office. Also in 1967, the annual Sir Mackenzie Bowell Award was introduced to recognize an individual who had made an outstanding contribution to local education. The first recipient was E. Arnold Orr, retiring superintendent of education.

Many Belleville residents today fondly recall the contribution of Don and Rita Foster to Belleville celebrations. The Fosters operated a clown/costume agency, and their volunteers and costumes were found at Santa Claus parades and similar events for many years. To the delight of children of all ages, Don appeared as Bozo the Clown. In memory of their son, Billy, the Fosters also set up an ever-growing Christmas display around their Emily Street home. In recent years, the display can be found at the Alemite Park every Christmas season. Many other residents have set up their own Christmas displays, which are highlights of the annual seniors' bus tour, when the city's bus drivers volunteer one evening to drive hundreds of seniors to some of the exciting holiday displays.

The 1960s saw a continuation of the building boom that had begun after the war. A new post office was constructed in 1960 at the corner of Pinnacle and Station streets. In 1961, a twelve-year dream was realized when the Victoria and Grey Trust Company opened a new office building (now the site of a Scotiabank office) immediately north of City Hall. The East End branch library followed in 1964, the same year as the YMCA moved from its downtown Campbell Street location to its present location on Victoria Avenue. In 1965, the police moved from the Market Square Building into the former YMCA, and the new home of the *Intelligencer*, which housed CJBQ for several years, opened at the corner of Pinnacle and East Bridge.

Belleville's industrial base was also growing. The Northeast Industrial Park, which had seemed a deserted commons prior to the mid-sixties, had five industries on site by the summer of 1968. One of the most important plants would be Procter and Gamble, arriving in 1975.

A significant change in retail marketing in Belleville was witnessed in 1971. On August 18, Mayor Russell Scott cut the ribbon officially opening the Quinte Mall on North Front Street, and 10,000 people surged into the main concourse as the red and white ribbon parted. The continued expansion of the mall, and the subsequent proliferation of retail businesses along North Front Street and Bell Boulevard, was a serious blow to the downtown.

With the city's changing business pattern, several long-time Front Street businesses closed or moved over time. These included Walker's Hardware, James Texts, McIntosh Brothers, Leslie's Shoes, and Stroud's. It would be several years before the downtown would revive.

Fire also decimated some downtown businesses. A major loss occurred on May 1, 1972, when fire destroyed five downtown businesses, lawyers' offices, and apartments on the northeast corner of Front and Victoria streets. Lost in the blaze were the historic Victoria Block (housing King Sol Discount), and Stephen Licence Bicycle Shop. Fortunately, Stephen Licence was able to relocate, first to the former McCarthy Theatre (now the Empire Theatre), and still later to another Front Street location. Fires affected more than the downtown area. In the mid-1970s, St. Thomas' Church was destroyed almost a century after the previous devastating fire. Again, the church was restored. This time, interior columns supported the weight of the roof, since the weakened walls could not do so.

Major changes took place in Foster Ward during the early 1970s. The waterfront began to take on added importance, as residential development began to replace industrial usage. Improvements included sewers and improved roads. Building projects included Maurice Rollins' Anchorage (with 89 luxury condominiums overlooking the harbour), and Pier 31, at the eastern end of Keegan Parkway on the site of a former Graham Food Processing plant.

Women continued to join professions previously open only to men. In June 1972, two women made local history when they were sworn in as the first female officers in the Belleville Police Department (now known as the Belleville Police Service).

Belleville's first business with both an elevator and an escalator was built in the mid-1970s. As construction got under way, the *Ontario Intelligencer* reported on June 12, 1975, that the addition of Century Place at the corner of Bridge and Front streets would be "a shot of adrenalin for downtown." The president of the Merchants' Association noted that "Century Place is the first step in city core re-development — a step that must be followed by the rest of the downtown community."[33]

One celebration in the 1970s that made all others pale by comparison, was the one-hundredth anniversary of Belleville's incorporation as a city. As the year approached, city council set up a committee to help organize the celebration. With Tom Baird and others leading the way, the committee scheduled events throughout the year, rather than on a single day as in 1878. One part of the celebration that almost didn't happen was the giant parade on July 1. It was to resemble the 1878 parade, though on a smaller scale. Fortunately, parade planning came together at the last moment and the event was a great success.

Belleville's centennial year saw the first event held in the new Quinte Sports Centre, constructed at no cost to the taxpayers through funds donated by the provincial lottery and through fundraising by members of the Belleville Yardmen Benefit Fund. Although the Yardmen had also contributed funds to many other local groups, the last roll of the drum took place on July 26, 1979, after the volunteer Yardmen lottery-ticket sellers found it impossible to compete with the expanding provincial lottery.[34] Nevertheless, the Quinte Sports Centre was to serve the community well, becoming the site of many leagues and tournaments, and the home of the Belleville Bulls junior hockey team.

The enthusiasm generated by Belleville's centennial year and the other events of this period would carry through the remaining years of the century.

The Old and New City Hall[35]

IT WAS A sunny but very chilly autumn afternoon when several hundred guests gathered on the Market Square behind City Hall to witness history in the making. The event, on October 30, 1988, marked the official opening of the restored/renovated Belleville City Hall.

A heritage building erected in 1872–73, the Belleville landmark had fallen on difficult times. Not only were interior and exterior repairs essential, but working conditions for the growing city staff were becoming unpleasant, despite periodic efforts to improve them. For example, for two years after the Second World War, a critical housing shortage led to a few families living in the auditorium. When they left on June 6, 1948, council directed that "the City Hall not again be used as living quarters." Staff had found it very difficult to work while trying to ignore the sounds of young children crying or playing, as well as the smells of cabbage and other foods cooking. By the early 1950s, the auditorium at the east end of the second floor had been completely converted to offices, and the large stage curtain (dating back to the time of the First World War) was stored in the attic, sharing that space with pigeon visitors. Similarly, council gradually converted the indoor market for office use and closed it altogether in 1961. No longer could the building be known as the *market building and City Hall*. Now it was simply the *City Hall*.

Renovations and repairs were carried out from time to time, and there were several proposals for dealing with the shortage of space. In 1956, a committee considered renovating the largely unused basement to provide space for recreation groups. Alderman Claude Tice thought that this renovation could provide an auditorium to seat 350 persons. In 1975, council employed architect Paul Wiegand to prepare a feasibility study on improvements needed to enhance public approaches inside the building. Wiegand was especially critical of the long, central staircase that posed a safety hazard and made access difficult. Mayor J. Ben Corke agreed with this view. He noted that the long staircase led not to the imposing council chambers, but rather to two small rooms marked "Staff Only Men" and "Staff Only Women." Mayor Corke summed up council's position in 1977: "It's difficult to decide how to re-arrange a 104-year-old building that's been repeatedly hashed about to accommodate the growth of City Hall services."

Meanwhile, staff continued to work under difficult conditions. The Hastings County Public Institutions Panel warned that safety was a serious issue, and pieces of masonry continued to fall from the tower. In 1985, the firm of Noble Lambooy Greer Galloway Architects and Engineers suggested several options. These ranged from the creation of an additional third floor within City Hall (and the building of a 10,000-square foot addition, on supports, over the Market Square, to the restoration of both the existing City Hall and the city-owned Cablevue Building across Front Street. The company estimated the overall cost at $2,700,000. This was double the figure council had contemplated the previous year.

Belleville aldermen Bob Dolan (left) and Ross McDougall (centre) listen to Bel-Con Engineering President Bill White explain how he could provide 10,000 additional square feet of space inside City Hall by adding a third floor and renovating the attic. Courtesy of Hastings County Historical Society, Mika Collection.

Early in 1986, Bel-Con Engineering Ltd. entered the picture. Company president Bill White was the lead player in the plan that would lead to the highly successful restoration and renovation of City Hall. White's imagination had been fired after he climbed the tower-access stairs to the attic space and was astounded to see, for the first time, the giant twelve-foot deep timber trusses spanning the full width of the building. Finding a hole in the ceiling, he climbed down a ladder into a ten-foot-deep void. A dim light revealed a suspended ceiling ten feet below. His measurements showed that not one, but two additional floors (with generous headroom) could be created within the existing building.

White was a dreamer, but a very practical one, and this dream would soon be realized. On July 4, 1986, he presented council with a seventy-six-page report concluding that Belleville "had the opportunity to renovate the roof space … and to expose the magnificent and historical structure contained within to combine the past with the present in a way which could rival the Kingston City Hall." This was the answer that Mayor George Zegouras and his council had been looking for. By a 7–3 vote, council approved Bel-Con's plans to renovate City Hall, to add 10,000 additional feet of floor space, and to restore the exterior. Because the building was designated under the Ontario Heritage Act, the Ontario Ministry of Culture and Communications agreed to fund half of the exterior restoration.

While Bel-Con was doing the work, City Hall operations would move into King George Public School, recently closed by the Hastings County Board of Education.

Demolition of the interior of City Hall took most of the fall of 1987. Meanwhile, Bel-Con was completing design work, with Barry Johnson in charge of this phase. A five-minute encounter between White and engineering consultant Arnold Vandermeer assisted in the planning. Vandermeer suggested that everyday functions involving taxpayers should be on the ground floor, and executive functions, such as the mayor's office and council chambers, should be on the top floors. White "twigged" to this common-sense idea, and City Hall incorporated it.

As the restoration and renovation proceeded in 1988, the area's citizens — both corporate and individual — were given the opportunity to assist. A special fundraising sub-committee chaired by Alderman Selma Bochnek sought financial help to provide furnishings for special areas. There was a good response, and plaques throughout the building recognize the generosity of citizens who contributed.

City Hall from the south. The direction of the cars is a reminder that Front Street was one-way for many years. Courtesy of Hastings County Historical Society, Mika Collection.

Meeting rooms were named after several distinguished local citizens, such as Captain John W. Meyers (a founder of Belleville), Sir Mackenzie Bowell (editor of the *Intelligencer* and prime minister of Canada from 1894–96), John D. Evans (the original architect of City Hall) and John Forin (the original builder of City Hall).

Public response to the renovated/restored City Hall was overwhelming. Within a week of the opening on October 30, 1988, more than 2,000 people toured the building at four open houses. So great was the response that many people had to wait outside, braving showers and cool temperatures. Guided tours continue, upon request, to this day.

In the 1980s, when council was planning for improvements to City Hall, the hope was that the changes would accommodate staff for at least fifteen years. That time has passed, and the building is once again faced with space concerns, in part because of the amalgamation of Belleville and Thurlow Township. As a result, some former meeting areas (including the Corby Room and the Tower Room) have been converted to offices, and other spaces have been reconfigured. Nevertheless, City Hall remains as a major highlight of any visitor's tour of Belleville.[36]

A World-Famous Cemetery

QUESTION: HOW DO these books relate to Belleville?

    1. *Grave Reflections* (1995)
    2. *Bodies of Evidence* (1995)
    3. *The Backbone of History* (2002)

Answer: They all show how the study of cemeteries can be used to reconstruct history and portray the past, and they all have extensive chapters dealing with the importance of St. Thomas' Anglican Church Cemetery on Belleville's East Hill. They testify to the world attention that this cemetery has gained since 1989. That summer, a team of archaeologists, assisted by local volunteers, temporarily removed the skeletal remains of almost six-hundred individuals from the church burial ground. The subsequent study of the remains has added to anthropologists' knowledge of nineteenth-century life in Belleville.

The cemetery was one of Belleville's earliest, and was used from 1821–74. After the town council banned further burials within the town's boundaries in 1874 — largely for health reasons — the St. Thomas' congregation made good use of the unused portion of the burial ground, particularly the part lying on the north side of a small ravine that cut through the grounds. In 1887, they erected a two-storey, 30 x 60-foot "Sunday School House."[37] Then, on the eve of the First World War, when the congregation was preparing to build a new parish hall across from the church on Bridge Street, the northern section of the cemetery was sold to the Belleville School Board to provide more space for students attending the Union School (which housed Queen Victoria Public School and the Belleville High School) immediately to the north. The church received $4,500 for the land and building.[38] Another section was sold to school authorities in 1954 to "facilitate the parking of school busses [*sic*]."[39]

View of part of St. Thomas' Church Cemetery looking across Church Street to Bridge Street Methodist Church, circa 1890. Courtesy of Hastings County Historical Society, Neg. B-222.

Since 1874, almost all of the monuments in the St. Thomas' Church Cemetery have been moved from their original sites. A single stone remains *in situ*. Most surviving stones have been placed in brick cairns or fastened to the church's stone walls. Yet, the reason many of the memorials were moved from their original locations in 1989 was part of a project that helped make this cemetery one of the best known and most studied cemeteries, not only in Canada, but in all of North America.

The project had its beginning in the mid-1980s, when the congregation decided to erect a new parish centre, adjoining the church, on land that was then part of the consecrated cemetery. The decision was based on the fact that parishioners, including children and the elderly, had to cross Bridge Street to reach the parish hall. The old hall had been erected on the eve of the First World War, when Bridge Street was far less busy than it was in the 1980s. The decision was not unanimous. Some members felt that the nineteenth-century burials should not be disturbed, even though more than a century had passed since the last interment.

After the intention to clear part of the cemetery to prepare the way for the parish centre was advertised, and the approvals of the Anglican Diocese of Ontario and provincial cemetery authorities were obtained, the congregation was faced with a decision as to how the burials should be removed. According to the Ontario Cemeteries Act, whenever a cemetery has been legally closed, all bodies must be removed before the land can be used for other purposes, but the method of removal is not stipulated. A diviner (also known as a dowser) walked over the site and suggested that there would be only sixty to eighty burials affected. Based on that estimate, church authorities gave serious consideration to the possibility of excavating and studying the burials as an archaeological project, instead of the normal procedure, whereby a backhoe would remove the contents of the burial ground and the bones would be sifted out for reburial.

The Parish Centre Committee, chaired by Pam Tansley, invited Doctor Heather McKillop, an archaeologist from Trent University and a partner in Northeastern Archaeological Associates of Port Hope, to discuss the archaeological approach. The committee was enthusiastic about the prospect of important historical, cultural, and biological information being obtained from the archaeological excavation and subsequent study of the remains of the early members of the congregation and other early settlers. As a result, Doctor McKillop submitted a proposal to the committee for the archaeological excavation and study of the sixty to eighty burials from the churchyard. The committee agreed.

The contract with Northeastern Archaeological Associates called for a ten-week project with the remains to be reburied by mid-July so that construction on the parish centre could begin. The contract price was $34,000, and the project was initiated, under Doctor McKillop's direction, with a team of students and volunteers in May 1989.[40] Church authorities graciously allowed the main room in the church basement to be used as a laboratory, and the skeletal remains were stored in the basement choir rooms, which are still known as "The Bones Rooms."

It soon became apparent that there were far more than the expected sixty to eighty burials. Project historian Gerry Boyce found that the original St. Thomas' Church records in the Diocesan Archives in Kingston showed that there had been more than a thousand burials recorded from 1821–74. During the initial weeks of excavation, the archaeological team found dozens of graves, corroborating Boyce's findings. It became clear that almost no interments had been moved to the Belleville Cemetery after the church cemetery was officially closed in 1874.

A crisis ensued. The church needed the site to be cleared as quickly as possible in order to build the parish centre. Yet the Ontario Cemeteries Act made rigid demands on the parties. And the archaeologists needed to be paid for the extra time they were spending on the additional burials. In mid-July, when the in-ground part of the project should have been completed, work stopped. Northeastern Archaeological Associates insisted on a revised contract. Following intensive negotiations, the contract was amended. The original $34,000 figure was almost doubled, the size of the area to be excavated was reduced, and St. Thomas' Church agreed to begin fundraising to assist with the analysis of the bones.

Fieldwork in the churchyard was carried out over the course of four months (from May to August) in 1989. Before the fieldwork ended, the team had located 579 grave shafts and removed 577 burials. How many more burials remain on the site is difficult to say.[41] What we do know is that the burial records indicate the St. Thomas' clergy performed 1,564 burials during the period, and clergy from other denominations also used this burial ground.

The enlarged project was highly organized in a hierarchical, almost "militaristic" fashion. Doctor McKillop led a team of skilled students and volunteers assigned to specific tasks. After one team "shovel-shined" and located the graves, an expert group of trained student archaeologists excavated them and recorded vital information. Each grave was assigned a burial number, mapped using a surveying instrument, photographed, and described in detail on a summary sheet. All materials were carefully removed for cleaning in the church lab. Day by day, week by week, and month by month, the researchers uncovered and excavated graves, making their way across the churchyard until the site for the parish centre had been completely excavated.

A generous grant to Doctor McKillop from the Ontario Heritage Foundation supported the initial cleaning and sorting of the remains, a year-long, painstaking task carried out in the church basement by anthropologist Lorelyn Giese.

An archaeological "dig" at St. Thomas' Church in 1989 revealed the sandy nature of the area. This was the sandy, eastern shoreline of the old "misfit stream" that occupied a glacial spillway after the glacier that covered the area some 10,000 years ago began to melt and retreat. The stream's waters helped form Lake Iroquois. This high hill of sand continued almost to the Moira River, leading in 1816 to the proposed street that was to climb the hill being named Pinnacle Street. Photo by author.

While the fieldwork was in progress, Doctor McKillop invited Doctor Shelley Saunders, a biological anthropologist and professor from McMaster University's Department of Anthropology, to collaborate on the study of the skeletal remains.[42] As a result, the department's laboratories soon housed the skeletal remains from the cemetery. With the able assistance of fellow anthropologist Doctor Ann Herring, Doctor Saunders helped guide research conducted by graduate students. During the study's first year, a detailed series of skeletal analyses (including data collection, X-rays, photography, and tissue sampling) was carried out. Among the areas studied were age-at-death estimations of skeletons from known samples, and the state of dental health. Ultimately, researchers from a number of universities in Canada and the United States took part in the skeletal analysis.[43]

Several factors combined to focus the world's attention on St. Thomas' Church Cemetery:

1. The well-drained, sandy soil of the cemetery site (originally the sandy shore of a pre-historic waterway) promoted such excellent bone preservation that 87 percent of all adult skeletons were sufficiently complete to evaluate trauma and infection on all bones.
2. The skeletal remains were professionally removed and recorded.
3. This was a very large burial sample — almost six-hundred burials — perhaps the largest such sample in North America.
4. The church's burial records from 1821–74 were complete and well-kept.
5. Other valuable sources, such as newspapers, provided information.

6. About eighty burials could be positively identified because of coffin nameplates or other evidence.

7. More than 10,000 artifacts were recovered from the site. These ranged from 1,457 coffin handles, 555 buttons, and 183 hinges, to five dental appliances, four shoes, and three pipes. In short, this was an amazing collection of artifacts, one of the largest in Canada for that time period.

The project's importance had been recognized from the beginning of the preliminary archaeological work, when the Ontario Heritage Foundation provided Doctor McKillop with a much larger than usual grant. The Ontario Heritage Foundation, McMaster University's Arts Research Board, the Bridge Street United Church Foundation, and the Hastings County Historical Society were among the other financial supporters. The members and adherents of St. Thomas' Church provided financial and other support throughout the program. The largest grant came from the Social Sciences and Humanities Research Council of Canada. Consisting of $196,548, it provided for the creation of a master database including church, census, and other records.[44] This allowed McMaster anthropologists, working with Doctor Larry Sawchuk of the Scarborough campus of the University of Toronto and others, to expand the study in an effort to draw a "family tree" of the parish and the community.

There have been many positive achievements related to the St. Thomas' Cemetery project. Researchers have written chapters for three text/reference books.[45] In *Bodies of Evidence*, the research team focused on "the mortality of infants and children as a means of assessing how well skeletal analysis samples can represent the living populations they are drawn from."[46] In *Grave Reflections*, the researchers explored "the question of how representative the St. Thomas' data is of the once-living population from which it is derived, and wondering whether conclusions drawn from our analyses of demographic and health patterns can be generalized further than the borders of the parish to the population of the town as a whole and beyond."[47] In *The Backbone of History: Health and Nutrition in the Western Hemisphere*, researchers showed "that mortality rates, especially for infants, did not improve over the period of greatest cemetery use … [and considered] the importance of acute versus chronic infections and the significance of environmental conditions affecting infant morbidity and mortality…."[48] This volume is a major international project.

Several articles have appeared in leading archaeological and anthropological journals. For example, Doctor McKillop, now of the Louisiana State University in Baton Rouge, published an article "to evaluate whether or not there was a distinctive pattern in the archaeological record that could be used as a model for recognizing children's graves in the absence of historical records or skeletal remains."[49] This study, which focused on coffin handles and other coffin hardware, included a study of some of the personal items, notably the buttons, and was based on the material from the eighty personally identified graves. In addition, McMaster and Louisiana State University anthropologists have presented papers at international conferences in North America and Europe.

Graduate students have completed several theses on their research. Susan Jiminez of McMaster was among the first. She analyzed patterns of injury and disease.[50] Her findings highlighted the fact that 35 percent of men had healed fractures, double the percentage for women. These results reflected the differences between male and female activities in the pioneer community. Another graduate student, Sylvia Abonyi of the University of Calgary, examined local sources (including letters from Irish immigrant William Hutton), and reached conclusions on local dietary patterns.[51] She found that Belleville inhabitants "enjoyed access from an early date not only to the produce and livestock from local farms, but also to goods imported from the larger markets of Kingston and Toronto."[52] There was a heavy emphasis on meat protein (especially pork) and carbohydrates, but the diet was quite varied and not as monotonous as one might assume. In 1999, Chris Dudar earned his Ph.D. at McMaster University by relating DNA samples from the skeletal remains to vestry, land, and census records.[53] Indicative of the highly technical nature of the ongoing research is a 2007 article in the *American Journal of Physical Anthropology* entitled "Sexual Dimorphism of the Dental Tissues in Human Permanent Mandibular Canines and Third Premolars."[54]

The St. Thomas' Church Cemetery is a popular part of the curriculum at Louisiana State University, where Doctor McKillop includes the topic in two archaeological courses.[55] In addition, she and her students have been conducting ongoing studies on the artifacts, including those associated with the coffins (such as handles), and those associated with persons (such as buttons). A number of papers have been presented at professional conferences, two master's theses have been completed, and work on other papers and theses are underway.

There have been contributions to genealogists and general historians. Perhaps the most important has been the production of a CD-ROM containing all the data for Belleville from the Canadian census records for 1851, 1861, 1871, and 1881. Supervised by Doctor Larry Sawchuk and published by CITD Press in 2001, this is a major aid for genealogists and others seeking information on Belleville's population in the mid-nineteenth century.[56] Another positive benefit for genealogists has been the production of indexes for burials, marriages (for both grooms and brides), and deaths.

Researchers have also examined the causes of death. The St. Thomas' burial registers identified the causes for only 180 of the 1,500+ burials, and these were probably considered to be among the more unusual by the rectors. The breakdown is interesting, though by no means representative of the causes of death: disease (34 percent), accident (24 percent), drowning (23 percent), childbirth (8 percent), murder (2 percent), and other (9 percent). Doctor Sawchuk's ongoing research into the principal causes of death in mid-nineteenth century Belleville has identified tuberculosis as an important factor, especially among women. Supporting this finding was recent word from McMaster University that a graduate student has "identified the tuberculosis bacterium in one of the Belleville individuals."[57] Other continuing studies, based on census data, have identified differences between religious groups in Belleville in 1861 with respect to socio-economic conditions.

Unfortunately, the ongoing studies have not proceeded quite as well as the participants would have liked. Differences between church authorities and the archaeologists (largely because of the unforeseen costs created by the large number of skeletal remains), and between the archaeologists and some of the anthropologists, have hindered the exchange of information and the preparation of a detailed study on the project. Nonetheless, research continues in several places, on a wide variety of topics, and there is strong evidence of increased co-operation among the various parties recently. Certainly the complete story of the historical, archaeological, and anthropological importance of the St. Thomas' Cemetery deserves to be told. It should make compelling reading.[58]

The Last Thirty Years, 1978–2008

LIFE HAS BEEN good to Belleville over the last thirty years. In fact, it is generally conceded that the city and its citizens have fared better economically that most of eastern Ontario.

Although some prominent businesses (including American Optical, Mead Johnson, and Deacon Shirts) have closed, and some (such as Nortel) have downsized, others have opened or expanded. Prominent new industries include Halla Climate Control (1989), Sears Canada (1991), Stream International (1991), and Kellogg's. Arguably the most popular businesses, as far as the average consumer is concerned, would be W.T. Hawkins Ltd. (whose hallmark product is Cheezies, manufactured for more than fifty years with cornmeal and aged Canadian cheddar cheese), Reid's Dairy (home of the Loonie Milkshake), and Parmalat Canada/Black Diamond Cheese. Among the new state-of-the-art industries is Bioniche Life Sciences, Inc., a biopharmaceutical company that discovers, develops, manufactures, and markets proprietary products for human and animal health markets worldwide.

Given the community's central location, trucking has been an important industry, and, considering the increasing cost of fuel, rail travel for passengers and goods should continue to grow.

Students, staff, and friends of Belleville Collegiate Institute and Vocational School fought hard to keep their school open. However, faced with the choice of closing either Bayside Secondary School, a relatively new school in a rural setting, or BCIVS, a long-established urban school, the school board voted to close BCIVS in 1992. More than once, students marched on the board office to demonstrate their concern. "BCI Forever" was the group's slogan. Courtesy of Hastings County Historical Society, Mika Collection.

Over the last thirty years, Belleville's increasing population has necessitated new housing subdivisions in all suburban areas of the city. Home construction boomed, as did apartment and condominium construction. Reliable construction companies contributed to the city's prosperity.

There have been important changes in education. The overcrowding of Nicholson Catholic College led to the opening of St. Theresa Catholic Secondary School at the north end of Belleville Ward. Quinte Christian High School, which opened in 1977 on Pinnacle Street, recently moved to a new building on Wallbridge-Loyalist Road. Albert College added an excellent junior school facility and a resource centre to help educate its 300 students from some 43 countries. The Quinte Ballet School of Canada continued to add to its national and international reputation with the addition of a new 1,858 square metre facility, completed in January 2002. A few older elementary schools have been closed, and the city lost its senior public secondary school. Faced with declining enrolment, the school board voted to close BCIVS rather than Bayside Secondary School. Plans for a Quinte Cultural Centre that would use BCIVS to house a city library, a theatre, performing arts practice areas, an art gallery, archives, and other facilities were not successful.

Instead, city council built the new Belleville Public Library and John M. Parrott Art Gallery on Pinnacle Street (on the site of Belleville's first opera house). Concurrently, real-estate entrepreneur and musician Mark Rashotte turned the former McCarthy Theatre/Stephen Licence Bicycle Shop into the amazingly successful Empire Theatre. He also opened, and recently expanded, the adjacent Empire Square for outdoor use.

Many other organizations have played important roles in the city's cultural life. The Quinte Arts Council, whose membership includes more than eighty Belleville-area groups, celebrated its fortieth year of supporting the arts in 2007. In 2008, the Commodores Orchestra marked eighty years of providing big-band hits for area music-lovers.

The city's senior population has continued to expand, and various programs serve this group's needs. One of the most innovative was operated in the 1980s by BCIVS at the newly opened Quinte Living Centre. Regular high-school courses were offered to the students in their own building, and at least three received secondary school graduation diplomas and graduated with their fellow classmates at BCIVS. The first class was a local studies course, initiated by Gerry Boyce on September 8, 1982. Later courses included native studies, civics, geography, geology, and English. Students went on field trips to the nearby mining areas, the Tyendinaga Mohawk Territory, and the Parliament Buildings in Ottawa. During the American history course, students entertained Thomas Niles, the American ambassador to Canada, who signed their course certificates.

The Quinte Living Centre, established with the assistance of the Bridge Street United Church Foundation, funded by the Charlotte Sills Estate, was one of several retirement residences and homes that sprang up. The Bridge Street Retirement Home, Eden Place, Lakeview Manor, Quinte Gardens, and the Richmond Retirement Home are all recent additions. Aldersgate Village is an active retirement community for seniors who live independently. Newly built nursing homes include Hastings Manor and Belmont.

Seniors played a major role in the community's volunteer life. As the years passed, the Central Volunteer Bureau, founded in 1966 by Ruth Burrows, Belleville's volunteer extraordinaire, took on a greater role in co-ordinating volunteer activities. Many active volunteer groups owe their beginnings and continuing existence to the bureau, now known as Volunteer and Information Quinte. Deceased in 1999, Ruth's legacy lives on in the annual "Volunteer of the Year" award and in the Canadian Association of Volunteer Bureaus, which she helped found.

Heritage was not ignored. Several historically important buildings were preserved, often through the efforts of the Local Architectural Conservation Advisory Committee (LACAC), now known as Heritage Belleville, a committee of council, and local historians. Preserved structures included Belleville City Hall, the McIntosh-Ridley House on South Front Street (after a major struggle), the Billa Flint House on Coleman Street, and the Riverboat House on West Bridge Street, the latter two both saved by Brian Magee. Other heritage-minded businessmen who helped to preserve and improve the landscape included Richard Courneyea (Richard Davis Men's Clothing) and Paul Dinkel (Dinkel's Restaurant and other buildings), and Tom Boretski (the Boretski Gallery). In addition, several sites were plaqued, among them the former Methodist Church Cemetery on East Dundas Street, City Hall (1986), and the Moodie and Bowell residences. On the municipal side, thanks to the efforts of long-time mayor George Zegouras, several parks were named in honour of former mayors.

In 2007, citizens celebrated the 150th anniversary of the arrival of the first train. Annually, they celebrate the arrival of various immigrant groups as part of the Waterfront Ethnic Festival. And each July 1 since 2005, the Buy Locally Owned Group has sponsored a Canada Day celebration on Zwick's Island.

The Heritage movement was aided by the founding of a local branch of the Architectural Conservancy of Ontario. In 1997, murals depicting local historic scenes were erected in public places in Belleville's downtown. More recently, Paul Dinkel had an interior mural depicting Belleville's historic buildings installed in his restaurant. The recently improved Hastings and Prince Edward Regimental Museum and the Scout and Guide Museum at Sir James Whitney School are other important heritage sites.

During this period, a journalist born in Belleville gained national prominence as an award-winning author of several best-selling books. Arguably Canada's most famous investigative journalist, Stevie Cameron investigated Brian Mulroney in *On the Take: Crime, Corruption and Greed in the Mulroney Years* (1994), and Robert William Pickton in *The Pickton File* (2007), the story of the disappearances and murders of many female drug addicts and prostitutes in the Vancouver area. In connection with the first book, she allegedly served as a "confidential informant for the RCMP." Historians await the eventual opening of her records in the Clara Thomas Archives of York University.

Several changes occurred in religion. Some mainline religions suffered major setbacks. St. Margaret's on the Hill Anglican Church, on Oriole Park Avenue, closed, and is now a Montessori school. Tabernacle United Church, a bastion of Methodism for more than a century, was demolished and the site became a parking lot. The congregation united with Holloway United to form St. Matthew's. On the other hand, several churches grew, expanded, or were established. These included Calvary Temple, Desert Stream Christian Fellowship, First Pentecostal, Greek Orthodox, Holy Rosary Roman Catholic, and Maranatha Christian Reformed.

Sports continued to be an important part of Belleville life. In 1987, the Belleville Sports Hall of Fame inducted its first fifteen members at an emotion-filled ceremony at Sir James Whitney School. They included the legendary hockey player Bobby Hull (the Golden Jet), and his brother Dennis, both natives of Point Anne. Long the dream of Paul Kirby and others, the hall has since added many noted athletes, including blind master-athlete Sarah Thompson, the Belleville McFarlands, and martial-arts enthusiast Kenzo Dozono. As well, Doctor Bob Vaughan was honoured for bringing an Ontario Hockey League franchise to Belleville in 1981, and providing stability and strong leadership for the team, the Belleville Bulls.

The Bulls have earned a place in the city's sports elite, and have attracted national attention. Not only

Belleville native Stevie Cameron, prominent Canadian writer and alleged undercover agent for the Royal Canadian Mounted Police, signed copies of On the Take *at W & R Greenley's Booksellers in November of 1994, while Town Crier Al Kelleher and others looked on. Photo by author.*

did they advance to the Memorial Cup twice (the most recent time against the Kitchener Rangers in 2008), but many players have gone on to National Hockey League careers. When the Detroit Red Wings won the Stanley Cup in 2008, former Bull Dan Cleary became the first Newfoundlander to play on a Stanley Cup-winning team. Other noted Bull graduates have included Darren McCarty, who played on the 2008 Stanley Cup team, Dan Quinn, and Matt Stajan.

More important to the sporting community has been the proliferation of sports facilities over recent years. Soccer has replaced baseball as the most popular summer sport, and a growing number of soccer pitches annually attract almost 5,000 players of all ages. Similarly, thanks to artificial ice, almost an equal number of residents play hockey. These activities have been augmented by an increasing number of trails throughout the city, and particularly along the two waterways.

Belleville continued to enjoy the benefits of philanthropic citizens. What Senator Corby had done in providing a free library, a park, and public baths earlier, other citizens and former citizens continued to do. Charlotte "Lottie" Emma Martin (1873–1961) was one of the most generous. A native of Belleville for her early years, she moved to the United States after her marriage to Bill Sills in 1898. Her husband, educated in part at the Belleville Business College, was an accountant and eventually acquired all of General Motors' sales franchises in New England. After twelve years he retired a wealthy man. Following her death in 1961, her estate provided payments to several family members and her faithful chauffeur. The bulk of the estate was then allotted to the Bridge Street United Church and the Belleville General Hospital. Funds began to arrive in 1973.

The Bridge Street congregation created the Bridge Street Foundation and determined to use only the interest from the fund, which eventually totalled some $2,144,436 for grants and loans. Funding helped to erect the Quinte Living Centre. Seed money from the fund helped to establish several independent social agencies and programs in Belleville, including the First Adventure Child Development Centre, Serenity House, the Three Oaks Crisis Centre, and the Regional Hospice of Quinte.[59] Meanwhile, with its share of the estate, much swollen by interest, the Belleville General Hospital (now part of the Quinte Health Corporation) is constructing a convalescent wing.

Official opening of the new Belleville Public Library and John M. Parrott Art Gallery by Lieutenant-Governor James Bartleman, Bernice Parrott, and Mayor Mary Anne Sills, May 26, 2006. Photo by author.

Leona Riggs, Broadway
performer, Belleville musician,
and patron of the arts. Courtesy
of Hastings County Historical
Society (Riggs Collection),
HC-3466.

Other major philanthropists have included Jack and Bernice Parrott, whose Parrott Foundation helped the Belleville Public Library and the John M. Parrott Art Gallery, Albert College, Loyalist College, the Riverfront Trail, and other projects. Maurice Rollins contributed substantially to the Quinte Cultural Centre project, and the charitable foundation of the late Leona Riggs helped the Quinte Ballet School of Canada.

In the field of politics, the last few years saw good government and modest tax increases. Council meetings were not without the occasional controversy, and politicians such as the long-serving Stu Meeks tried to ensure that citizens received full benefit for their tax dollars. Remembered today as an outspoken alderman — he disliked being referred to as a councillor — Meeks was "a softy at heart" and loved to serve the community. He used his remuneration from the city to expand his business, LaSalle Ambulance, to include LaSalle Rescue Service. This would lead to the present Quinte Search and Rescue, an affiliate of the Canadian Coast Guard Auxiliary.

Meeks was still a member of council when he died in 2002, after twenty-seven years on council. Meanwhile, George Zegouras set a record for years in office as mayor, serving fourteen. His term would have been longer had he not been defeated in 1991 by a newcomer to political life, environmentalist Shirley Langer. Her term in office was one of the most controversial in the city's political history.

The period was to end with a major decision that would drastically alter the area's political map.

12
PAST, PRESENT, AND FUTURE

Why Not a "City of Quinte"?

WHEN HISTORIAN W.C. Mikel published his *City of Belleville History* in 1943, he concluded with a look at the future. He envisaged "Quinte City" as a very large entity. It would stretch from Trenton and Frankford in the west to Belleville and Point Anne in the east, and would also include the south shore of the Bay of Quinte from Rossmore to Carrying Place. Mikel did not live to see his dream realized, but municipalities in the area stretching from Murray Township in the west to Tyendinaga Township and Deseronto in the east did discuss the possibility of amalgamation in the mid-1990s. They were encouraged by the Ontario government, which felt that such amalgamations would bring about cost efficiencies and reduce the number of municipalities and municipal politicians. Longstanding rivalries — especially between Trenton and Sidney Township on the one hand and Belleville on the other — made the formation of Quinte City impossible. Nevertheless, Trenton, Sidney, Murray, and Frankford did come together to form the City of Quinte West.

Belleville and Thurlow Township were left out of the new city. They did, however, unite to form the enlarged City of Belleville, effective January 1, 1998. They were reunited after more than 150 years, having separated in 1836 when Belleville became a police village. Although somewhat reluctantly, Thurlow Council was motivated to enter union by several factors, including the provincial government's downloading of services and its decision that rural municipalities should start to pay for police services provided by the Ontario Provincial Police.

Initially, Belleville Ward of the new city would have seven councillors and Thurlow Ward would have three. The mayor would be elected at large. In 2000, council voted to reduce the

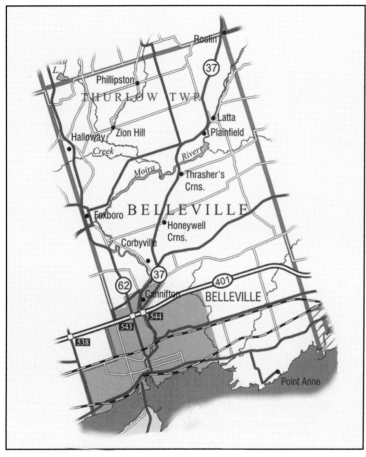

The amalgamation of Belleville and Thurlow Township, effective January 1, 1998, and the subsequent annexation of sections of Sidney Township (bounded by the western boundary of Belleville, the bay, Wallbridge-Loyalist Road and Highway 401) resulted in a larger city. Several historic Thurlow communities were now included in the city. Courtesy of County of Hastings and Development Department, June 2008.

number of councillors to eight — six from Belleville Ward and two from Thurlow Ward.

A major controversy erupted in the early summer of 2002, when city council considered abolishing the two-ward system and the removal of two councillors solely elected by Thurlow Ward residents. Thurlow residents turned out in large numbers at two public meetings and council backed down.[1]

The amalgamation of Belleville and Thurlow Township meant a new city that was about seven times larger in area than the old Belleville. The total land area now stood at 240.5 square kilometres Some 44,570 people lived in the new Belleville, and there were 424 kilometres of roads. Among the historic Thurlow communities included in the new city were Point Anne, Cannifton, Corbyville, Foxboro, Plainfield, and part of Roslin.

W.C. Mikel's dream of a large Quinte City had not been realized. Perhaps it will one day become a reality and questioners will not need to ask citizens of Quinte West: "So you're in Quinte West. Just where is Quinte East?"

Epilogue[2]

THERE HAS BEEN a recognized settlement at the mouth of the Moira River for more than two-hundred years. What began as an early Mississauga community and later became a Loyalist village (both with very small populations), has expanded to a modern city of almost 49,000.

Belleville is typical of many other Ontario communities. Its citizens have faced their share of challenges. While early settlers had to deal with the hardships of pioneer living, more recent immigrants have had to adjust to a new and different society.

Natural surroundings have been important to the city's development. The north-south waterway of the Moira River and east-west waterways of the Bay of Quinte and Lake Ontario were very significant to its growth. Belleville's relationship to, and use of, is natural attributes are echoed in all other Ontario towns and cities.

Each successive generation has found that the community had a need for social institutions to improve the lives of a growing population, and each generation has responded to those needs with determination and commitment, building upon the foundation established by its predecessor.

Belleville can also make various claims to fame, such as producing a prime minister, being the home of a famous regiment, supplying the National Hockey League with players, and being the hometown of Brian Price, gold medalist as coxswain for the Canadian men's eights rowing crew at the 2008 Beijing Olympics. While the specifics may be different, other large and small communities can also make such claims.

But being typical of other cities, towns, and villages does not detract from the sense of pride that Bellevillians should feel. In developing a city, they have been full partners in the growth of the province and the nation, and they will continue to play their full role.

Water holds the future to successful Belleville tourism. Former Belleville resident and present Florida resident, Bob Sears, is a regular summer visitor to the harbour at Meyers Pier, one of the area's prime tourist attractions. Belleville is host to several bass, pickerel, and pike fishing derbies. Photo by author, 2007.

APPENDIX A

Belleville's Growth in Population, 1818–2006

AT BEST, POPULATION statistics are educated guesses. No amount of searching, surveying, interviewing, and rechecking can guarantee 100 percent accuracy. Consider Stephen Leacock's comments on population statistics for the imaginary town of Mariposa, as described at the beginning of *Sunshine Sketches of a Little Town* (1912). According to Leacock, the federal census taker would determine the population to be about 5,000. Over the next ten years, two local newspapers, the undertaker, the bar owner, and various citizens would estimate that the population was increasing dramatically and would soon reach 10,000. The census taker's next visit, and his figure of 5,000, brought everyone back down to earth.

Nevertheless, the following figures (provided by Statistics Canada and John Lowry, local historical researcher) do show Belleville's general population trends, including the rapid growth of the city in the 1840s, 1850s, 1860s, and 1950s. The figures are from three sources: (1) the Canadian census (2) municipal enumeration records (3) various visitors, newspapers, and books.

YEAR	POPULATION		
	Official Canadian Census	Municipal Enumeration Records	Unofficial Sources and Estimates
1818			150
1824			500
1829			700
1836			1,000
1850			2,200
1851	4,569		
1861	6,277		
1871	7,305		
1878			11,000
1881	9,516		
1884			11,000
1891	9,916		
1901	9,117		
1910			9,800
1911	9,876		
1921	12,206		
1931	13,790		
1935			14,500
1941	15,710		
1943		15,642	
1949		18,274	
1951	19,519		
1956	20,605		
1958		21,394	
1961	30,655		
1964		30,610	
1966	32,785		
1971	35,128		
1974		35,125	
1976	35,331		
1979		34,989	

YEAR	POPULATION		
	Official Canadian Census	Municipal Enumeration Records	Unofficial Sources and Estimates
1981	34,923		
1985		36,720	
1986	36,041		
1991	37,243		
1996	37,083		
2001	45,986		
2006	48,821		

APPENDIX B

Belleville's Boundary Changes

BELLEVILLE HAS GROWN greatly in physical size. The original town plot was only on the east side of the Moira River on the southern part of lot 4 in the first concession of Thurlow Township.

The government had purchased 428 acres from the Mississauga First Nation just prior to 1816, and the town plot occupied less than half of the acreage. Today, the city has grown to 246.76 square kilometres (about 60,800 acres or 95 square miles). This map shows the principal expansion steps. Although some of the acquisitions were very small, such as the 1930 bayshore section to provide a site for the water filtration plant, others were much larger. The largest came in 1998, with the amalgamation of the city with Thurlow Township. *(Courtesy of Belleville Development Services Department)*

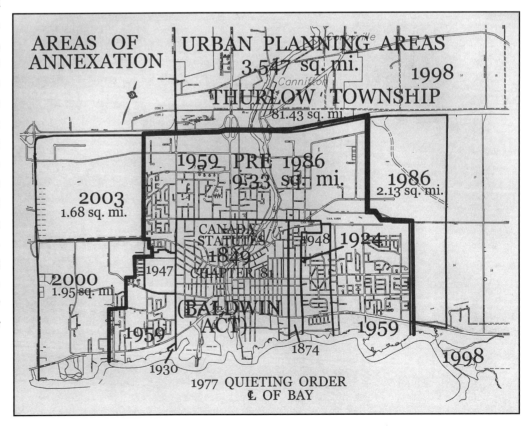

NOTES

One: The Beginning

1. For a detailed, attractively illustrated view of the geology of Hastings County and the Belleville area, see Orland French, ed., *Heritage Atlas of Hastings County* (Belleville: The County of Hastings, 2006) 10–27.
2. Gerald E. Boyce, *Historic Hastings* (Belleville: Hastings County Council, 1967), 7.
3. Russell J. Barber submitted two reports to the Ontario Ministry of Culture and Recreation in 1976, where they are available in manuscript form.
4. An excellent description of the various archaeological periods in aboriginal Ontario is found in Edward S. Rogers and Donald B. Smith, eds., *Aboriginal Ontario: Historical Perspectives on the First Nations* (Toronto: Dundurn Press, 1994). For a more local approach, see also Nick Adams, "The Pre-Contact Occupation of the Kingston Area: An Archaeological Consultant's View," in *Historic Kingston*, vol. 54, 85–98.
5. Hugh J. Daechsel, *Moira Archaeological Survey, 1984: Report for Archaeological Licence 84–05* (Hamilton: the author, 1985).
6. *Ibid.*, 18.
7. Captain John W. Meyers, often regarded as the founder of Belleville, negotiated with the Mississauga First Nation for permission to establish the community's first industries on this land, but was refused by the government. The reference to "Reserved for Indian Burying Ground" was found on Plan B45 in the Ontario Ministry of Natural Resources (consulted in the 1960s), and entitled: "Plan of the Township of Thurlow in the District of Mecklenburg surveyed in 1787 by Lewis Kotte with the Names of the Proprietors inserted on the Lots." A notarized copy

of the plan is found in the Hastings County Historical Society Archives, File 2863.

8. Susanna Moodie, *Life in the Clearings*, edited and introduced by Robert L. McDougall (Toronto: The Macmillan Co. of Canada Ltd., 1959), 6.

9. David A. Robertson, "Mourning, Curing, Feasting or Industry? The Interpretation of the Quinte and Perch Lake Mounds," in *Ontario Archaeology* No. 7 (2001) 38, describing T.C. Wallbridge, "On Some Ancient Mounds upon the Shores of the Bay of Quinte," in *The Canadian Journal,* vol. 2, no.9 (September 1860) 408–17.

10. W.C. Mikel, *City of Belleville History* (Picton: Picton Gazette Publishing Co., 1943), 1, 6, 7.

11. Michael Macklem, trans., *Voyages to New France (Samuel de Champlain: Voyages to New France 1615–1618)* (Canada: Oberon Press, 1970), 45.

12. Joe C.W. Armstrong, *Champlain* (Toronto: Macmillan of Canada, 1987), 166.

13. W.S. Herrington makes a strong case for the Cataraqui River as the river ascended, and Long Lake in Lennox and Addington County as being near the site of the encampment in his *History of the County of Lennox and Addington* (Toronto: Macmillan Co. of Canada Ltd., 1913) 1–5.

14. Armstrong, *Champlain,* 17–19.

15. An excellent account of the mission is to be found in Richard A. Preston and Leopold Lamontagne, *Royal Fort Frontenac* (Toronto: University of Toronto Press, 1958), the second volume in the Champlain Society's series for the Government of Ontario, 3–16, with relevant documents on 85–101.

16. Bishop Laval's letter of instruction quoted in Preston and Lamontagne, 87.

17. Wallace Havelock Robb pamphlet attached to his 1951 Christmas card in author's possession.

18. Wallace Havelock Robb, *Thunderbird* (Kingston: Abbey Dawn Press, 1949), 17.

19. *Ibid.*, 5.

20. From Dawn Cove Abbey Empowerment Outreach, http://www.dawncoveabbey.org, accessed April, 20, 2008. The site describes Robb as "a deeply artistic, poetic, spiritual man, with a deep reverence for life."

21. Library and Archives Canada (LAC), National Map Collection (NMC), "Plan of the Township of Thurlow in the District of Mecklenburg surveyed in 1787 by Lewis Kotte with the Names of the Proprietors inserted in the Lots," identified as B45–No. 5.

22. Donald B. Smith, *Sacred Feathers: The Reverend Peter Jones (Kahkewaquonaby) & the Mississauga Indians* (Toronto: University of Toronto Press, 1987). This is an excellent source of information on the Mississauga First Nations.

23. *Ibid.*, 20.

24. *Ibid.*, 24.

25. The actual deeds for some of these early treaties have not survived. In addition, some treaties were incomplete. Treaty Number 13 (The Gunshot Treaty), negotiated at the Carrying Place, at the head of the Bay of Quinte, on September 23, 1787, had the totems or emblems of the Mississauga leaders, but no signatures for the British delegates. Also, it failed to describe the boundaries for the lands and the payments for the Mississauga. The British planned to fill in these "details" later.

26. R.J. Surtees, *Land Surrenders in Ontario 1763–1867* (Ottawa: Indian and Northern Affairs Canada, 1983), 23–24.

Two: Settlement Problems

1. A more detailed account of Captain George Singleton, with source references, is to be found in Gerald E. Boyce, "George Singleton," in *Dictionary of Canadian Biography, Vol. IV, 1771 to 1800* (Toronto: University of Toronto Press, 1979), 710–11.

2. The major historical works are: Jane Bennett Goddard's *Hans Waltimeyer* (Cobourg: author, 1980) and Mary Beacock Fryer's *Loyalist Spy* (Brockville: Besancourt Publishers, 1974), republished as *John Walden Meyers: Loyalist Spy* (Toronto and Charlottetown: Dundurn Press, 1983). Connie Brummel Crook has written several historical-fiction novels about John Meyers, the most recent one being *Meyers' Rebellion* (Markham: Fitzhenry & Whiteside, 2006). All three authors are Loyalist descendants, and Goddard and Crook are descendants of Meyers.

3. Jane Bennett Goddard, flyer, *circa* 1980, announcing the publication of *Hans Waltimeyer*.

4. Robert J.M. Shipley, "Meyers, John Walden," in *Dictionary of Canadian Biography, Vol. VI, 1821 to 1835* (Toronto: University of Toronto Press, 1987), 502–04.

5. William Canniff, *History of the Settlement of Upper Canada (Ontario) With Special Reference to the Bay Quinte* (Toronto: Dudley & Burns, 1869), 496; *Moira Valley Conservation Report* (Toronto: Department of Planning and Development, 1950), 36.

6. See "Government by the People" for Meyers' political role.

7. For differing versions of the legend see Goddard, *Hans Waltimeyer*, 491–99; Grace Maidens Bennett, "Silver Cache Legend Part of Family Lore," *The Globe and Mail*, October 23, 1954; and Merrill Denison, "The Bon Echo Story," *The Tweed News*, August 6, 1964.

8. Shipley, "Meyers, John Walden," 503.

9. McNabb is spelled in several ways, such as McNab and Macnab.

10. Hastings County Historical Society (HCHS), Phyllis H. White, "Dr. James Macnab — The Lost Loyalist" (typed manuscript, January 2, 2007) n.p.

11. *Ibid.*, 1.

12. *Ibid*, 13

13. William Canniff, *History of the Settlement of Upper Canada*, 589, based on letter of July 22, 1791, in Bell Papers in Lennox and Addington County Historical Society Archives.

14. This section is largely based upon the research of Lois Foster, Belleville historian and a great-great-great-granddaughter of Margaret Simpson.

15. Archives of Ontario (OA), Canniff Papers, G4, MS768, reel 2, 34th frame (approx.).

16. Lennox and Addington Historical Society, *Papers and Records,* vol. IX (1917), 44.

17. Alexander Oliphant Petrie, quoted in Canniff, *History of the Settlement of Upper Canada*, 576.

18. OA, RG1, Upper Canada Land Papers, L3, v, 456(a), Petition of Margaret Simpson, Moira Village, to Lieutenant-Governor Francis Gore, July 17, 1816.

19. HCHS, Lois Foster's Notes on the Simpson Family for the society's newsletter, *Outlook*, n.d.

20. The *Daily Intelligencer,* November 18, 1869.

21. Jane Bennett Goddard, *Hans Waltimeyer,* (Cobourg: Jane Bennett Goddard, 1980), 365, based on Hugh Judge, *Memoirs & Journal…* (Philadelphia: 1841).

22. Tom Ransom, "150 Years Ago," *Ontario Intelligencer,* April 7, 1960.

23. Lenny Williamson, "Our Architectural Heritage," *Ontario Intelligencer,* May 21, 1964.

24. Carol Randolph, "Margaret Johnson Russell Simpson, born 1750s," in The Canadian Federation of University Women Belleville and District, *Quinte Women of Distinction* (Cobourg: Haynes Printing Co. [Cobourg] Ltd., 2002), 32.

25. Benzie Sangma, "Remember When," the *Intelligencer,* April 26, 2003.

26. Canniff, *History of the Settlement of Upper Canada,* 548–49.

27. *Kingston Gazette,* May 19, 1812.

28. *Upper Canada Gazette,* March 4, 1812.

29. Mikel, *City of Belleville History,* 84–85.

30. Library and Archives Canada (LAC), 12305–12312, Upper Canada Sundries, March 20, 1816,

31. LAC, 8186–8198, Upper Canada Sundries, April 7, 1814.

32. *Kingston Gazette,* October 17, 1812.

33. LAC, 6813, Upper Canada Sundries, June 8, 1814.

34. *Ibid.*, 12890–12894, 1816.

35. William Canniff, *Settlement of Upper Canada,* 382.

36. LAC, 5080–5082, Upper Canada Sundries, November 8, 1810.

37. *Ibid.,* 5708–5710, September, 5, 1811.

38. For the local contribution to the war effort, see Boyce, *Historic Hastings,* 36–40.

39. LAC, RG7, G16C, vol. 7, 15.

40. HCHS, file 698, notes and documents by Tom Ransom.

41. Redrawn copies of this original plan found in the Ministry of Natural Resources, Toronto, were printed by the Hastings County Historical Society some years ago.

42. HCHS, file 698, notes by Tom Ransom.

43. Canniff, *History of the Settlement in Upper Canada*, 501; Thomas Rolph, *A Brief Account, Together with Observations, Made during a Visit in the West Indies, and a Tour through the United States of America, in Parts of the Years 1832–3 together with a Statistical Account of Upper Canada* (Dundas: Hackstaff, 1836), 157.

44. *Kingston Gazette,* August 24, 1816.

45. *Ibid.,* September 7, 1816.

46. OA, RG1–A–1–6, August 3, 1816, letter announcing Lieutenant-Governor Francis Gore's pleasure "that the New Town laid out at the River Moira shall be called Bellville [*sic*]."

47. Upper Canada Legislative Assembly Journals, February 27, 1818.

48. Ontario Department of Planning and Development, *Moira Valley Conservation Report* (Toronto: Department of Planning and Development, 1950).

49. *Ibid.,* Chapter 1, "The River," 5.

50. Moodie, *Life in the Clearings,* 19–28.

51. *Ibid.,* 21.

52. *Ibid.,* 26.

53. *Ibid.,* 27.

54. *Moira Valley Conservation Report,* 7.

55. *Ibid.,* 10.

56. *Ibid.,* 15.

57. Wilma Alexander, *And the Boats Go Up and Down* (Toronto: General Paperbacks, 1991).

58. Canniff, *History of the Settlement of Upper Canada,* 332.

59. *Ibid.,* 333.

60. *Ibid.,* 330.

61. *Kingston Gazette,* November 16, 1816.

62. LAC, 1818, 17756, Upper Canada Sundries, Report of Board of Education for the Midland District.

63. Robert Gourlay, *Statistical Account of Upper Canada,* vol.1 (London: Simpkin and Marshall, 1822), 610.

64. LAC, 14429–14433, Upper Canada Sundries, Report of the Midland District Board of Education, February 1, 1817.

65. Canniff Haight, *Country Life in Canada Fifty Years Ago* (Toronto: Rose, 1885), reprinted by Mika Silk Screening Ltd., Belleville, 1971, 16–17.

66. *Kingston Chronicle and Gazette,* August 9, 1834.

67. *Ibid.*

68. *Ibid.,* August 30, 1834.

69. The *Patriot,* November 17, 1835.

70. HCHS, Ponton Papers, William Hutton to his mother, February 24, 1835.

71. HCHS, Ponton Papers, William Hutton to John McCrea, Belleville, June 26, 1834, and William Hutton to Fanny Hutton, Belleville, June 8, 1834.

72. LAC, MG24, B35, John Holmes to Henry Yager, Belleville, April 3, 1835.

73. Canniff, *History of the Settlement of Upper Canada,* 284.

74. J. William Lamb, *Bridging the Years: A History of Bridge Street United/Methodist Church, Belleville, 1815–1990* (Winfield, BC: Wood Lake Books Inc., 1990), 20. Lamb's book is exceptionally well researched and captures the flavour of religious and community life in Belleville over two centuries.

75. *Ibid.,* 27.

76. Class Leader John Reynolds would become the first Methodist bishop in Canada.

77. Interview with long-time Belleville postmaster James H. Meacham, the *Intelligencer,* December 28, 1895, quoted in Lamb, *Bridging the Years,* 17.

78. Lamb, *Bridging the Years,* 29.

79. *Ibid.,* 49.

80. *Ibid.,* 32–33.

81. *Ibid.,* 68. Note the original spelling of *Bellville* without the middle *e.*

82. *Ibid.,* 69–70. Lamb offers compelling evidence to support this somewhat controversial claim.

83. LAC, RG 1, L3, Upper Canada Land Petitions; B11/213, Petition of James McNabb & others, Belleville, December 28, 1818.

84. Canniff, *History of the Settlement of Upper Canada,* 268–69.

85. *Ibid.,* 283.

86. Reminiscences of Allan Taylor Petrie, *Daily Intelligencer,* November 16, 1901.

87. Ina Bellstedt, *St. Thomas' Anglican Church 1818–1968: The Parish Story* (Belleville: St. Thomas' Church, 1969), 5.

88. Quoted in Edward J. Buckley, *A History of the Parish of St. Michael The Archangel, Belleville, Ontario 1829–1993* (Belleville: author, 1993), 7.

89. LAC, RG.1, L3, vol. 44, B13/46.

90. Buckley, *A History of the Parish,* 11, contains an interesting discussion of the possible origins of the first building.

91. "Reminiscences of Mrs. White, of White's Mills, near Cobourg, Upper Canada, formerly Miss Catherine Chrysler of Sydney, near Belleville, aged 79," in *Ontario Historical Society Papers and Records,* vol. VII (Toronto: The Ontario Historical Society, 1906), 155.

92. Gerald E. Boyce, *The St. Andrew's Chronicles* (Belleville: St. Andrew's Presbyterian Church, 1978), 24–26.

93. *Ibid.,* 31–33. The Presbyterian Church in Canada published a four-page history of this event by Gerald E. Boyce in May 1981, as part of its Presbyterian History series.

94. Canniff, *A History of the Settlement of Upper Canada,* 270. For a nicely written account of Baptist efforts in the Belleville area, see Veva L. Robson, *Victoria Avenue Baptist Church, Belleville, Ontario 1872–1973: A Century of Service* (Belleville: Victoria Avenue Baptist Church, 1973).

95. Canniff, *A History of the Settlement of Upper Canada,* 280.

96. *Kingston Chronicle and Gazette,* September 13, 1837.

97. *A Letter to the Right Honourable the Earl of Liverpool, K.C., First Lord Commissioner of the Treasury. Relative to the Rights of the Church of Scotland in British North America from a Protestant of the Church of Scotland* (Kingston: James MacFarlane, 1826), 17.

98. *Kingston Chronicle,* July 7, 1826.

99. *The Patriot,* February 1, 1833.

100. Sir Richard Henry Bonnycastle, *Canada and the Canadians in 1846* (London: Coborn, 1846), 224.

101. *Kingston Chronicle and Gazette,* October 11, 1837. The Reverend Bill Lamb presents an exciting account of the Belleville Chapel case in *Bridging the Years,* 73–80.

102. LAC, RG5, B26, vol. 2, Statistical Return by Edmund Murney, 1840.

Three: Law and Order

1. A detailed history of the May 15 meeting is found in Gerald E. Boyce et al., *Sidney Township 1790–1990* (Belleville: Hastings County Historical Society, 1990), 3–4. A highlight of the bicentennial celebrations in May 1990 was a re-enactment by Bayside Secondary School students of the original bylaw appointing fence viewers. Immediately thereafter, the 1990 council approved an actual bylaw appointing replacement fence viewers.

2. Leading military officers, including Captain Meyers, are said to have exercised an unofficial judicial function.

3. Gerald E. Boyce, "James Hunter Samson," in *Dictionary of Canadian Biography, Vol. VII, 1836–1850* (Toronto: University of Toronto Press and Les Presses de l'université Laval, 1988), 772.

4. *Hallowell Free Press*, 1832.

5. LAC, Upper Canada Sundries, June 29, 1832, letter from Samuel Wilmot.

6. *Ibid.*, October 29, 1832.

7. For a more complete history of early Belleville newspapers see Boyce, *Historic Hastings*, 211–215, and J. Owen Herity, "Journalism in Belleville," in *Ontario Historical Society Papers and Records*, vol. XXVII (Toronto: The Society, 1931), 400–06.

8. *Kingston Chronicle,* March 5, 1831.

9. *Hallowell Free Press,* July 17, 1832.

10. *Kingston Chronicle and Gazette*, August 30, 1834.

11. Canniff, *Settlement of Upper Canada*, 360.

12. *The Patriot*, November 4, 1834; November 25, 1834.

13. *Ibid.*, November 4, 1834, quoting the *Intelligencer.*

14. Sheldon and Judith Godfrey, *Burn this Gossip: The True Story of George Benjamin of Belleville, Canada's First Jewish Member of Parliament 1857–1863* (Toronto: The Duke & George Press, 1991), vii.

15. *Ibid.*, 23–28.

16. *Ibid.*, 29.

17. *Ibid.*, 84–85.

18. *Hastings Chronicle*, October 22, 1856.

19. Reverend James Gardiner, *My Life Story,* extracts in HCHS prepared by Gerald E. Boyce, 1960, from a manuscript in possession of Percy G. Anderson of California, USA, loaned to Lennox and Addington County Historical Society, 66.

20. *Belleville Intelligencer,* quoted in *Kingston Chronicle and Gazette,* October 10, 1835. Perhaps a hint of the violence associated with political rallies is reflected in the question periods of Canadian legislatures.

21. Quoted in *Kingston Chronicle and Gazette,* July 26, 1834.

22. Rolph, *Upper Canada,* 158.

23. *Kingston Chronicle and Gazette*, November 8, 1834.

24. LAC, 37159–37160, Upper Canada Sundries, Petition of Reverend Thomas Campbell and others, January 24, 1825.

25. *Kingston Chronicle and Gazette,* April 29, 1837.

26. LAC, MG24, B35, John Holmes to Henry Yager, April 3, 1835.

27. Gordon Dodds, "Sir James Buchanan Macaulay," in *Dictionary of Canadian Biography, Vol. VIII, 1851–1860* (Toronto, Buffalo, London: University of Toronto Press, 1985), 512.

28. For further information, see Heritage Belleville, *Heritage Buildings East of the Moira River* (Belleville: Heritage Belleville, 1991); article on 67 South Front Street and the related files are located in the Heritage Belleville office.

29. HCHS, Rebellion Losses Papers. The collection is also available on microfilm in LAC, MF 971.Has.

30. LAC, MG24, B35, Henry Yager Papers, John Holmes to Henry Yager, MLA, April 3, 1835.

31. Betsy Dewar Boyce, *The Rebels of Hastings* (Toronto; University of Toronto Press, 1992). Betsy and I shared a Hamilton background, a degree in history from McMaster University, a love of local history, and similar initials (G.E.B); however, we are not related.

32. Gerald M. Craig, *Upper Canada: The Formative Years 1784–1841* (Toronto: McClelland & Stewart Ltd., 1963), 92.

33. Robert Gourlay, *Statistical Account of Upper Canada,* vol. 2 (London: Simpkin and Marshall, 1822), 616.

34. *Kingston Gazette,* September 29, 1818.

35. *Ibid.*, September 29, 1818.

36. *Ibid.*, March 10, 1832 ; March 17, 1832.

37. *Ibid.*, December 20, 1837.

38. Many records spell McNabb's name with a single "b."

39. *Kingston Chronicle and Gazette,* December 13, 1837.

40. LAC, RG 9, 1B1, Adjutants General's Correspondence, vol. 22, Hastings file, Colonel Thomas Coleman to Colonel Richard Bullock, Belleville, October 19, 1837.

41. *Kingston Chronicle and Gazette,* December 9, 1837.

42. *Ibid.*, February 21, 1838.

43. Richard Henry Bonnycastle, *Canada, As It Was, Is, And May Be*, vol. 2 (London: Colborn, 1846), 79.

44. *Ibid.*, vol. 2, 89.

45. Richard Henry Bonnycastle, *The Canadas in 1841,* vol. 2 (London: Colborn, 1841), 65.

46. Bonnycastle, *Canada, As It Was, Is, And May Be,* vol. 2, 93, contradicted somewhat in vol. 2, 314–15.

47. *Kingston Chronicle and Gazette,* June 6, 1838.

48. LAC, Upper Canada Sundries, George Benjamin letter, June 13, 1838.

49. *Ibid.*, Letter from Hastings County Justices of the Peace re: Bill Johnson, June 11, 1838.

50. LAC, "C" Series, vol. 611 (Militia, 1794–1870), Major Warren to Colonel Halkett, Belleville, 234–38.

51. AO, Mackenzie-Lindsey Papers, Correspondence, Clifton McCollom to W.L. Mackenzie, Johnstown, Montgomery Township, New York, January 30, 1838.

52. Arthur Papers, no. 362, Sir George Arthur to Sir John Colborne, Cobourg, October 17, 1838.

53. *Kingston Chronicle and Gazette,* October 20, 1838, November 21, 1838.

54. LAC, Upper Canada Sundries, October 11, 1838, July 6, 1839, July 11, 1839, etc.

55. HCHS, Reverend James Gardiner Papers, Extracts from *My Life Story* file.

56. LAC, "C" Series, vol. 611 (Militia 1794–1870), Baron de Rottenburg to Sir George Arthur, Belleville, November 27, 1838.

57. HCHS, Reverend James Gardiner Papers, Extracts from *My Life Story*.

58. HCHS, Hastings County Rebellion Losses Claims, John O'Carroll file.

59. *Kingston Chronicle and Gazette*, May 19, 1839.

60. Moodie, *Life in the Clearings,* 35–36.

61. *Ibid.,* xix.

62. Boyce, *The Rebels of Hastings,* 172–73.

63. See Boyce, *Rebels of Hastings,* 173–86, for a complete list of claims and awards.

64. *The Patriot,* January 29, 1836.

65. LAC, MG24, B35, Benson to Henry Yager, Belleville, March 20, 1835.

66. *Ibid.,* April 2, 1835.

67. *Kingston Chronicle and Gazette,* March 2, 1837.

68. LAC, RG1, Report of Justices of the Peace of the Midland District, 133–34.

69. LAC, Legislative Council, *Journal of Upper Canada* (February 21, 1823).

70. LAC, 4334–4335, Upper Canada Sundries, November 1826.

71. Thurlow Township Minute Book, January 4, 1836.

72. "An Act to ... establish a Board of Police in the Town of Belleville" (passed April 20, 1836), quoted in Mikel, *City of Belleville History,* 196–201.

73. HCHS, "Police Regulations of the Town of Belleville" (1840; repr. Hastings County Historical Society, ca. 1980).

74. Moodie, *Life in the Clearings,* 13.

Four: The 1840s and 1850s

1. Gerald E. Boyce, *Hutton of Hastings* (Belleville: Hastings County Council, 1973), 7–8.

2. *Ibid.*, 13–14.

3. *Ibid.*, 29.

4. *Ibid.*, 34.

5. *Ibid.*, 224–45 contains the complete text of his second award-winning essay.

6. Michael Peterman, *Sisters in Two Worlds: A Visual Biography of Susanna Moodie and Catharine Parr Traill* (Doubleday Canada, 2007), 98. This is the most recent and most lavishly illustrated of the Moodie books.

7. *Ibid.*, 110.

8. *Ibid.*, 111.

9. *Ibid.*, 35.

10. Moodie, *Life in the Clearings,* (Toronto: Macmillan Co. of Canada Ltd., 1959).

11. *Ibid.,* 16.

12. Glanmore National Historic Site, Minute Book of the Congregational Church of Belleville 1844–1847, April 2, 1845.

13. Although Susanna could not identify the source of the raps, the Fox sisters later confessed they had made the sounds. Charlotte Gray, *Sisters in the Wilderness,* (Toronto: The Penguin Group, 1999), 256–57.

14. Carl Ballstadt, Elizabeth Hopkins, and Michael Peterman, eds., *Letters of a Lifetime* (Toronto: University of Toronto Press, 1985), 156–57.

15. Carl Ballstadt, Elizabeth Hopkins, and Michael Peterman, eds., *Letters of Love and Duty: The Correspondence of Susanna and John Moodie* (Toronto: University of Toronto Press, 1993), 240–44.

16. AO, A.N. Buell Papers.

17. Stan McMullin, *Anatomy of a Séance: A History of Spiritual Communication in Central Canada* (Montreal & Kingston: McGill-Queen's University Press, 2004), xvi. A fascinating account of the role of Spiritualism in Ontario after the Fox sisters heard their first raps in Hydesville, New York, in 1848.

18. Moodie, *Life in the Clearings,* 29.

19. Nick Mika and Helma Mika, *Mosaic of Belleville* (Belleville: Mika Silk Screening Ltd., 1966), 32.

20. E.C. Guillet, *Pioneer Inns and Taverns*, vol. 3, (Toronto: Guillet, 1952), 108.

21. Quoted in *Kingston Chronicle and Gazette,* September 26, 1840.

22. Moodie, *Life in the Clearings,* 157.

23. *Victoria Chronicle,* September 10, 1846.

24. *Hastings Chronicle,* August 30, 1855.

25. Buckley, *A History of the Parish of St. Michael,* 349–55.

26. Smith, *Albert College,* 6–7, ff.

27. HCHS, Library Annual Report, January 4, 1848.

28. Moodie, *Life in the Clearings* 6.

29. Plumpton, *The Rambling River,* 167.

30. *Victoria Chronicle,* March 11, 1847.

31. Guillet, *Pioneer Inns,* vol. 3, 109.

32. OA, RG2, F-3–E, Minutes of the Belleville Board of Education, September 14, 1850.

33. *Ibid.,* January 17, 1851. Fees would still be charged for students living outside the town limits.

34. *Ibid.,* June 30, 1852.

35. *Ibid.,* December 31, 1853.

36. *Ibid.,* October 21, 1852.

37. *Ibid.,* August 7, 1852.

38. *Ibid.,* July 26, August 18, September 29, 1853.

39. *Ibid.,* August 11, September 8, 1853.

40. *Ibid.,* April 7, 1856.

41. *Ibid.,* January 19, 1854.

42. *Ibid.,* October 18, 1854, December 26, 1854.

43. *Ibid.,* November 1, 1855.

44. *Ibid.,* December 31, 1855.

45. The provincial government transferred the hospital reserve lots and the building to Belleville when they were found to be unsuited for hospital use. Upper Canada Statutes 14–15, Victoria., ch. 140 (Assented to August 30, 1851).

46. OA, RG2, F-3–E, Minutes of the Belleville Board of Education, July 7, 1856.

47. OA, RG2, F-3–F, Box 1, Reports from on Belleville Separate School Board, 1860, 1862.

48. OA, RG2, G-1–A, Report by the Reverend William Ormiston, November 5, 1855.

49. J. George Hodgins, *Historical and Other Papers and documents illustrative of the Educational System of Ontario, 1858–1876* (Toronto: L.K. Cameron, 1911), Chief Superintendent of Education Egerton Ryerson's Circular to the Boards of Trustees of Grammar Schools in Upper Canada, vol. 4, 41.

50. J. George Hodgins, *Documentary History of Education in Upper Canada from the passing of the Constitutional Act of 1791, to … 1870,* vol. 20 (Toronto, Warwick Bros. & Rutter, 1894), 237.

51. *Ibid.,* vol. 23, 169–70.

52. *Ibid.,* vol. 20, 248–56.

53. OA, RG2, F-3–E, Minutes of the Belleville Board of Education, July 8, 1868.

54. *Ibid.,* July 14, 1868.

55. OA, RG2, G-1–A, Report of Grammar School Inspector Mackenzie, June 18, 1869.

56. OA, RG2, F-3–E, Minutes of the Belleville Board of Education, August 2, 1870.

57. *Ibid.*, April 12, 1870.

58. *Ibid.*, October 4, 1870.

59. *Journal of Education, Ontario*, May 1869, 66.

60. The quotations and much of the information are from Carl Ballstadt, "Alexander Milton Ross," in *Dictionary of Canadian Biography, Vol. XII, 1891–1900,* (Toronto: University of Toronto Press, 1990), 924–28. See also Steven Duff, *Hunter of Dreams: A Story of the Underground Railroad* (Victoria, BC: Trafford Publishing, 2002).

61. Boyce, *Hutton,* 181.

62. Quoted in *Kingston Chronicle and Gazette*, December 17, 1836.

63. *Ibid.*, October 29, 1845.

64. Peterman et al, *Susanna Moodie, Letters of a Lifetime,* 173.

65. David B. Knight, *Choosing Canada's Capital: Conflict Resolution in a Parliamentary System* (Ottawa: Carleton University Press, 1991), xiii.

66. *Ibid.*, 18.

67. In 1956, while researching links between the Province of Canada and the Great Northwest in the Public Archives of Canada (now Library and Archives Canada) in Ottawa, I came across official government correspondence indicating the reason that the petition was not forwarded. Unfortunately, despite a subsequent search, I have been unable to locate the petition or the correspondence.

68. LAC, PRO, CO42/611, B-227, 404.

69. Undated confidential memorandum quoted in Knight, *Choosing Canada's Capital,* 254.

Five: The Confederation Era

1. For a detailed and entertaining description of the Prince of Wales' tour, see Ian Radforth, *Royal Spectacle: The 1860 Visit of the Prince of Wales to Canada and the United States* (Toronto: University of Toronto Press, 2004). Pages 186–87 describe the actual visit, and pages 196–97 relate to the subsequent apology in Toronto. For more detailed, and somewhat contradictory, coverage see the Belleville newspapers.

2. *Ibid.*, 186.

3. *Ibid.*, 124–25.

4. H.E.D. (Formerly Reporter to the Press), *The Aylwards and Their Orphans: Unjust Hanging of*

Prisoners at Belleville, C.W., Trial for Murder and Proofs of Their Innocence. A Full Report of all the Facts. (Quebec: L.P. Normand, St. Roch, 1863). Other excellent sources are Albert R. Hassard, "A Norland Nemesis," in *Not Guilty and Other Trials* (Toronto: Lee Collins, 1926) and contemporary newspaper accounts, as well as a review of the event as seen through the eyes of the 1862 *Chronicle* reporter and reporter Harry Mulhall of the *Intelligencer,* January 6, 1965. In the 1980s, I used these document and newspaper clippings to develop a script for a successful simulation of the Aylward trial and execution for high school and community college students.

5. Buckley, *A History of the Parish*, 35.

6. Quoted in Harry Mulhall's article in the *Intelligencer,* January 6, 1965.

7. Bob Lyons, "The Trouble Just Began," the *Bancroft Times*, November 21, 1984.

8. Quoted in Buckley, *A History of the Parish,* 37.

9. *Ibid.*, November 27, 1984.

10. Legislation mandating that executions be moved behind jail walls came into effect January 1, 1870, as the result of Canada, Act 32–33 Victoria, ch. 29. It is interesting that John Melady, a former vice-principal at Bayside Secondary School near Belleville, wrote a fascinating book about the last public hanging. It was entitled *Double Trap: The Last Public Hanging in Canada* (Toronto: The Dundurn Group, 2005). It followed the murder of a wealthy farmer, his wife, and her unborn child in western Ontario on June 6, 1868.

11. The story of this discovery is told in detail in Gerry Boyce, *Eldorado: Ontario's First Gold Rush* (Toronto: Natural Heritage/Natural History Inc., 1992).

12. C.F. Aylsworth, "Madoc Gold Excitement of 1866–67," in *Annual Report of the Association of Ontario Land Surveyors 1919,* 134.

13. *Madoc Mercury,* October 20, 1866; *Weekly Intelligencer*, October 26, 1866.

14. Details of the meeting are to be found in C.F. Aylsworth, "Madoc Gold Excitement of 1866–67."

15. *Madoc Mercury*, November 10, 1866.

16. *Weekly Intelligencer,* December 7, 1866.

17. *Ibid.*, December 7, 1866.

18. *Hastings Chronicle,* December 12, 1866; *Weekly Intelligencer,* December 14, 1866.

19. *Daily Intelligencer,* January 12, 1867.

20. *Weekly Intelligencer,* December 21, 1866.

21. *Hastings Chronicle,* January 9, 1867.

22. A. Michel, "Report on the Gold Region of Hastings," January 20, 1867, in Canada, Geological Survey, *Reports of Dr. T. Sterry Hunt and Mr. A. Michel on the Gold Regions of the County of*

Hastings, (Montreal: M. Longmore & Co., 1867), 10–11.

23. AO, MU 307 (Buell Papers), Delia O'Hare to A.N. Buell, Belleville, March 29, 1867.

24. *Madoc Mercury*, February 9, 1867.

25. *Daily Intelligencer*, July 25, 1867.

26. *Madoc Mercury*, February 13, 1867.

27. *Toronto Leader*, February 20, 1867.

28. *Weekly Intelligencer*, March 22, 1867.

29. Hastings Land Registry Office, Joint Stock Declaration, Madoc A-13, June 13, 1867.

30. Hastings County Clerk's Office, County Council Minute Book 3, January 26, 1869.

31. *Daily Intelligencer*, January 17, 1868.

32. From Opawica Explorations Inc., http://www.opawica.com/projects/madocdingman.php, accessed April 10, 2008.

33. AO, MU307 (Buell Papers), Dora O'Hare to A.N. Buell, Belleville, March 18, 1867.

34. LAC, RG1, E1, vol. A-E, 112, quoting Campbell's memorandum March 18, 1867.

35. *Weekly Intelligencer*, March 29, 1867; *Madoc Review*, March 30, 1867.

36. Canadian Mining Journal, *Centenary Flashback to the Year of the Birth of Canada 1867*. Compiled by J.V. Deragon. (Gardenvale, Quebec: National Business Publications Limited, 1967), 44.

37. *Madoc Mercury*, April 27, 1867.

38. *Daily Intelligencer*, May 31, 1867.

39. *Madoc Mercury*, June 15, 1867.

40. Gerald E. Boyce, *Belleville City Hall from 1873 to 1989,* with coloured picture portfolio by Roger Pensom (Belleville: Mika Publishing Company, 1988), 13.

41. For a detailed study of the Fenians' impact on Belleville, see Boyce, *Historic Hastings*, 134–38.

42. Barbara Wilson, "The Grand Trunk Railway Brigade," in *Canadian Army Journal,* vol. XVII, no. 2, 1963.

43. HCHS, Ponton Papers, file 17, copy of letter from Colonel W.N. Ponton to Militia Headquarters, re: Fenian medal for William Clarke, 1896.

44. Belleville Town Council Minute Book, September 3, 1867.

45. *Ibid.*, June 25, 1867.

46. Don Akenson, *At Face Value: The Life and Times of Eliza McCormack/John White* (Montreal and Kingston: McGill-Queen's University Press, 1990).

47. *Weekly Intelligencer,* October 11, 1894.

Six: The Early Dominion

1. Circus Historical Society, Brown's Burnt Cork Activity, http://www.circushistory.org/Cork/BurntCork, accessed April 20, 2008.

2. For a detailed history of many early sports, see Paul Kirby, *Champions All: A Sports History of Belleville Part One* (Belleville: Dharma Publishing, 1986).

3. George Carver's column, the *Intelligencer*, May 26, 1911.

4. *Ibid.*

5. *Ibid.*, April 5, 1904.

6. The *Hastings Chronicle*, July 21, 1858.

7. *Daily Ontario*, July 22, 1887.

8. James S. Gilchrist, *Marchmont Distributing Home, Belleville, Ontario 1870–1925*, (Belleville: Epic Press, 2003).

9. Both local newspapers, the *Intelligencer* and the *Chronicle*, covered this story in considerable detail.

10. Paul Kirby offers an excellent account of the early years of the Bay of Quinte Yacht Club in *Champions All: A Sports History of Belleville, Part One*, 12–28.

11. *Toronto Mail*, September 17, 1873.

12. *Daily Ontario*, September 23, 1873.

13. *Daily Intelligencer*, September 22, 1881. See also Kirby, *Champions All Part One*, 16–19.

14. For a detailed study of Belleville City Hall, see Gerald E. Boyce, *Belleville City Hall from 1873 to 1989*, with coloured picture portfolio by Roger Pensom (Belleville: Mika Publishing Company, 1988).

15. For a detailed study of Belleville's cemeteries, see Gerry Boyce, *Conflict and Co-operation: The Cemeteries of Belleville, Ontario*, a paper presented to the annual meeting of the Canadian Historical Association in Halifax on May 29, 2003.

16. Part of concession 1, lot 5 in Thurlow Township.

17. Canniff, *History of the Settlement of Upper Canada*, 248. Ferguson was Captain Singleton's brother-in-law and trading partner.

18. Ontario Diocesan Archives, Kingston, Parish Records for St. Thomas' Church.

19. The family's position is supported by a reference in Canniff, *History of the Settlement of Upper Canada*, 248.

20. In 1904, St. Michael's opened St. James Cemetery, adjacent to the Belleville Cemetery.

21. Historical plaque erected in 1993 on the site of the Dundas Street Burying Ground from wording based on research by the Reverend J. William Lamb, author of *Bridging the Years: A*

History of Bridge Street United/Methodist Church, Belleville 1815–1990. (Belleville: Bridge Street United Church, 1990).

22. Telephone conversation with the Reverend Bill Lamb, summer of 1993.

23. HCHS, file 141–1, article quoting the *Intelligencer*, August 14, 1847.

24. Moodie, *Life in the Clearings*, 7. Susanna Moodie was aware of a spring-fed stream that flowed through a small ravine in the middle of the Anglican cemetery. Its waters were collected at the foot of the hill for use in homes and businesses.

25. *Hastings Chronicle*, February 14, 1856.

26. Town of Belleville Council Minutes, March 5, 1856.

27. The *Daily Intelligencer*, September 9, 1870.

28. *Ibid.*, August 1, 1871.

29. *Ibid.*, August 15, 1871.

30. *Ibid.*, August 24, 1871.

31. *Ibid.*, August 25, 1871.

32. Belleville Cemetery Company Archives.

33. Mackenzie Bowell was a director from 1872–78 and served as president in 1878. John Bell was a director from 1872–79 and served as president in 1879.

34. First Annual Report of the Belleville Cemetery Company, quoted in the *Daily Intelligencer*, January 24, 1873.

35. H.A. Engelhardt, *The Beauties of Nature Combined with Art* (Montreal: Lovell, 1872). Pleasance Crawford of Toronto is the acknowledged authority on Engelhardt's life. See her article, *H.A. Engelhardt (1830–1897): Landscape Designer*, a paper prepared for a symposium of the German-Canadian Historical Association at the University of Guelph on June 5, 1984.

36. The *Daily Intelligencer*, July 18, 1873.

37. *Ibid.*, August 26, 1873.

38. HCHS, file 313, *Rules and Regulations of the Belleville Cemetery*. (Belleville: The *Daily Intelligencer* Office, 1873).

39. The *Daily Intelligencer*, January 20, 1874.

40. *Ibid.*, July 17, 1890.

41. HCHS, W.N. Ponton Papers, Minutes of Meeting of Grounds Committee, May 20, 1903.

42. *Rules and Regulations of the Belleville Cemetery and Crematorium* (Belleville: The Belleville Cemetery Company, 1999), 2.

43. HCHS, Town of Belleville Bylaw 287, November 3, 1873.

44. HCHS, Town of Belleville Bylaw 356, May 29, 1876, and the *Daily Intelligencer*, May 30, 1876.

45. Donald Creighton, *John A. Macdonald: The Old Chieftain* (Toronto: Macmillan Co. of Canada, 1955) 223–25.

46. Toronto *Mail,* September 13, 1876.

47. Belleville Town Council Minutes, September 10, 1876.

48. *Toronto Globe,* November 29, 1876.

49. *Ibid.,* December 27, 1876.

50. *Montreal Gazette*, December 29, 1876.

51. *Ibid.,* December 25, 1876.

52. *Ibid.,* January 1, 1877.

53. A.W. Currie, *The Grand Trunk Railway of Canada* (Toronto: University of Toronto Press, 1957), 153.

54. *Toronto Globe,* December 20, 1876.

55. *Montreal Gazette,* January 1, 1877.

56. *Toronto Globe*, December 13, 1876.

57. *Ibid.,* January 24, 1877.

58. Canada, *Correspondence respecting disturbances on the line of the Grand Trunk Railway, Jan. 1st, 1877* (Ottawa: Printed by Order of Parliament, 1877), 14.

59. *Ibid.,* 13.

60. *Ibid.,* 15.

61. *Ibid.,* 47.

62. *Ibid.,* 14.

63. *Ibid.,* 10.

64. Lieutenant Colonel W.T. Barnard, The *Queen's Own Rifles of Canada 1860–1960: One Hundred Years of Canada.* (Toronto: The Ontario Publishing Company, 1960), 41.

65. Canada, *Correspondence respecting disturbances on the line of the Grand Trunk Railway*, 10.

66. *Ibid.,* 10.

67. *Montreal Gazette*, January 4, 1877.

68. Currie, *The Grand Trunk Railway of Canada,* 1953, 153.

69. Canada, *Correspondence respecting disturbances on the line of the Grand Trunk Railway*, 12.

70. *Daily Ontario,* October 6, 1877.

71. For a detailed study of the events of July 1, 1878, see Gerald E. Boyce, *Belleville: Birth of a City, July 1, 1878* (Belleville: Quinte Kiwanis Club, 1978).

72. The medical terms listed included Seminal Weakness (involuntary ejaculation of semen during sleep), Spermatorrhea (abnormally frequent or excessive loss of semen without orgasm), and Self Abuse (masturbation).

73. The *Intelligencer*, April 20, 1878.

74. *Ibid.*, April 27, 1878, and the *Daily Ontario,* April 26, 1878.

75. The *Intelligencer*, April 1878.

76. The trial of Dr. A. lasted from April 2–8, 1878, and accounts appeared in the *Daily Ontario* on several days.

77. *Daily Ontario*, April 18, 1878.

78. It is interesting to note that in the early months of 2008, police charged two women for soliciting on Front Street.

79. The *Intelligencer*, April 8, 1878.

Seven: End of the Victorian Era

1. The *Intelligencer*, July 12, 1872, quoted in Nick Mika and Helma Mika, *A Dream Accomplished: The Founding of the Belleville General Hospital* (Belleville: Mika Publishing Co., 1985), 20. Belleville teacher Francis Buckley later wrote *Belleville General Hospital: One Hundred Years* (Belleville: Hospital Board of Governors, 1986), a more detailed history of the hospital covering 1886–1986.

2. Nick Mika and Helma Mika, *A Dream Accomplished,* 25.

3. *Ibid.*, 36. The annual report for the year that ended October 1884 indicated that the home was a government institution and eligible to receive 7¢ per day for each inmate.

4. In 1963, under the Belleville General Hospital Act, the hospital came under the joint ownership of Belleville and the County of Hastings.

5. The donations in 2008 included a $100,000 gift to the Foundation Endowment Fund to be used for essential equipment needs. For an updated account of the group's activities, see HCHS, manuscript by Diane Sule, *Women's Christian Association of Belleville,* 2008.

6. The *Intelligencer*, April 9, 1880.

7. Merrill Denison's letter to the author, Bon Echo, August 17, 1968. The "thinly disguised biography" was Flora MacDonald's *Mary Melville The Psychic* (Toronto: Austin Publishing Co. Ltd., 1900).

8. Cyril Greenland, "Mary Edwards Merrill, 'The Psychic' 1858–1880," in *Ontario History,* June 1976. Greenland is currently professor emeritus of McMaster University.

9. MacDonald, *Mary Melville: The Psychic,* foreword, ii.

10. Ramsay Cook, "Spiritualism, Science of the Earthly Paradise," in *Canadian Historical Review,* vol. LXV, no.1 (March 1984), 9.

11. Kevin O'Brien, *Oscar Wilde in Canada,* (Toronto: Personal Library, 1982) 94.

12. *Ibid.*, 192.

13. Robert M. Stamp, "Teaching the Children of Silence: Samuel Greene and the Hearing-Impaired," in *Historical Studies in Education* (Spring 2005); an excellent, but brief, account of Greene's career. For a more detailed account, see the enthralling biography by Clifton F. Carbin, *Samuel Thomas Greene: A Legend in the Nineteenth Century Deaf Community* (Belleville: Epic Press, 2005).

14. The *Daily Intelligencer*, October 19, 1890; *The Daily Intelligencer*, October 14, 1890.

15. Stamp, "Teaching the Children of Silence," 2.

16. The *Daily Ontario*, February 17, 1890.

17. Carole Gerson, "Gilbert Parker," in *Dictionary of Literary Biography* (Thomson Gale, 2005–06). Online edition at http://www.bookrags.com/biography/gilbert-parker-dlb, accessed April 1, 2008.

18. "Sir Gilbert Parker in 'The Car,'" quoted in the *Daily Intelligencer*, November 5, 1903.

19. Information on recent iceboating based on a telephone conversation with Richard Bird, June 5, 2008, and Kirby, *Champions All Part One*, 39–41.

20. Betsy Dewar Boyce, *The Accidental Prime Minister: The Biography of Sir Mackenzie Bowell* (Ameliasburgh: Seventh Town Historical Society, 2001), ISBN 0–9691935–5–6. The society hopes to produce printed copies of the book in the near future. P.B. Waite, professor emeritus of Dalhousie University, Halifax, has written an excellent, though somewhat less complete and less sympathetic, account of Bowell in the *Dictionary of Canadian Biography Vol. XIV, 1911–20*, 120–24.

21. Waite, *Biography*, 122.

22. John T. Saywell, ed., *The Canadian Journal of Lady Aberdeen, 1893–1898* (Toronto: The Champlain Society, 1960), 161.

23. LAC, MG 26E 3 (a) vol. 114. Bowell Papers, article from the Winnipeg *Daily Nor'Wester*, February 20, 1894. Founded in Winnipeg in 1894, the *Nor'Wester* was a partisan Conservative paper.

24. Saywell, *Canadian Journal of Lady Aberdeen*, 245.

25. Boyce, *Historic Hastings*, 186.

26. Friends of Glanmore National Historic Site, *Glanmore National Historic Site of Canada* (Belleville: Friends of Glanmore National Historic Site, 2003) is an excellent, well-illustrated history of the site.

27. HCHS, fonds 10, W.N. Ponton Papers, file 77.

28. *Ibid.*, W.N. Ponton to G. Gillies, Detroit, April 11, 1893.

29. Lamb, *Bridging the Years*, 185.

30. *Ibid.*, 221.

31. Buckley, *A History of the Parish*, 53.

32. HCHS, *The Seaview Gazette*, vol. 1, no. 7 (January 1893), 53. Recent residents of 215 Charles Street have also reported unusual events.

33. *Ibid.*, 53.

34. The *Intelligencer*, June 7, 1882, quoted in Mikel, *City of Belleville History*, 171.

35. William Canniff, *The Medical Profession in Upper Canada 1783–1850* (Toronto: William Briggs, 1894), reprinted with a new introduction by Charles G. Roland by The Hannah Institute for the History of Medicine, 1980.

36. Purists, who believe that a century is not over until a full one-hundred years have elapsed, believe that the nineteenth century ended on December 31, 1900.

Eight: Dawn of a New Century

1. Mikel, *City of Belleville History*, 280.

2. See Kirby, *Champions All Part One*, 69–86 for a detailed outline of George Pepper's exciting career.

3. *Daily Intelligencer*, June 25, 1907; June 12, 1907.

4. *Ibid.*, October 25, 1911.

5. HCHS, Chamber of Commerce Scrapbook, vol. 5, 138, 185.

6. "The Gateway to Central Ontario" won the $10 prize. Second prize of $3 went to "Belleville — The City of Opportunity," and third prize of $2 went to "Why Not Belleville?" The complete list of entries is found at the Hastings Heritage Centre in a circular (May 14, 1923) inside the back cover of Chamber of Commerce Scrapbook 6. Information on the winning entries is found in clippings in Scrapbook 5, 185.

7. *Ibid.*, Scrapbook 4, August, 1925, and October 8, 1925.

8. *Ibid.*, December 31, 1910.

9. *Ibid.*, December 30, 1910.

10. C.W. Hunt, *Dockside Democracy*, (Belleville: Billa Flint Publications, 2000), 39.

11. *Ibid.*, 43–44.

12. *Ibid.*, 44.

13. *Ibid.*, 45 quoting the *Daily Intelligencer*, January 2, 1915.

14. *Ibid.*, 45.

15. Beatrice Lillie, John Philip, and James Brough told her fascinating story in *Every Other Inch a Lady* (New York: Doubleday & Co., Ltd., 1972). Subsequent to her death in January 1989, Bruce Laffey did an excellent summary of her life in *Beatrice Lillie: The Funniest Woman in the World,* (New York: Wynwood Press, 1989).

16. HCHS, *St. Agnes' School, Elmpool, Belleville*, 5.

17. Beatrice Lillie, *Every Other Inch a Lady*, 58.

18. *Ibid.*, 59.

19. *Ibid.*, 62.

20. Mikel, *City of Belleville History*, 4.

21. The *Intelligencer*, June 4, 1914.

22. From NASA History Division Centennial of Flight, http://www.centennialofflight.gov/essay/ExplorersRecordSettersDaredevils/early exhibition/EX7.htm, accessed April 1, 2008.

Nine: The First World War and Its Aftermath

1. Quinte Writers' Guild, Ruth Howard, ed., *Dare We Forget? Stories By and About Those Who Were There, Book 1* (Belleville: Quinte Writers' Guild, 1995) is a good example. See also William D. Mathieson, *My Grandfather's War: Canadians Remember the First World War 1914–1918* (Toronto: Macmillan of Canada, 1981). Garn Dobbs' daughter, Dorothy Bowes, made the forty unpublished Garn Dobbs letters (consisting of four-hundred pages) available to the Hastings County Historical Society in 2005.

2. Hunt, *Dockside Democracy*, 111.

3. The *Daily Intelligencer*, quoted in Brian D. Tennyson, "Premier Hurst, the War, and Votes for Women," in *Ontario History* (September 1965), 115–16.

4. HCHS, Garn Dobbs letters.

5. HCHS, file 825, W.C. Mikel Collections, minutes of the meeting were recorded by a court reporter.

6. *Ibid.*, 20–21.

7. *Ibid.*, 136–137.

8. Paul Kirby, *A History of the Rotary Club of Belleville 1920–1989* (Belleville: Dharma Publishing, 1989), 5.

9. *The Ontario*, October 19, 1922.

10. *The Financial Post,* February 27, 1930.

11. *The Ontario,* July 26, 1922; the *Intelligencer*, July 21, 1922.

12. *Ibid.*, July 19, 1922.

13. C.W. Hunt, *Dockside Democracy*, 29–32.

14. *Ibid.*, 67–68.

15. *Ibid.*, 107.

16. *Ibid.*, 152.

17. Mikel, *City of Belleville History,* 290–301.

18. See Lamb, *Bridging the Years*, 248–253, for a detailed account of deliberations in the Belleville churches.

19. A memorial window on the north side of the church commemorates the Ponton family.

20. A few years ago, descendants of Reverend Kerr inquired if there was a plaque in the church to commemorate his ministry. Given the circumstances of 1925, it is easy to see why no plaque was installed.

21. Mrs. Everett (Flora) Bell to Gerry Boyce, Belleville, June 8, 1959, letter in possession of the author.

22. Jeannine Locke, "When the Ku Klux Klan rode in Saskatchewan," in *Canadian Weekly* (June 19–25, 1965), 2.

23. Rick Mofina, "Ku Klux Klan: City's skyline didn't escape burning crosses," the *Intelligencer,* December 11, 1982.

24. Quoted in Buckley, *A History of the Parish*, 106.

25. The *Daily Intelligencer*, June 28, 1926.

26. Lenny Williamson, telephone conversation with author, January 28, 2008.

27. *The Community Press*, March 6, 1990.

28. Eldon Barton, "Canadian KKK organization fizzled-out fast," *The Community Press*, March 27, 1990.

29. Extensively quoted in Buckley, *A History of the Parish,* 107–109.

30. *Ibid.*, 107.

31. *Ibid.*, 108.

32. *Ibid.*, 409.

33. C.W. Hunt, *Booze Boats and Billions* (Toronto: McClelland & Stewart, 1988).

34. *Toronto Star Review Magazine* (June 3, 1989), M9.

35. Hunt, *Booze,* 229.

36. *Daily Intelligencer*, May 27, 1927.

37. *Ibid.*, October 17, 1926.

38. The Welbanks' House at 190 James Street is also noteworthy. It was the only Belleville structure to be included in *The Ancestral Roof,* a groundbreaking study of Ontario architecture by Marion MacRae and Anthony Adamson (Toronto: Clarke, Irwin & Company Ltd., 1963), 236.

39. *Toronto Globe,* October 19, 1928, quoted in *The Ontario*, October 19, 1928.

40. *The Ontario,* November 7, 1928.

41. *Ibid.*, November 11, 1928.

42. *Ibid.*, November 15, 1928.

43. *Ibid.*, November 20, 1928.

44. *The Ontario*, August 21, 22, 1929.

Ten: Depression, Royalty, and War

1. Kirby, *Champions All Part One*, 130–31.

2. *Ontario Intelligencer*, August 19, 1933.

3. *The Financial Post*, February 27, 1930.

4. *Intelligencer*, February 25, 1930.

5. *Ontario Intelligencer*, June, 1931.

6. HCHS, file 153, Aqua Vita Company.

7. HCHS, Chamber of Commerce Scrapbook 4, 125, *Ontario Intelligencer* clipping.

8. Kirby, *Champions All Part One*, 35.

9. *Ontario Intelligencer*, September 8, 1936. See also Kirby, *Champions All Part One,* 69–86.

10. Kirby, *Champions All Part One*, 32–34.

11. *Ibid.*, 87–99.

12. Farley Mowat, *Born Naked* (Toronto: Key Porter Books Ltd., 1993), 46.

13. *Ibid.*, 53.

14. *Ibid.*, vi.

15. The *Intelligencer*, October 15, 1901.

16. *Ibid.*, May 22, 1939.

17. Fortunately, the school (opened in 1922 and closed in June 1987) had been spared long enough to serve for a year as the temporary home of Belleville's municipal government while Belleville City Hall was undergoing extensive renovation.

18. Outstanding books that describe the local impact include Farley Mowat, *The Regiment* (Toronto: McClelland & Stewart, 1955); Kenneth B. Smith, *Duffy's Regiment* (Don Mills: T.H. Best Printing, 1983); and the Quinte Writers' Guild, Ruth Howard, ed., *Dare We Forget? Books 1 and 2* (Belleville: Quinte Writers' Guild, 1995). In addition, *Plough Jockey: the Journal of the Hastings and Prince Edward Regiment* (Belleville: The Regiment) has promoted the regimental family and its activities since the summer of 1993.

19. Mowat, *The Regiment,* viii.

20. *Ibid.*, xviii.

21. Kenneth B. Smith, *Duffy's Regiment*, Foreword, ii-iii.

22. *Ibid.*, iv.

23. Mowat, *The Regiment*, 173.

24. James J. McKever, "Lieutenant-General Chester Hull," in *Dare We Forget, Book 2*,160–173.

25. Private conversations with the author, 1990–2007.

26. Andrew Clark, *A Keen Soldier: The Execution of Second World War Private Harold Pringle* (Canada: Alfred A. Knopf, 2002).

27. Mikel, *City of Belleville History*, 165.

28. *Ibid.*, 239.

29. *Ontario Intelligencer*, July 9, 1944.

Eleven: The Post-War Era

1. Smith, *Duffy's Regiment*, 160.

2. Buckley, *A History of the Parish*, 443–45.

3. The *Ontario Intelligencer*, October 18, 1956.

4. Francis Buckley, *Belleville General Hospital,* 61.

5. The *Ontario Intelligencer*, quoted in Nick and Helma Mika, *Belleville: Portrait of a City*, (Belleville: Mika Publishing Co., 1983), 420.

6. Wren Blair, *The Bird: The Life and Times of Hockey Legend Wren Blair* (Etobicoke: Quarry Press Inc., 2002), 60–1.

7. Nick and Helma Mika, *Belleville: Portrait of a City*, 420.

8. HCHS, Mayor A.M. Haig Papers, A.R. Willmott, *Royal Commission: Report of the Commissioner Respecting the Financial Affairs of the Corporation of the City of Belleville* (October 31, 1959) 47.

9. *Ibid.*, 3.

10. *Ibid.*, 4.

11. *Ibid.*, 6.

12. *Ibid.*, 7.

13. *Ibid.*, 11.

14. *Ibid.*, 16.

15. *Ibid.*, 20.

16. *Ibid.*, 19.

17. *Ibid.*, 21.

18. *Ibid.*, 20.

19. *Ibid.*, 20.

20. *Ibid.*, 23.

21. *Ibid.*, 36.

22. *Ibid.*, 33.

23. *Ibid.*, 34.

24. *Ibid.*, 32.

25. *Ibid.*, 46.

26. *Ibid.*, 47.

27. *Ibid.*, 41–42.

28. *Ibid.*, 38–39.

29. *Ibid.*, 45.

30. Nick Mika and Helma Mika, *Places in Ontario: Their Name Origins and History Part One A-E,* (Belleville: Mika Publishing Co., 1977), 5. Morley was curator of special collections at the Douglas Library of Queen's University.

31. Stuart Laidlaw, "Unforeseen reward for Belleville 40 years later," the Star.com, May 3, 2008.

32. Orland French, *Pioneering: A History of Loyalist College* (Belleville: Loyalist College, 1992) is an excellent history of Loyalist College.

33. Mika, *Belleville Centenary Flashback*, 74.

34. *Ontario Intelligencer,* July 27, 1979.

35. This section is based on Gerald E. Boyce, *Belleville City Hall from 1873 to 1989* (Belleville: Mika Publishing Company, 1988), especially 48–80.

36. See Gerald Boyce, *Belleville City Hall,* 81–94, for a series of beautiful colour photographs by Roger Pensom showing City Hall soon after the completion of the restoration/renovation.

37. Diocese of Ontario Archives, St. Thomas' Church Vestry Minutes, 7–BM-2, February 7, 1887.

38. *Ibid.*, May 16, 1911 ff.

39. *Ibid.*, box 7–B-1, item 97.

40. The provincial licence to conduct this archaeological exploration was number 89–101B, and was issued April 16, 1989.

41. The question of the location of burials was more than academic. Plans to convert the nearby former Belleville Collegiate Institute and Vocational School into the Quinte Cultural Centre could have been affected by the presence of burials on that part of the school property purchased from the church almost a century ago. However, plans for this centre were not realized, and the grounds were turned into playing fields for separate school students.

42. Dr. Shelley Saunders was the Canada Research Chair in Human Disease and Population Relationships and a fellow of the Royal Society of Canada.

43. These included McMaster University, the University of Guelph, Queen's University, and the University of Toronto in Ontario; the University of Manitoba; the University of Northern British Columbia; and the University of Tennessee.

44. The extensive computer database created at McMaster University for the years 1821–74 included 1,564 burials, 4,153 baptisms, and 1,522 marriages.

45. See: Shelley R. Saunders, D. Ann Herring, and Gerald Boyce, "Can Skeletal Samples Accurately Represent the Living Populations They Come From? The St. Thomas' Cemetery Site, Belleville, Ontario," 69–89, in Anne L. Grauer, ed., *Bodies of Evidence: Reconstructing History Through Skeletal Analysis* (New York: Wiley-Liss, 1995); Shelley R. Saunders, Ann Herring, Lawrence A. Sawchuk and Gerry Boyce, "The Nineteenth-Century Cemetery at St. Thomas' Anglican Church, Belleville: Skeletal Remains, Parish Records and Censuses," 92–117, in Shelley R. Saunders and Ann Herring, eds., *Grave Reflections: Portraying the Past through Cemetery Studies* (Toronto: Canadian Scholars' Press Inc., 1995); and Shelley R. Saunders, Ann Herring, Larry Sawchuk, Gerry Boyce, Rob Hoppa, and Susan Klepp, "The Health of the Middle Class: The St. Thomas' Anglican Church Cemetery Project," 130–161, in Richard H. Steckel and Jerome C. Rose, *The Backbone of History: Health and Nutrition in the Western Hemisphere* (Cambridge: Cambridge University Press, 2002).

46. Grauer, *Bodies of Evidence*, 71.

47. Shelley R. Saunders and Ann Herring, *Grave Reflections*, 93–94. This book arose from an international symposium co-organized and co-chaired by Doctors Saunders and Herring for the sixtieth annual meeting of the American Association of Physical Anthropologists in April 1993.

48. Rose, *The Backbone of History*, 130.

49. Heather McKillop, "Recognizing Children's Graves in Nineteenth-Century Cemeteries: Excavations in St. Thomas' Anglican Churchyard, Belleville, Ontario, Canada," in *Historical Archaeology*, vol. 29, no. 2 (1995), 77.

50. Susan B. Jiminez, *Analysis of Patterns of Injury and Disease in an Historic Skeletal Sample from Belleville, Ontario*, MA Thesis, McMaster University, 1991.

51. Sylvia Abonyi, "The Effects of Processing on Stable Isotope Levels and Mineral Concentration in Foods: Implications for Paleodietary Reconstruction" (master's thesis, University of Calgary, 1993). The large sample of infants and young children made it possible to detect breast-feeding and weaning patterns. William Hutton's letters from the Belleville area are found in Gerald E. Boyce, *Hutton of Hastings: the Life and Letters of William Hutton, 1801–1861* (Belleville: Hastings County Council, 1972).

52. *Ibid.*, 46–7.

53. Chris Dudar, "Reconstructing Population History from Past Peoples Using Ancient DNA and Historic Records Analysis: The Upper Canadian Pioneers and Land Resources" (Ph.D. thesis, McMaster University, 1998).

54. The authors are Shelley R. Saunders, Andrea H.W. Chan, Bonnie Kahlon, Hagen F. Kluge, and Charles M. FitzGerald.

55. Dr. McKillop developed and regularly teaches two courses: "The Archaeology of Death" and "Archaeology and Death" (a graduate seminar). In 1990, she accepted a tenure-track position in the Department of Geography and Anthropology at Louisiana State University, and is currently the William G. Haag Professor of Archaeology in that department, continuing both her Mayan studies and research on St. Thomas' Church Cemetery artifacts.

56. L.A. Sawchuk, S. Sharma, W. Grainger & G. Boyce, *Belleville Family History Project* (Toronto: CITD Press, University of Toronto at Scarborough, 2001), ISBN: 0–7727–6304–6. The disk also contains a brief, illustrated history of Belleville and the St. Thomas' Church Cemetery, and links to relevant websites.

57. E-mail from Doctor Shelley Saunders, April 9, 2003.

58. Although the St. Thomas' Cemetery Project is well-known by archaeologists and anthropologists, it has been given little attention in historical circles. One exception was at the "Celebrating One Thousand Years of Ontario's History Symposium," sponsored by the Ontario Historical Society at Willowdale in April 2000. Gerry Boyce and Ann Herring (on behalf of co-authors Shelley Saunders and Larry Sawchuk) gave an illustrated presentation on the project, the outline for which was subsequently included in *Celebrating One Thousand Years of Ontario's History: Proceedings of the Celebrating One Thousand Years of Ontario's History Symposium* (Willowdale: The Ontario Historical Society, 2000).

59. For a detailed description of the Bridge Street Foundation and its activities see Mary-Lynne Morgan, *On Silver Pond: Reflections on the Twenty-Fifth Anniversary of the Bridge Street United Church Foundation* (Belleville: Bridge Street United Church Foundation, 1998).

Twelve: Past, Present, and Future

1. The same summer, city councillors voted themselves a 76-percent pay hike and the mayor a 33-percent pay hike (covering the period from December 2000 to January 1, 2002). Many residents felt the increases had been approved without proper consultation with the voters, and many letters to the editor were written in protest.

2. Thanks to former history teacher Bruce Retallick for suggesting the wording of the Epilogue.

BIBLIOGRAPHY

Archives

Belleville Cemetery Company Office
Annual reports and burial records (1874–1900).

City of Belleville Archives
City of Belleville Minute Books, 1960–2006.
Thurlow Township Minute Book, 1836.

Glanmore National Historic Site, Belleville
Minute Book of the Congregational Church of Belleville, 1844–47.

Hastings County Clerk's Office
Hastings County Council Minute Books, 1842–1965.

Hastings County Historical Society (Hastings Heritage Centre)
Aqua Vita Company (Hastings County Historical Society, file 153).
Belleville Chamber of Commerce Scrapbooks, 1920–40, 5 vols.
City of Belleville Minute Books, 1836–1950.
Dobbs, Garn, Letters from World War One, 1917–19.
Foster, Lois, "Notes on the Simpson Family" *Outlook* (n.d.).
Gardner, Reverend James, *My Life Story,* extracts prepared by Gerry Boyce, 1960.

Haig Papers: A.R. Willmott, *Royal Commission: Report of the Commissioner Respecting the Financial Affairs of the Corporation of the City of Belleville* (October 31, 1959).

Hastings County Rebellion Losses Papers.

Mikel, W.C. Collection (Minutes of Better Understanding Meeting, 1925, etc.).

Ponton Family Papers.

The Seaview Gazette (Private family newspaper of the Bancroft Family), 1893.

White, Phyllis H., *Dr. James Macnab: The Lost Loyalist* (typed manuscript), 2007.

Library and Archives Canada (LAC)

Legislative Council, Journal of Upper Canada, 1823.

National Map Collection.

MG24: Henry Yager Papers.

MG26: Mackenzie Bowell Papers.

RG1, L3, UC Land Petitions, Reports of Justices of the Peace.

RG5, A1 Upper Canada Sundries.

Ontario Archives (OA)

A. N. Buell Papers.

Canniff Papers.

Mackenzie-Lindsey Papers.

RG1 Upper Canada Land Papers.

RG2 Education Records for Belleville Schools, Reports of Grammar School Inspectors.

RG9, 1B1 Adjutants General's Correspondence.

Upper Canada Legislative Assembly Journals.

Ontario Diocesan Archives of the Anglican Church of Canada

Parish Records for St. Thomas' Church, Belleville. 1825–76.

Newspapers

Bancroft: The *Bancroft Times,* 1984.

Belleville: *Hastings Chronicle*, 1850s.

              Intelligencer, 1834–2008 (known as the *Ontario Intelligencer* for many years after

1930).

The Ontario, 1870–1930.

Victoria Chronicle, 1840s.

Kingston: *Kingston Chronicle,* 1819–33.

Kingston Chronicle and Gazette, 1833–47.

Kingston Gazette, 1810–18.

Madoc: *Madoc Mercury,* 1866–71.

Montreal: *Gazette,* 1876–77.

Picton: *Hallowell Free Press,* 1832.

Stirling: The *Community Press,* 1990–2008.

Toronto: *Financial Post,* 1930.

Globe, 1876–77.

Leader, 1867.

Mail, 1876.

The Patriot, 1833–36.

Star Review Magazine, 1989.

Books and Publications

Adams, Nick. "The Pre-Contact Occupation of the Kingston Area: An Archaeological Consultant's View." *Historic Kingston,* vol. 54 (2006).

Akenson, Don. *At Face Value: The Life and Times of Eliza McCormack/John White.* Montreal and Kingston: McGill-Queen's University Press, 1990.

Armstrong, Joe C.W. *Champlain.* Toronto: Macmillan of Canada, 1987.

Aylsworth, C.F. "Madoc Gold Excitement of 1866–67." *Annual Report of the Association of Ontario Land Surveyors 1919.*

Ballstadt, Carl, "Alexander Milton Ross." *Dictionary of Canadian Biography, Vol. XII, 1891–1900.* Toronto: University of Toronto Press, 1990.

Ballstadt, Carl, Elizabeth Hopkins, and Michael Peterman, eds. *Letters of a Lifetime*. Toronto: University of Toronto Press, 1985.

_____. *Letters of Love and Duty: The Correspondence of Susanna and John Moodie*. Toronto: University of Toronto Press, 1993.

Bellstedt, Ina. *St. Thomas' Anglican Church 1818–1968: The Parish Story*. Belleville: St. Thomas' Church, 1968.

Blair, Wren. *The Bird: The Life and Times of Hockey Legend Wren Blair*. Etobicoke: Quarry Press, Inc., 2002.

Bonnycastle, Sir Richard Henry. *Canada and the Canadians in 1846*. London: Colborn, 1846.

_____. *Canada, As It Was, Is, And May Be*. London: Colborn, 1846.

_____. *The Canadas in 1841*. London: Colborn, 1841.

Boyce, Betsy Dewar. *The Accidental Prime Minister: The Biography of Sir Mackenzie Bowell*. Ameliasburgh: Seventh Town Historical Society, 2001.

_____. *The Rebels of Hastings*. Toronto: University of Toronto Press, 1992.

Boyce, Gerald E. *Belleville: Birth of a City, July 1, 1978*. Belleville: Quinte Kiwanis Club, 1978.

_____. *Belleville City Hall*. Belleville: Mika Publishing Co., 1988.

_____. *Historic Hastings*. Belleville: Hastings County Council, 1967.

_____. *Hutton of Hastings*. Belleville: Hastings County Council, 1973.

_____. "James Hunter Samson" *Dictionary of Canadian Biography, Vol. VII, 1836–50*. Toronto: University of Toronto Press and les Presses de l'université Laval, 1988.

_____. *The St. Andrew's Chronicles.* Belleville: St. Andrew's Presbyterian Church, 1978.

_____. "George Singleton" *Dictionary of Canadian Biography, Vol. IV, 1771–1800.* Toronto: University of Toronto Press, 1979.

Boyce, Gerald E., et al. *Sidney Township 1790–1990.* Belleville: Hastings County Historical Society, 1990.

Boyce, Gerry. *Conflict and Co-operation: The Cemeteries of Belleville, Ontario*, a paper presented to the annual meeting of the Canadian Historical association in Halifax on May 29, 2003.

_____, *Eldorado: Ontario's First Gold Rush.* Toronto: Natural History/Natural Heritage, 1992.

Boyce, Gerry, et al. "The St. Thomas' Church Cemetery Project, Belleville, Ontario" *Celebrating One Thousand Years of Ontario's History Symposium.* Toronto: The Ontario Historical Society, 2000.

Buckley, Edward C. *A History of the Parish of St. Michael The Archangel Belleville, Ontario 1829–1993.* Belleville: Edward Buckley, 1993.

Buckley, Frank. *Belleville General Hospital: One Hundred Years.* Belleville: Hospital Board of Governors, 1986.

Canada. *Correspondence respecting disturbances on the line of the Grand Trunk Railway, Jan. 1st, 1877.* Ottawa: Printed by Order of Parliament, 1877.

Canadian Federation of University Women, Belleville and District. *Quinte Women of Distinction.* Belleville: CFUW, 2002.

Canadian Mining Journal, J.V., Deragon (compiler). *Centenary Flashback to the year of the birth of Canada 1867.* Gardenvale, QC: National Business Publications Ltd., 1967.

Canniff, William. *History of the Settlement of Upper Canada with special reference to the Bay Quinte.* Toronto: Dudley & Burns, 1869; reprinted by Mika Silk Screening Ltd., Belleville, 1971.

_____, *The Medical Profession in Upper Canada 1783–1850*. Toronto: William Briggs, 1894; reprinted with new introduction by Charles G. Roland by the Hannah Institute for the History of Medicine, 1980.

Carbin, Clifton F. *Samuel Thomas Greene: a Legend in the Nineteenth Century Deaf Community*. Belleville: Epic Press, 2005.

Clark, Andrew. *A Keen Soldier: The Execution of Second World War Private Harold Pringle*. Toronto: Alfred A. Knopf, 2002.

Cook, Ramsay. "Spiritualism, Science of the Earthly Paradise" in *Canadian Historical Review* (March 1984).

Craig, Gerald M. *Upper Canada: The Formative Years 1784–1841*. Toronto: McClelland & Stewart Ltd, 1963.

Creighton, Donald. *John A. Macdonald: The Old Chieftain*. Toronto: Macmillan Co. of Canada, 1955.

Currie, A.W. *The Grand Trunk Railway of Canada*. Toronto: University of Toronto Press, 1957.

Daechsel, Hugh J. *Moira Archaeological Survey, 1984: Report for Archaeological Licence 84-05*. Hamilton: the author, 1985.

Dodds, Gordon. "Sir James Buchanan Macaulay" *Dictionary of Canadian Biography Vol. VIII, 1851–60*. Toronto: University of Toronto Press, 1985.

Englehardt, H.A. *The Beauties of Nature Combined with Art*. Montreal: Lovell, 1872.

French, Orland. *Heritage Atlas of Hastings County*. Belleville: The County of Hastings, 2006.

_____. *Pioneering: A History of Loyalist College*. Belleville: Loyalist College, 1992.

Friends of Glanmore National Historic Site. *Glanmore National Historic Site of Canada*. Belleville: Friends of Glanmore National Historic Site, 2003.

Fryer, Mary Beacock. *Loyalist Spy*. Brockville: Besancourt Publishers, 1974.

Gerson, Carole. "Gilbert Parker" *Dictionary of Literary Biography*. Thomson Gale, 2005–2006. Online edition at http://www.bookrags.com/biography/gilbert-parker-dlb (accessed April 1, 2008).

Gilchrist, James S. *Marchmont Distributing Home, Belleville, Ontario 1870–1924*. Belleville: Epic Press, 2003.

Goddard, Jane Bennett. *Hans Waltimeyer*. Cobourg: the author, 1980.

Godfrey, Sheldon, and Judith Godfrey. *Burn this Gossip, The True Story of George Benjamin of Belleville, Canada's First Jewish Member of Parliament 1857–1863*. Toronto: The Duke & George Press, 1991.

Gourlay, Robert. *Statistical Account of Upper Canada*. London: Simpkin and Marshall, 1822.

Gray, Charlotte. *Sisters in the Wilderness*. Toronto: The Penguin Group, 1999.

Greenland, Cyril. "Mary Edwards Merrill, 'The Psychic' 1858–1880" *Ontario History* (June 1976).

Guillet, Edwin C. *Early Life in Upper Canada*. Toronto: The Ontario Publishing Co. Ltd, 1933.

Haight, Canniff. *Country Life in Canada Fifty Years Ago*. Toronto: Rose, 1885; reprinted by Mika Silk Screening Ltd., Belleville, 1971.

Hastings County Historical Society. *Outlook* (newsletter). Belleville: The Society, 1980–2008.

Heritage Belleville. *Heritage Buildings East of the Moira River*. Belleville: Heritage Belleville, 1991.

Herity, J. Owen. "Journalism in Belleville" *Ontario Historical Society Papers and Records,* vol. XXVII. Toronto: The Society, 1931.

H.E.D. (Formerly Reporter to the Press). *The Aylwards and Their Orphans: Unjust Hanging of Prisoner at Belleville, C.W., Trial for Murder and Proofs of Their Innocence. A Full Report of all the Facts*. Quebec: L.P. Normand, St. Roch, 1863.

Herrington, W.S. *History of the County of Lennox and Addington.* Toronto: Macmillan Co., of Canada Ltd., 1913.

Hodgins, J. George. *Documentary History of Education in Upper Canada from the passing of the Constitutional Act of 1791, to … 1870,* vol. 20. Toronto: Warwick Bros. & Rutter, 1894.

_____. *Historical and Other Papers and documents illustrative of the Educational System of Ontario, 1858–1876.* Toronto: L.K. Cameron, 1911.

Hunt, C.W. "Bill." *Booze Boats and Billions: Smuggling Liquid Gold.* Toronto: McClelland & Stewart, 1988.

_____. *Dockside Democracy; Women, Foster Ward & The Wharf Street Debating Club.* Belleville: Billa Flint Publications, 2000.

Journal of Education Ontario (1869).

Kirby, Paul. *A History of the Rotary Club of Belleville 1920–1989.* Belleville: Dharma Publishing, 1989.

_____. *Champions All: A Sports History of Belleville Part One.* Belleville: Dharma Publishing, 1986.

Knight, David B. *Choosing Canada's Capital: Conflict Resolution in a Parliamentary System.* Ottawa: Carleton University Press, 1999.

Laffey, Bruce. *Beatrice Lillie: The Funniest Woman in the World.* New York: Wynwood Press, 1989.

Lamb, J. William. *Bridging the Years: A History of Bridge Street United/Methodist Church, Belleville, 1815–1990.* Winfield, BC: Wood Lake Books Inc., 1990.

Lennox and Addington Historical Society. *Papers and Records,* 1912–1920.

Lillie, Beatrice, John Philip, and James Brough. *Every Other Inch a Lady.* New York: Doubleday & Co. Ltd., 1972.

MacDonald, Flora. *Mary Melville The Psychic.* Toronto: Austin Publishing Co. Ltd., 1900.

Macklem, Michael, trans. *Voyages to New France (Samuel de Champlain: Voyages to New France 1615–1618).* Canada: Oberon Press, 1970.

McMullin, Stan. *Anatomy of a Séance: History of Spiritual Communications in Central Canada.* Montreal and Toronto: McGill-Queen's University Press, 2004.

Michel, A. "Report on the Gold Regions of Hastings." in Canada, Geological Survey, *Reports of Dr. T. Sterry Hunt and Mr. A. Michel; on the Gold Regions of the County of Hastings.* Montreal: M. Longmore & Co., 1867.

Mika, Nick and Helma Mika. *A Dream Accomplished: The Founding of the Belleville General Hospital.* Belleville: Mika Publishing Co., 1985.

_____. *Belleville: Friendly City.* Belleville: Mika Publishing Co., 1973.

_____. Belleville: *Portrait of a City.* Belleville: Mika Publishing Co., 1983.

_____. *Historic Belleville.* Belleville: Mika Publishing Co., 1977.

_____. *Mosaic of Belleville.* Belleville: Mika Silk Screening Ltd., 1966.

_____. *Places in Ontario: Their Name Origins and History Part One A-E.* Belleville: Mika Publishing Co., 1977.

Mikel, W.C. *City of Belleville History.* Picton: Picton Gazette Publishing Co. Ltd., 1943.

Moodie, Susanna. *Life in the Clearings.* Toronto: Macmillan Co. of Canada Ltd., 1959, edited and introduced by Robert L. McDougall.

Morgan, Mary-Lynne. *On Silver Pond: Reflections on the Twenty-Fifth Anniversary of the Bridge Street United Church Foundation.* Belleville: Bridge Street United Church Foundation, 1998.

Mowat, Farley. *Born Naked*. Toronto: Key Porter Books Ltd., 1993.

_____. *The Regiment*. Toronto: McClelland & Stewart, 1955.

O'Brien, Kevin. *Oscar Wilde in Canada*. Toronto: Personal Library, 1982.

Ontario Department of Planning and Development. *Moira Valley Conservation Report*. Toronto: Department of Planning and Development, 1950.

Peterman, Michael. *Sisters in Two Worlds: a Visual Biography of Susanna Moodie and Catharine Parr Traill*. Toronto: Doubleday Canada, 2007.

Plumpton, Mary. *The Rambling River*. Belleville: Township of Thurlow, 1967.

Preston, Richard A. and Leopold Lamontagne. *Royal Fort Frontenac*. Toronto: University of Toronto Press, 1958.

Quinte Writers' Guild, Ruth Howard, ed. *Dare We Forget? Stories by and About Those Who Were There Books 1 and 2*. Belleville: Quinte Writers' Guild, 1995.

Radford, Ian. *Royal Spectacle: The 1860 Visit of the Prince of Wales to Canada and the United States*. Toronto: University of Toronto Press, 2004.

Robb, Wallace Havelock. *Thunderbird*. Kingston: Abbey Dawn Press, 1949.

Robertson, David A. "Mourning, Curing, Feasting or Industry? The Interpretation of the Quinte and Perch Lake Mounds" in *Ontario Archaeology*, no. 7 (2001).

Rogers, Edward S. and Donald B. Smith. *Aboriginal Ontario: Historical Perspectives on the First Nations*. Toronto: Dundurn Press, 1994.

Rolph, Thomas. *A Descriptive and Statistical Account of Canada Shewing its great adaptation for British Emigration preceded by an account of a Tour through portions of the West Indies and the United States*. London: Smith, Elder, 1841.

Sangma, Benzie (successor to reporter "Bill" Hunt). "Remember When" weekly column in the *Intelligencer,* 2000s.

Saywell, John T., ed. *The Canadian Journal of Lady Aberdeen, 1893–1898.* Toronto: The Champlain Society, 1960.

Shipley, Robert J.M. "Meyers, John Walden" *Dictionary of Canadian Biography, Vol. VI, 1821–35.* Toronto: University of Toronto Press, 1987.

Smith, Donald B. *Sacred Feathers: The Reverend Peter Jones (Kahkewaquonaby) & the Mississauga Indians.* Toronto: University of Toronto Press, 1987.

Smith, Waldo E.L. *Albert College 1857–1957.* Belleville: Albert College, 1957.

Stamp, Robert M. "Teaching the Children of Silence: Samuel Greene and the Hearing-Impaired" in *Historical Studies in Education* (Spring 2005).

Surtees, R.J. *Land Surrenders in Ontario 1763–1867.* Ottawa: Indian and Northern Affairs Canada, 1984.

Tennyson, Brian D. "Premier Hurst, the War, and Votes for Women" in *Ontario History* (September 1965).

Waite, P.B. "Mackenzie Bowell" *Dictionary of Canadian Biography, Vol. XIV, 1911–20.* Toronto: University of Toronto Press, 1998.

Wallbridge, T.C. "On Some Ancient Mounds upon the Shores of the Bay of Quinte." *The Canadian Journal,* no. 2 (September 1860).

Williamson, Lenny. "Our Architectural Heritage" series in *Intelligencer,* 1964.

Note: Several other useful sources have been acknowledged in the endnotes beginning on page 252.

INDEX

ABOUT THE AUTHOR

GERRY BOYCE HAS been active in historical circles, especially in the Belleville-Quinte area of Ontario, for more than fifty-five years. His books include *Historic Hastings,* a history of the county, which sold 8,000 copies after 1967; *Hutton of Hastings*, the life and letters of William Hutton, whose letters described life in Ontario from 1834 to 1861; and *Eldorado: Ontario's First Gold Rush*. He was instrumental in establishing the Hastings County Historical Society (1957), the first Hastings County Museum (1961), Glanmore National Historic Site (1973), and the Hastings Heritage Centre (1999). A former city councillor, and an active jogger until recently, he lives in Belleville with his wife Bev, one of Canada's senior lifeguards.